# PERSPECTIVES ON EARLY CHILDHOOD PSYCHOLOGY AND EDUCATION

SPECIAL FOCUS

Enhancing Behavioral Outcomes in Early Childhood

Volume 7, Issue 1
Spring 2022

Copyright © 2022
Pace University Press
41 Park Row
15th floor
New York, NY 10038

ISBN: 978-1-935625-72-8
ISSN: 2471-1527

Member

Council of Editors of Learned Journals

# PERSPECTIVES on EARLY CHILDHOOD PSYCHOLOGY and EDUCATION

### EDITOR
Maria Hernández Finch, *Ball State University*

### GUESTS EDITORS
Kayla Bates-Brantley, Ph.D., *Mississippi State University*
Zachary C. LaBrot, Ph.D., *University of Southern Mississippi*
Sarah Wright Harry, Ph.D., *Ball State University*

### ASSOCIATE EDITORS
Tammy Hughes, *Duquesne University*
Barbara A. Mowder, *Pace University*
Flo Rubinson, *Brooklyn College*

### EDITORIAL REVIEW BOARD
Vincent C. Alfonso, *Gonzaga University*
Stephen Bagnato, *University of Pittsburgh*
Renee Bergeron, *Consultant*
Zeynep Biringen, *Colorado State University*
Bruce A. Bracken, *College of William & Mary*
Melissa Bray, *University of Connecticut*
Victoria Comerchero, *Touro College*
Gerard Costa, *Montclair State University*
Grace Elizade-Utnick, *City University of New York at Brooklyn College*
Nancy Evangelista, *Alfred University*
Kathryn Fletcher, *Ball State University*
Randy Floyd, *University of Memphis*
Gilbert Foley, *New York Center for Child Development*
Laurie Ford, *University of British Columbia*
Pamela Guess, *University of Tennessee*
Robin Hojnoski, *Lehigh University*
Paul McCabe, *Brooklyn College*
Sara McCane-Bowling, *University of Tennessee*
Geraldine Oades-Sese, *Rutgers Robert Wood Johnson Medical School*
Matt Reynolds, *University of Kansas*
Gail Ross, *NY Presbyterian Hospital*
Susan Ruby, *Eastern Washington University*
Mark Sossin, *Pace University*
Esther Stavrou, *Yeshiva University*
Mark Terjesen, *St. John's University*
Lea A. Theodore, *College of William and Mary*
Mary Ward, *Weill Cornell Medical College*
Adriana Wissel, *Gonzaga University*

# TABLE OF CONTENTS

Editor's Note .................................................... 1
*Maria Hernández Finch*

## SPECIAL FOCUS:
## ENHANCING BEHAVIORAL OUTCOMES IN EARLY CHILDHOOD

Introduction to Special Focus: Enhancing Behavioral Outcomes in Early Childhood ...................................................... 3
*Kayla Bates-Brantley, Zachary C. LaBrot, and Sarah Wright Harry*

An Evaluation of a Teaching Interaction Procedure Implemented in a Recess Setting ........................................................ 11
*Kate A. Helbig, Stefanie R. Schrieber, Keith C Radley, and James R. Deriuex*

An Intervention Targeting Academic and Behavioral Skill Deficits in Early Childhood: A Case-Study .......................................... 35
*Kayla Bates-Brantley, Mallie Donald, Jasmine Sorrell, Meredith Staggers, Rylee McHenry, and Sarah Wright Harry*

Strategies to Promote Positive Mealtime Behavior in Early Childhood ... 59
*Hailey E. Ripple, Hallie M. Smith, and Kayla Bates-Brantley*

The Effect of Token Economies on Student Behavior in the Preschool Classroom: A Meta-Analysis........................................... 83
*Lynda B. Hayes, Brad A. Dufrene, Crystal Taylor, D. Joe Olmi, Leonard Troughton, Evan H. Dart, and Caitlyn M. Weaver*

Universal Screening in Early Childhood Populations: A Systematic Review .............................................................. 109
*Mikayla Drymond, Alexis Sanchez, Nathaniel von der Embse, Gabrielle Francis, Dorie Ross, and Samin Khallaghi*

Social-Emotional Interventions for Young Children in Rural Areas: A Single-Case Design Meta-Analysis............................................ 135
*Tyler E. Smith, Melissa Stormont, Marina Antonova, Emily Singell, Wendy M. Reinke*

Addressing Barriers to Universal Screening for Social, Emotional, and Behavioral Risk in Elementary Schools .................................. 163
*Crystal N. Taylor, Rebecca W. Lovelace, Caitlyn M. Weaver, Sarah W. Harry, Terreca A. Cato, and Meleah M. Ackley*

Building Foundations for Friendship: Preventing Bullying Behavior in Preschool ............................................................ 187
*Kara E. McGoey, Allison Aberson, Bridget Green, and Seana Bandi Stewart*

Impact of Kindergarten Transition Practices in Promoting Positive Behavioral School Readiness Skills ..................................... 207
*Tyler M. Szydlo, Elyse M. Farnsworth*

**LIST OF CONTRIBUTORS** ............................ 241

**EDITORIAL POLICY** .................................. 249

SPECIAL FOCUS
===

# Enhancing Behavioral Outcomes in Early Childhood

# Editor's Note

*Maria Hernández Finch*

    This issue includes manuscripts focused on social, emotional, and behavioral interventions that can be implemented with young children. Specifically, psychologists, early childhood teachers, special education teachers, and school counselors can gain knowledge from the meticulously selected topics covered in this issue on social, emotional, and behavioral (SEB) interventions and early childhood. The manuscripts in this issue cover the topics of SEB universal screeners, bullying prevention, the teaching interaction procedure, and addressing challenging behavior.

The journal welcomes submissions of manuscripts for general issues that focus on early childhood assessment, intervention, and prevention. Also, authors are encouraged to submit manuscripts for possible special articles, including manuscripts on the topics of early childhood neurodiversity and of play therapy from an assessment, parent empowerment or new developments in the field perspective. Experienced researchers in the fields of education and psychology are welcome to submit proposals to serve as guest editors for special sections of the journal. In the coming months we will have announcements regarding applying to join the expanding editorial board, additional ways for early career and graduate students to become involved with the journal, and a journal mission that more clearly centers equity, inclusion, diversity, and justice.

# Introduction to Special Focus

*Kayla Bates-Brantley, Zachary C. LaBrot, and Sarah Wright Harry*

## Abstract

Early childhood is a period that is marked by rapid changes in development. Exposure to enriched experiences such as positive family interactions, participation in early childhood education, and community engagement can foster healthy development and prevent many behavioral and mental health difficulties. Conversely, young children's development can be negatively influenced by a variety of risk-factors that have unfortunate long-term outcomes. Given the pervasive impact of behavioral development on young children's overall developmental outcomes, research examining strategies to enhance young children's positive behavioral outcomes is needed. The purpose of this paper is to introduce Part 1 of a two-part special issue in Perspectives on Early Childhood Psychology and Education that pertains to enhancing young children's behavioral outcomes. Rationale for the special issue, content of included articles, and special considerations for readers are described.

***Keywords:*** *Early childhood; early childhood education; behavioral assessment; behavioral interventions; behavioral outcomes; early childhood development.*

## Introduction

Early childhood is a period that is marked by rapid changes in development. Enriched experiences provided through family, early childhood education programs, and the community have potential to bolster developmental competencies, such as cognitive abilities, social skills, effective communication, and activities of daily living (Bick & Nelson, 2017; McWayne et al., 2004). Conversely, early exposure to various risk factors can negatively impact children's development. Poverty, family discord, exposure to violence, and low parental education place young children at high risk for the development of internalizing (e.g., anxiety, depression) and externalizing (e.g., oppositional defiant disorder, conduct problems) problems (Carter et al., 2010; Egger & Angold, 2006; Wichstrom et al., 2012). These risk factors are even more pronounced for young children with neurodevelopmental disabilities (e.g., autism, ADHD; Flouri et al., 2015; Midouhas et al., 2013). As such, it is imperative that these risk factors are mitigated through evidence-based practices.

Fortunately, a variety of strategies have been empirically evaluated and found to be effective for altering young children's behavior and subsequent developmental trajectory (e.g., Filcheck et al., 2004; Kuhn et al., 2020; LaBrot et al., 2018; Pasqua et al., 2021; Radley et al., 2017; Trimlett et al., 2021; von Schulz et al., 2018). This is often accomplished by directly targeting young children's behavioral outcomes in home, school, and clinic. Because young children are sensitive to the effects of their immediate environment, arranging antecedents and providing contingencies to occasion and reinforce adaptive behaviors are ideal strategies to promote behavioral outcomes that lead to healthy development (LaBrot et al., 2018; LeGray et al., 2013; von Schulz et al., 2018). Relevant behavioral outcomes include appropriate behavior (e.g., compliance with instructions), social skills, and academic responding.

Despite the plethora of empirical studies that demonstrate the effectiveness of various behavioral interventions that target these relevant outcomes, risk factors that threaten healthy development persist (Carter et al., 2010; Egger & Angold, 2006; Wichstrom et al., 2012), especially in the wake of the COVID-19 pandemic. Further, parents and teachers in early childhood programs often report feeling ill-equipped to address young children's unique developmental and behavioral needs (Snell et al., 2012; Worcester et al., 2008). As such, additional research examining effective, efficient, and novel assessment and intervention techniques to address common presenting concerns in early childhood is needed.

The primary aim of Part 1 of this two-part special issue is to introduce research on assessment and intervention strategies that directly impact young children's behavioral outcomes. More specifically, this special issue will provide practitioners and researchers who work with early childhood populations tools to improve a variety of behavioral outcomes that have been demonstrated to prevent difficulties and promote long-term, healthy development. Articles in this issue range from empirical to conceptual and have implications for both school and clinic.

Two articles in this issue provide insights on universal screening practices in early education settings. Taylor et al. (2022) thoroughly discusses recommendations to overcome barriers to universal screening practices in kindergarten through fifth grade educational settings. Drymond et al. (2022) reviews commonly utilized early childhood universal screening tools for their usability, technical adequacy, and appropriateness. Collectively, these articles provide evidence-based insights and strategies for using universal screening to identify young children at risk for social-emotional, behavioral, and academic difficulties. Further, implications for using universal screening data to inform effective intervention is discussed.

Four articles in this issue provide empirical evaluations of behavioral interventions utilized with young children in early childhood education settings. McGoey et al. (2022) examined the effectiveness of an eight-lesson curriculum designed to improve young children's social skills and behavior with a primary objective of bullying prevention. Similarly, Helbig et al. (2022) evaluated the effects of a social skills intervention for improving eight children's social skill use on the playground and in classroom settings. Hayes et al. (2022) conducted a systematic review of the literature to determine whether implementation of token economy interventions in preschool settings meet design standards to be considered an evidence-based practice and further discuss methodological limitations to be addressed in future research. Finally, Smith et al. (2022) conducted a meta-analysis of single-case design research studies that evaluated social-emotional interventions implemented in rural settings, with a focus on assessing the effects on teacher and parent practices to support young children. Given their empirical nature, these articles offer evidence for effective and practical strategies that can be used in educational settings for directly enhancing young children's behavioral outcomes.

In addition to examining behavioral interventions for enhancing behavioral outcomes, this issue also contains two articles that examine strategies for improving young children's academic outcomes. Bates-Brantley et al. (2022) examined the effectiveness of a novel early literacy intervention and found that it was useful for improving both early literacy skills and behavior in a seven-year-old student. Szydlo and Farnsworth (2022) conducted a systematic review of the literature to synthesize research evaluating kindergarten readiness transition practices. They found that multi-component interventions that target children's self-regulation skills in addition to parent involvement can lead to children's successful transition to kindergarten. Together, these two studies highlight the importance of interventions that target relevant behavioral outcomes (i.e., academic skills) for enhancing early academic success in early childhood populations.

Finally, Ripple et al. (2022) provides evidence-based interventions to address young children's picky eating and disruptive behaviors during mealtimes. Specifically, recommendations for parents and teachers to prevent and address tantrums and food refusal during mealtimes are described. This article provides valuable insights into approaches that are beneficial to promote behavioral outcomes for common presenting concerns that often occur during mealtimes.

Taken together, the findings and insights from the articles in Part 1 of this special issue enhance our understanding of strategies to promote young children's behavior outcomes across school, home, and even clinical settings. Furthermore, this special issue delineates strategies that are not only effective, but practical to implement. Because some of the articles in this issue focus on enhancing behavioral outcomes in early elementary age children, we encourage readers to consider the components of each article in the context of a broad range of early childhood (i.e., birth to 8). It is our hope that this collection of articles emphasizes the impact of the various strategies discussed to promote young children's behavioral and subsequent development outcomes.

### References

* Denotes articles included in Part 1 of the special issue

*Bates-Brantley, K., Donald, M., Sorrell, J., Huff, M., McHenry, R., & Harry, S. W. (2022). An early childhood intervention targeting academic and behavioral skill deficits. *Perspectives on Early Childhood Psychology and Education.*

Bick, J., & Nelson, C. A. (2017). Early experience and brain development. *Wiley Interdisciplinary Reviews: Cognitive Science*, 8(1-2), 1-12.

Carter, A. S., Wagmiller, R. J., Gray, S. A. O., McCarthy, K. J., Horwitz, S. M., & Briggs-Gowan, M. J. (2010). Prevalence of DSM-IV disorder in a representative, healthy birth cohort at school entry: Sociodemographic risks and social adaptation. *Journal of the American Academy of Child and Adolescent Psychiatry*, 49, 686–698. https://doi.org/10.1016/j.jaac.2010.03.018

*Drymond, M., Sanchez, A., von der Embse, N., Francis, G., Ross, D., & Khallaghi, S. (2022). University screening in early childhood populations: A systematic review. *Perspectives on Early Childhood Psychology and Education.*

Egger, H. L., & Angold, A. (2006). Common emotional and behavioral disorders in preschool children: Presentation, nosology, and epidemiology. *Journal of Child Psychology and Psychiatry*, 47(3), 313-337. https://doi.org/10.1111/j.1469-7610.2006.01618.x

Filcheck, H. A., McNeil, C. B., Greco, L. A., & Bernard, R. S. (2004). Using a whole-class token economy and coaching of teacher skills in a preschool classroom to manage disruptive behavior. *Psychology in the Schools*, 41(3), 351-361. https://doi.org/10.1002/pits.10168

Flouri, E., Midouhas, E., Charman, T., & Sarmadi, Z. (2015). Poverty and the growth of emotional and conduct problems in children with autism with and without comorbid ADHD. *Journal of Autism and Developmental Disorders*, 45(9), 2928-2938. https://doi.org/10.1007/s10803-015-2456-z

*Hayes, L. B., Dufrene, B. A., Taylor, C., Olmi, J. D., Troughton, L., Dart, E. H., & Weaver, C. M. (2022). The effect of token economies on student behavior in the preschool classroom: A meta-analysis. *Perspectives on Early Childhood Psychology and Education.*

*Helbig, K. A., Schrieber, S. R., Radley, K. C., & Deriuex, J. R. (2022). An evaluation of a teaching interaction procedure implemented in a recess setting. *Perspectives on Early Childhood Psychology and Education.*

Kuhn, B. R., LaBrot, Z. C., Ford, R., & Roane, B. M. (2020). Promoting independent sleep onset in young children: Examination of the excuse me drill. *Behavioral Sleep Medicine,* 18(6), 730-745. https://doi.org/10.1080/15402002.2019.1674852

LaBrot, Z. C., Dufrene, B. A., Pasqua, J., Radley, K. C., Olmi, J., Bates-Brantley, K., … & Murphy, A. (2018). A comparison of two function-based interventions: NCR vs. DRO in preschool classrooms. *Preventing School Failure: Alternative Education for Children and Youth,* 62(3), 161-175. https://doi.org/10.1080/1045988X.2017.1408054

LeGray, M. W., Dufrene, B. A., Mercer, S., Olmi, D. J., & Sterling, H. (2013). Differential reinforcement of alternative behavior in center-based classrooms: Evaluation of pre-teaching the alternative behavior. *Journal of Behavioral Education,* 22(2), 85-102. https://doi.org/10.1007/s10864-013-9170-8

*McGoey, K. E., Aberson, A., Green, B., & Stewart, S. B. (2022). Building foundations for friendship: Preventing bullying behavior in preschool. *Perspectives on Early Childhood Psychology and Education.*

McWayne, C. M., Fantuzzo, J. W., & McDermott, P. A. (2004). Preschool competency in context: An investigation of the unique contribution of child competencies to early academic access. *Developmental Psychology,* 40(4), 633-645.

Midouhas, E., Yogaratnam, A., Flouri, E., & Charman, T. (2013). Psychopathology trajectories of children with autism spectrum disorder: The role of family poverty and parenting. *Journal of the American Academy of Child & Adolescent Psychiatry,* 52(10), 1057-1065. https://doi.org/10.1016/j.jaac.2013.07.011

Pasqua, J. L., Dufrene, B. A., LaBrot, Z. C., Radley, K., Dart, E. H., & Lown, E. (2021). Evaluating the independent group contingency: "Mystery Student" on improving behaviors in head start classrooms. *Psychology in the Schools.* https://doi.org/10.1002/pits.22540

Radley, K. C., Dart, E. H., Moore, J. W., Lum, J. D., & Pasqua, J. L. (2017). Enhancing appropriate and variable responding in young children with autism spectrum disorder. *Developmental Neurorehabilitation,* 20(8), 538-548. https://doi.org/10.1080/17518423.2017.1323973

*Ripple, H. E., Smith, H. M., & Bates-Brantley, K. (2022). Strategies to promote positive mealtime behavior in early childhood. *Perspectives on Early Childhood Education and Psychology.*

*Smith, T. E., Stormont, M., Antonova, M., Singell, E., & Reinke, W. M. (2022). Social-emotional interventions for young children in rural areas: A single-case design meta-analysis. *Perspectives on Early Childhood Psychology and Education.*

Snell, M. E., Berlin, R. A., Voorhees, M. D., Stanton-Chapman, T. L., & Hadden, S. (2012). A survey of preschool staff concerning problem behavior and its prevention in Head Start classrooms. *Journal of Positive Behavior Interventions, 14*(2), 98-107. https://doi.org/10.1177%2F1098300711416818

*Szydlo, T. M., & Farnsworth, E. M. (2022). Impact of kindergarten transition practices in promoting positive behavioral school readiness skills. *Perspectives on Early Childhood Psychology and Education.*

*Taylor, C. N., Lovelace, R. W., Weaver, C. M., Harry, S. W., Cato, T. A., & Ackley, M. A. (2022). Addressing barriers to universal screening for social, emotional, and behavioral risk in elementary schools. *Perspectives on Early Childhood Psychology and Education.*

Trimlett, G. M., Barton, E. E., Baum, C., Robinson, G., Shulte, L., & Todt, M. (2021). Teaching board game play to young children with disabilities. *Journal of Positive Behavior Interventions,* 1-14. https://doi.org/10.1177%2F1098300720985287

von Schulz, J. H., Dufrene, B. A., LaBrot, Z. C., Tingstrom, D. H., Olmi, D. J., Radley, K., ... & Maldonado, A. (2018). An evaluation of the relative effectiveness of function-based consequent and antecedent interventions in a preschool setting. *Journal of Applied School Psychology, 34*(2), 134-156. https://doi.org/10.1080/15377903.2017.1403400

Wichstrom, L., Berg-Nielsen, T. S., Angold, A., Egger, H. L., Solheim, E., & Sween, T. H. (2012). Prevalence of psychiatric disorders in preschoolers. *The Journal of Child Psychology and Psychiatry, 53*(6), 695-705. https://doi.org/10.1111/j.1469-7610.2011.02514.x

Worcester, J. A., Nesman, T. M., Mendez, L. M. R., & Keller, H. R. (2008). Giving voice to parents of young children with challenging behavior. *Exceptional Children, 74*(4), 509-525. https://doi.org/10.1177%2F001440290807400406

# An Evaluation of a Teaching Interaction Procedure Implemented in a Recess Setting

*Kate A. Helbig, Stefanie R. Schrieber, Keith C Radley, and James R. Deriuex*

## Abstract

The teaching interaction procedure (TIP) is a strategy that has been demonstrated as effective in promoting social skill acquisition in school settings for young students with social communication deficits (Leaf et al., 2009; Leaf et al., 2010). However, a frequently cited criticism of social skills training is the lack of generalizability of target skills to novel contexts (Bellini et al., 2007). The purpose of the study was to evaluate a TIP-based social skills intervention conducted on the playground, intended to promote generalizability through training in naturalistic settings and to evaluate generalizability of skill acquisition to the classroom. Eight students 5-8 years old with an educational classification of autism or developmental delay participated in the study. The primary dependent variable was skill acquisition in the playground setting, and a secondary measure was generalized skill acquisition to the classroom setting. Target skills included appropriate body language, participation, and responding to initiations. A multi-probe design embedded within a multiple baseline design across target skills with concurrent replication across participants was used to evaluate the primary and secondary measures. Overall, results suggest that increases in skill acquisition were observed during implementation of the TIP across most participants and skills in both training and generalization phases. However, substantial variability was noted across participants related to maintaining skill acquisition during maintenance and follow-up phases in both the training and generalization settings. Limitations of these results are discussed as well as implications for school practitioners.

**Keywords:** *social skills, developmental delay, special education, modeling, performance feedback.*

Deficits in social and communication skills are defining features of autism spectrum disorder and developmental delays (American Psychiatric Association, 2013; IDEA, 2004). A lack of social communication skills is often associated with a host of undesirable outcomes (Garrison-Harrell et al., 1997; Locke et al., 2013; McConnell, 2002). During preschool, social deficits may appear as lack of response to name, poorly modulated eye contact, and difficulty with joint attention skills. These skills are often prerequisites to more complex and advanced social skills; therefore, it is critical that they are acquired early on. Further, acquisition of these foundational skills has been linked to stronger social, cognitive, and language repertoires (Dawson, 2013; Neimy et al., 2017).

Given the impact of these outcomes, it is imperative to identify strategies to support social skill development. Early intervention has been identified as an effective means to improve social communication skills (Kasari et al., 2010). Based on an operant learning perspective, provision of social skills training during early childhood development can potentially prevent or reduce the likelihood that children with autism spectrum disorder and other developmental delays experience social and communication deficits through shaping, prompting, and reinforcing prosocial skills (Neimy et al., 2017). An operant learning-based intervention focuses on events that precede and follow the occurrence of a behavior (Neimy et al., 2017). More specifically, this type of intervention focuses on teaching various cues in the environment to elicit corresponding social skills, and provides direct reinforcement following the demonstration of a social skill, thus increasing the likelihood of those social skills occurring in the future.

One strategy that fits within an operant learning category and has been demonstrated to be effective in promoting social skill acquisition for young students with social communication deficits is the teaching interaction procedure (TIP; Leaf et al., 2009; Leaf et al., 2010). TIP is comprised of various intervention strategies, including description of the specific target skill, rationale for using the skill, breaking the target skill into discrete steps, inappropriate and appropriate modeling of the skill, opportunity for students to role-play the skill, and provision of feedback (Bedlington et al., 1978; Minkin et al., 1976). Although similar to behavioral skills training, TIP has two unique features: (a) provision of a rationale for students to engage in the specific skill or behavior, and (b) an inappropriate demonstration of skill during the modeling phase of the intervention (Leaf et al., 2015). The effectiveness of TIP has been evaluated in the context of increasing social skills acquisition (Leaf et al., 2010; Leaf et al., 2009). Both of these studies evaluated the effectiveness of TIP on increasing acquisition of social skills for young students with autism spectrum disorder. Results of both studies demonstrated the effectiveness of TIP on promoting social skills acquisition. Readers should see full studies for procedural details.

A frequently cited criticism of social skills training is the lack of generalizability of target skills to novel contexts (Bellini et al., 2007). This limitation extends to TIP, as evidenced by limitations noted within Leaf et al. (2010). Specifically, although generalization to a novel person was evaluated, this was measured in the same room where training was conducted. There is a further need for evaluation of social skills teaching and the generalization of social skills to a novel environment. It has been suggested that social skills interventions be implemented within naturalistic settings to improve the likelihood of generalization of skill acquisition (Bellini et al., 2007; Gresham et al., 2001). The purpose of the current study was to evaluate a TIP-based social skills intervention on social skill acquisition conducted on the playground, intended to promote generalizability through training in a naturalistic setting, and additionally to evaluate generalization of skill acquisition to the classroom environment.

## Methods

### Participants and Setting

The study took place at a public elementary school in a suburban area in the southeastern United States. Racial make-up of the student population was 85% Black, 6% White, and 5% multiracial.

Additionally, 100% of students received free or reduced lunch. Participants included eight Black male students who were receiving special education services full-time in a behavior support classroom.

All students received services under the primary disability category of developmental delay (DD) or autism (AU). The special education teacher held a bachelor's degree and had approximately ten years of previous teaching experience. She requested assistance with social skills programming to meet students' Individualized Educational Plan (IEP) goals. Every student in her classroom had a broad goal related to improving social interaction skills on their IEP. All eight students participated in the group to increase the number of social opportunities students, and to mimic the natural environment of class recess on the playground. The special education teacher and all parents/guardians provided informed consent prior to participation in the study. Data were collected as a means to monitor student progress on IEP goals.

Social skills groups were conducted at the school's playground, which consisted of a play set with a slide, playhouse, tricycles, and a picnic table. Group sessions and data collection were facilitated by doctoral school psychology graduate students and were conducted during the participants' recess. Sessions were conducted 1-2 times per week for ten weeks with each session lasting approximately 35 minutes, including intervention time and data collection. Materials required for the intervention included a playground area, "fun-ties" (e.g., a small band that students could wear around their wrist), small edible items (e.g., candy), and data collection sheets.

Students IEPs were reviewed for their present level of performance. Only data related to students' social/emotional, communication, and cognitive abilities was reported below. Psudonyms are used for student names.

Landon was a 6-year-old Black male with a special education classification of DD. Limited data were provided in his IEP regarding current social-emotional capabilities. Anecdotally, Landon had a limited verbal repertoire comprised of single word phrases, and his teacher reported that he had minimal interactions with peers on the playground.

Lance was a 5-year-old Black male with a special education classification of DD and a secondary classification of Language/Speech Impairment (L/S). A review of his IEP indicated that his language and social-emotional skills were in the "significant delay" range on the Learning Accomplishment Profile, 3rd Edition (LAP-3). Additionally, Lance was performing below the first percentile for social-emotional and cognitive abilities on the Developmental Profile, Third Edition (DP-3), His cognitive capabilities as measured by the LAP-3 were significantly below those of same-aged peers.

Stephen was a 6-year-old Black male receiving services under the special education category of AU. Based on his performance on the Battelle Developmental Inventory, 2nd Edition (BDI-2; Newborg, 2005), he was performing below the first percentile in personal social skills. His cognitive capabilities as measured by the Stanford-Binet, Fifth Edition (SB-5; Roid, 2003) were reported in the mildly impaired range when compared to same-aged peers.

Jay was a 5-year-old Black male receiving special education services under the category of DD. A review of his IEP indicated that his social-emotional and communication skills were in the below average range on the DP-3. His cognitive capabilities, as measured by the SB-5, were reported in the low average range.

Bray was a 5-year-old Black male with an AU special education classification. LAP-3 results, as reported in his IEP, indicated that he was significantly delayed in language and personal social skills. Additionally, his performance on the DP-3 indicated that his cognitive, communication abilities, and social-emotional skills were at or below the first percentile.

Joe was a 6-year-old Black male receiving special education services under the eligibility category of DD. According to the data reported in his IEP, Joe was performing below the first percentile in personal-social, and communication skills on the BDI-2. No other information was documented regarding Joe's cognitive abilities.

Matthew was a 9-year-old Black male receiving special education services under the DD category. There were no test scores or measures to indicate his current level of social-emotional skills or cognitive capabilities. Anecdotally, Matthew often used two to three word phrases and had minimal appropriate social interactions with peers.

Kevin was a 7-year-old Black male with a special education classification of AU. According to his IEP, his scores on the BDI-2 indicated that his personal-social, communication skills, and cognitive abilities were below the first percentile.

## Measures

Target skills were selected based on teacher report. Skills included body language, participation, and responding to initiations. Cues (i.e., signals for the participants to engage in a target skill) and task analyses (i.e., a breakdown of discrete steps within each target skill) were developed to systematically collect data (see Table 1).

*Table 1*

*Target Skill Cues and Task Analyses*

| Body Language | Participate | Responding to Initiations |
|---|---|---|
| *Engage in Conversation with Participant* | "(Name) go play with (Name of student/group)" | *Student invited to play with another student or group* |
| 1. Face the person (orient head & shoulders w/i 3s) | 1. Physical Proximity (within 5 ft of partner) | 1. Use all steps in Body Language |
| 2. Make eye contact (w/i 3s, and maintain for 5s) | 2. Face the person (orient head and shoulders w/i 3s) | 2. Listen to the interaction (do not talk over anyone) |
| 3. Use appropriate volume (appropriate for outside) | 3. Make eye contact (within 3s, and maintain for 5s) | 3. Decide if you want to play (make eye contact) |
| 4. Use appropriate expression that matches how he/she is feeling | 4. Wait for an opportunity to engage without interrupting others/skipping someone's turn | 4. Give a clear and appropriate response (yes or no, thank you) |
| 5. Relaxed Position (shoulders down and within 3ft of conversation partner) | 5. Join by engaging in activity without disrupting progression | |

The primary dependent variable was the percent of accurate skill demonstration in the playground setting (i.e., training setting), with a secondary dependent variable of percent of accurate skill demonstration in the classroom setting (i.e., generalization setting). Percent of accurate skill demonstration was calculated by dividing the total number of steps the participant performed correctly by the total possible number of steps and multiplying by 100. A second independent observer (i.e., doctoral school psychology student) simultaneously recorded the accurate and inaccurate steps for a minimum of 30% of probes across participants, skills, and phases. Observers were trained using behavioral skills training led by the primary author. Observers were required to meet a minimum of 80% agreement across all skills before their training was completed. Interobserver agreement was calculated by dividing the number of agreements by the total agreements and disagreements. The average of the interobserver agreement across all participants, skills, and phases was 99.39% (range 80-100%).

Treatment integrity data were also collected to measure the degree to which the social skills intervention was implemented correctly. The intervention was broken down into 15 different steps, and graduate student researchers recorded whether each component was implemented, not implemented, or not applicable for the current phase. The intervention was implemented with 100% integrity. A second, independent observer also recorded the treatment integrity for 30% of all sessions and was noted to have 100% agreement.

Social validity data were also collected to evaluate teacher and student perceptions of the intervention. The teacher completed the Usage Rating Profile-Intervention Revised (URP-IR; Chafouleas et al., 2011), and students completed a modified Children's Inventory Rating Profile (CIRP; Witt & Elliot, 1985). The CIRP was adapted to best match the participants' cognitive abilities. It was composed of six questions, each with a 6-point "smiley-face" Likert scale. At the conclusion of the study, a graduate student researcher met with each student individually, read each question aloud, and asked the participants to circle the face that best matched their agreement with the statement.

## Design

A multi-probe design across skills with concurrent replication across participants (Cooper et al., 2019) was used to evaluate the effectiveness of the intervention. A multi-probe design was used for its flexibility to evaluate student response to cues intermittently. With this design, a series of probes is provided prior to intervention of the target skill until stability in performance is achieved. Phases included baseline, intervention, generalization, maintenance, and follow-up.

## Baseline

During baseline, graduate student researchers provided the cues on the playground and in the classroom to signal each student to engage in the target skills. Student researchers allowed the students 10 seconds to initiate a response to the cue. If no response was initiated, all steps were scored as inaccurate. A minimum of 60 seconds was required between the provision of cues. Instruction, corrective feedback, or reinforcement was not provided during baseline sessions.

**Intervention**

Participants were directed to the picnic table on the playground where they were welcomed to the group, reviewed the schedule of the social skills lesson, and discussed the group rules (i.e., voices off when the teacher is talking, keep hands and feet to yourself, participate, and follow directions). Next, the graduate student researchers utilized TIP (Leaf et al., 2015) to teach the target skills. This procedure involved the graduate student researcher (a) stating the target skill, (b) providing a rationale explaining why engaging in the target skill is important, (c) listing the discrete steps in the task analysis, (d) modeling an inaccurate and accurate demonstration of the skill and requiring participants to identify the correct and incorrect steps, (e) role-playing, and (f) giving corrective feedback until the skill was demonstrated with 100% accuracy two consecutive times. These procedures were conducted as a group, with students having the opportunity to observe their peers practice and receive feedback. Student researchers then explained the "fun-tie contingency". Specifically, participants were told that if they demonstrated the skill correctly, they would be provided with a fun-tie that they could wear on their wrist. If they earned at least four fun-ties, they would receive a prize. Once the contingency was explained, participants were dismissed from the picnic table and provided a minimum of 5 minutes on the playground prior to the start of data collection for the target skill. Data collection procedure was identical to baseline, with a 10 second allotment for initiation of the target skill and 60 seconds between the provision of cues. Each student was provided a minimum of five opportunities to engage in the target skill. Decisions to provide additional cues were determined on an individual basis using visual analysis. If data were not stable (e.g., trending, but with an outlying or inconsistent data point), additional cues were provided. Students were not provided explicit corrective feedback for inaccurate demonstrations but were provided a fun tie for 100% accurate demonstrations of the target skill. After data collection was complete, participants with four or more fun-ties could exchange their fun-tie for a small edible item (i.e., candy). At the conclusion of recess, participants returned to their classroom settings where graduate student researchers provided the same cues to collect generalization data on the target skill. There was no provision of reinforcement or corrective feedback during generalization data collection. Mastery of the target skill was defined as 100% accurate demonstration across three consecutive cues.

***Maintenance***

After participants mastered the target skill and TIP intervention was completed, maintenance data were collected during all subsequent sessions. A minimum of one probe was collected for each skill in both settings during the maintenance phase. Data collection was identical to baseline sessions (i.e., no provision of instruction, corrective feedback, or reinforcement). Data were collected in both the playground and classroom settings.

### *Follow-Up*

Follow-up data collection occurred one month after the completion of the intervention phase. Data collection was identical to baseline sessions (i.e., instruction, corrective feedback, and reinforcement were not provided). Data were collected in both the playground and classroom settings. A minimum of one probe was administered for each skill and setting.

## Data Analysis

Data were analyzed using visual analysis of level, trend, variability, immediacy of effect, and magnitude of change. A secondary statistic, baseline-corrected tau (Tarlow, 2017), was also calculated to estimate the effectiveness of the intervention. Phase change decisions were made based on stability of data and mastery of target skills.

## Results

### Landon

Landon demonstrated variable levels of skill accuracy for the body language skill during baseline, and low to moderate levels of skill accuracy for the participation and responding to initiations skills (Figure 1). Intervention resulted in large and immediate increases in skill accuracy in training and generalization settings for body language, moderate yet variable increases in participation in the training setting with no changes for generalization, and large and immediate increases in training and generalization settings for responding to initiations. Whereas increases in skill accuracy were maintained for body language and responding to initiations during the maintenance phase, decreases in accuracy were observed for training setting probes for participation and increases in accuracy for generalization setting probes. Follow-up was associated with maintained levels of accuracy for body language and decreases in accuracy for participation and responding to initiations. Baseline-corrected tau effect size calculations indicated moderate to large effects for all skills across all phases for skill accuracy (Table 1), though smaller effects were observed.

**Figure 1**
*Percentage of Skill Steps Demonstrated Correctly, Landon*

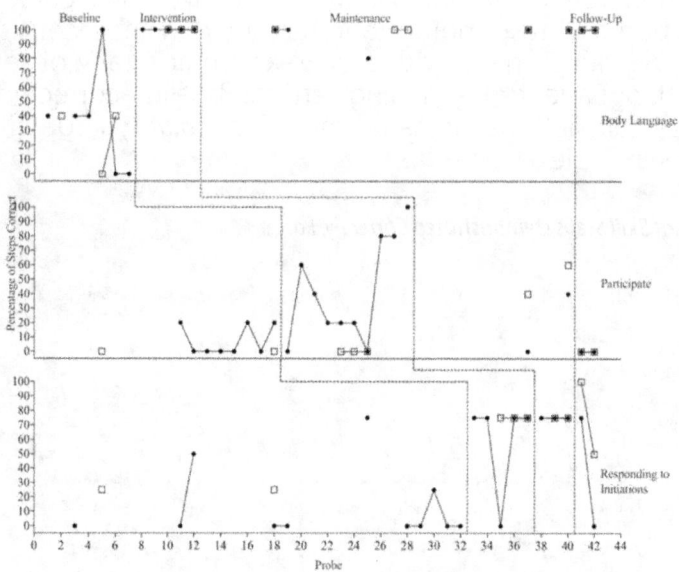

*Note. Filled circles = training setting; open squares = generalization setting.*

## Lance

Lance demonstrated low to moderate levels of skill accuracy for the body language and participation skills during baseline across both the training and generalization setting probes (Figure 2). For the responding to initiations skill, Lance demonstrated variable levels of skill accuracy for the training setting probes and a low level of skill accuracy for the single generalization setting probe. Across all skills, introduction of intervention was associated with immediate increases in skill accuracy in both training and generalization settings. During the maintenance phase, skill accuracy remained at high levels for training and generalization setting probes for body language and responding to initiations, with a decrease in skill accuracy from intervention phase levels observed for participation in the generalization setting. During follow-up, skill accuracy for participation and responding to initiations remained consistent with the previous phase, with a decrease in accuracy observed for body language in the training setting. Baseline-corrected tau effect size calculations indicated moderate to very large effects across skills (Table 1).

**Figure 2**
*Percentage of Skill Steps Demonstrated Correctly, Lance*

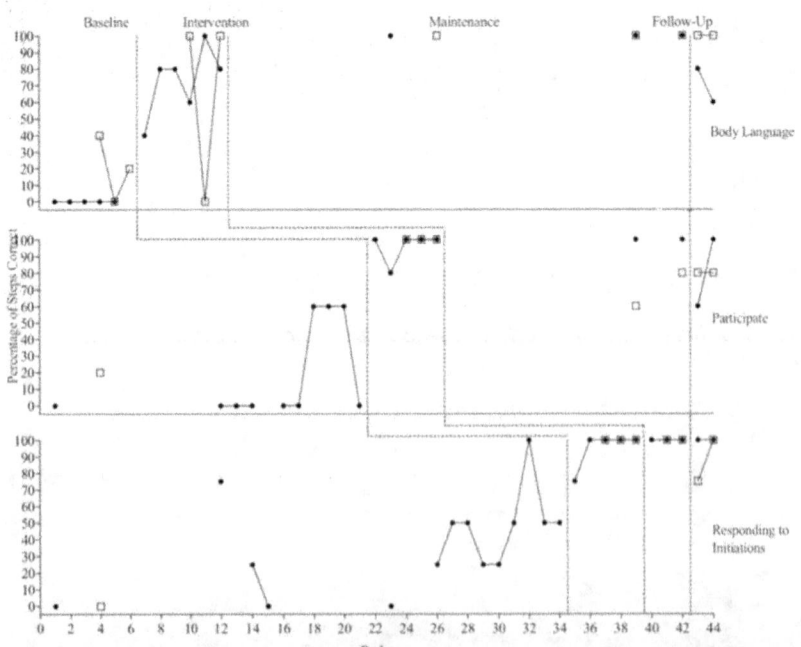

## Stephen

During baseline, Stephen's levels of skill accuracy were generally low to moderate across all skills in both training and generalization settings (Figure 3). Introduction of intervention was associated with increases in skill accuracy for training setting probes across skills. Generalization setting probes demonstrated increases for participation, with minimal change from baseline for body language and responding to initiations. During maintenance and follow-up, skill accuracy was observed to remain at similarly high accuracy levels for training setting probes across skills. Generalization setting data were high for body language and responding to initiations, and moderate for participation. Baseline-corrected tau effect size calculations indicated a range of effects across skills and settings, with small to large effects observed (Table 1).

**Figure 3**
*Percentage of Skill Steps Demonstrated Correctly, Stephen*

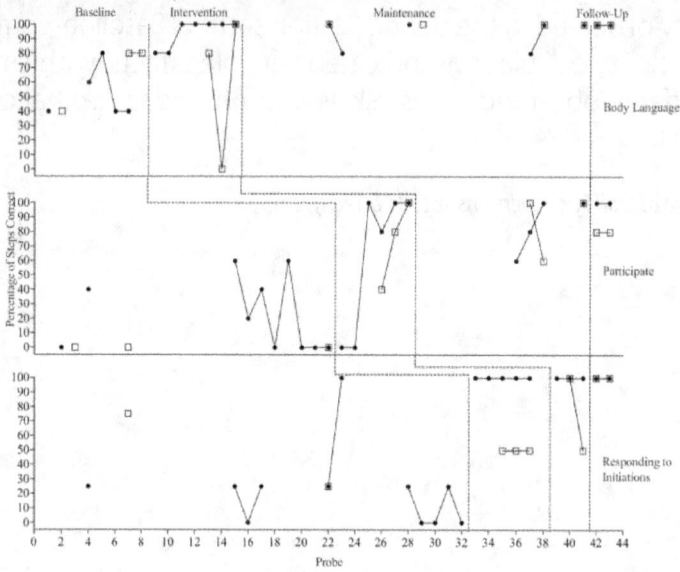

*Note. Filled circles = training setting; open squares = generalization setting.*

## Jay

Jay demonstrated variable levels of skill accuracy during baseline across all three skills for the training setting probes (Figure 4). Baseline levels of skill accuracy for the generalization setting probes were variable across all three skills with moderate to high levels for the body language skill, low levels for the participation skill, and low to high levels for the responding to initiations skill. Introduction of intervention was associated with immediate increases in skill accuracy across all skills in the training setting. Generalization data during the intervention phase also indicated increases in skill accuracy across skills, though a decreasing trend was observed for participation. High levels of skill accuracy continued to be observed during the maintenance phase in the training setting. Generalization data for the maintenance phase were variable, with moderate to high levels of skill accuracy observed across skills. Data during follow-up indicated high levels of skill accuracy in the training setting across skills, with moderate to high levels of skill accuracy observed in the generalization setting. Baseline-corrected tau effect size calculations indicated variable effects, with small to large effects observed across skills and phases for skill accuracy (Table 1).

**Figure 4**
*Percentage of Skill Steps Demonstrated Correctly, Jay*

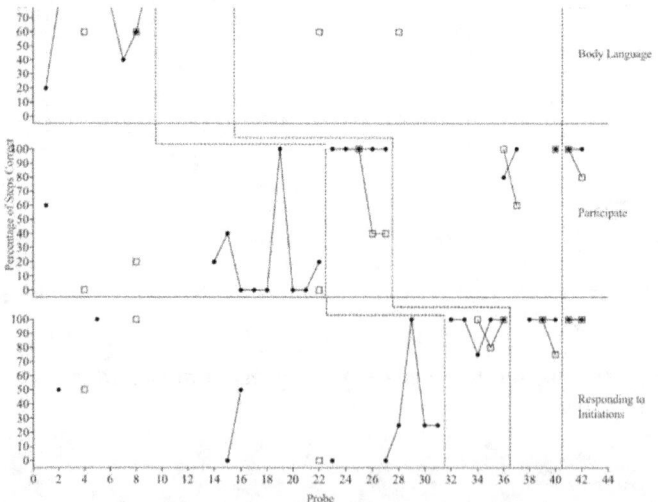

## Bray

During baseline, Bray's levels of skill accuracy were variable with low to moderate levels for all three skills in the training setting (Figure 5). In the generalization setting, baseline levels of skill accuracy were moderate to high for the body language skill, low to moderate for the participation skill, and low for the responding to initiations skill. Introduction of intervention was associated with immediate increases in skill accuracy in the training setting for body language and participation. No data were collected for responding to initiations due to inconsistent attendance. Maintenance data were variable and moderate to high for body language. For participation, training setting data returned to baseline levels and generalization setting data indicated highly accurate skill demonstration. During follow-up, training setting data were high for body language and at zero for responding to initiations. No data were collected for participation due to inconsistent attendance. Generalization setting data were high across skills. High levels were observed of responding to initiations although Bray did not receive intervention for this skill. Baseline-corrected tau effect size calculations were variable across skills and phases, with effects ranging from small to large (Table 1).

**Figure 5**
*Percentage of Skill Steps Demonstrated Correctly, Bray*

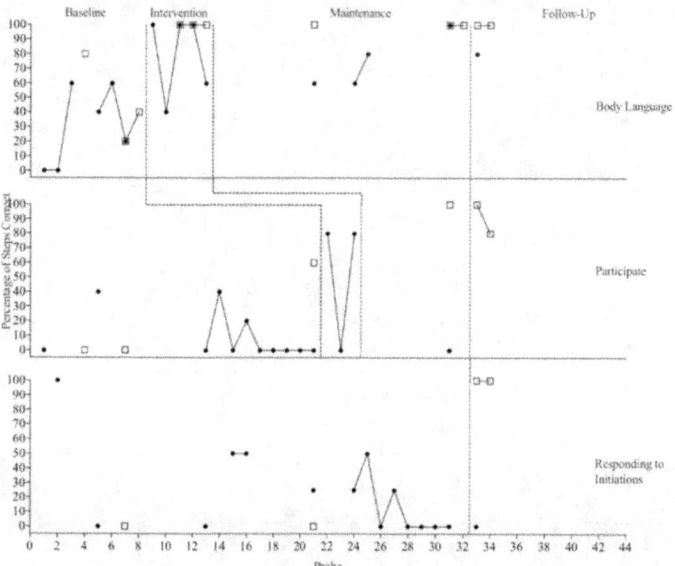

### Joe

Joe demonstrated variable (low to high) levels of skill accuracy during baseline across both the training and generalization setting probes for the body language skill, and also during the training setting probes for the responding to initiations skill (Figure 6). However, for the generalization setting probes for the responding to initiations skill, level of skill accuracy reached mastery levels. Levels of skill accuracy for the participation skill were low across baseline in both the training and generalization setting. For all skills, reductions in variability and increases in skill accuracy were observed in both training and generalization settings. Maintenance data were only collected for body language and participation, with body language skill accuracy being maintained from intervention and participation demonstrating a decrease in skill accuracy. For all skills, follow-up data were associated with high levels of skill accuracy in both training and generalization settings. Baseline-corrected tau effect size calculations indicated small to very large effects across skills and phases (Table 1).

**Figure 6**
*Percentage of Skill Steps Demonstrated Correctly, Joe*

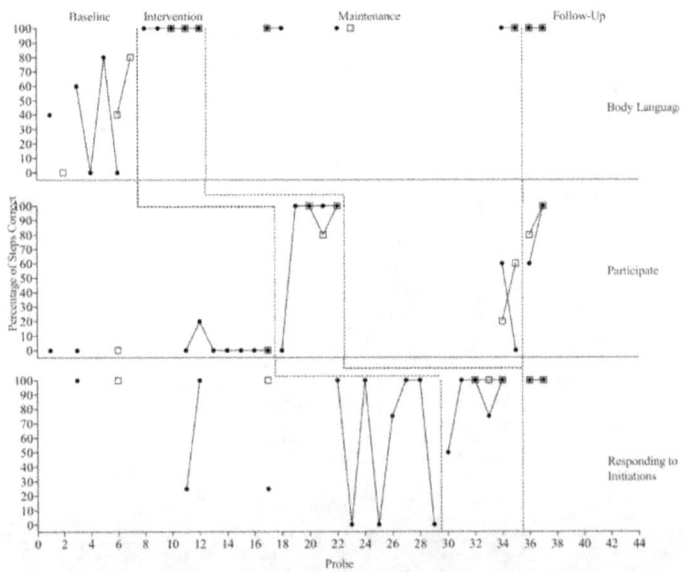

## Matthew

Matthew demonstrated variable levels of skill accuracy during the baseline phase across all skills in both training and generalization settings (Figure 7). Intervention resulted in immediate increases in skill accuracy across skills in both training and generalization settings. During maintenance, skill accuracy was observed to increase in variability for body language and participation, though accuracy remained above baseline levels. Skill accuracy for responding to initiations remained at high levels. No follow-up data were collected due to inconsistent attendance. Baseline-corrected tau effect size calculations were variable across skills and conditions, with small to very large effects for all skills across intervention and maintenance phases for skill accuracy (Table 1).

*Figure 7*

*Percentage of Skill Steps Demonstrated Correctly, Matthew*

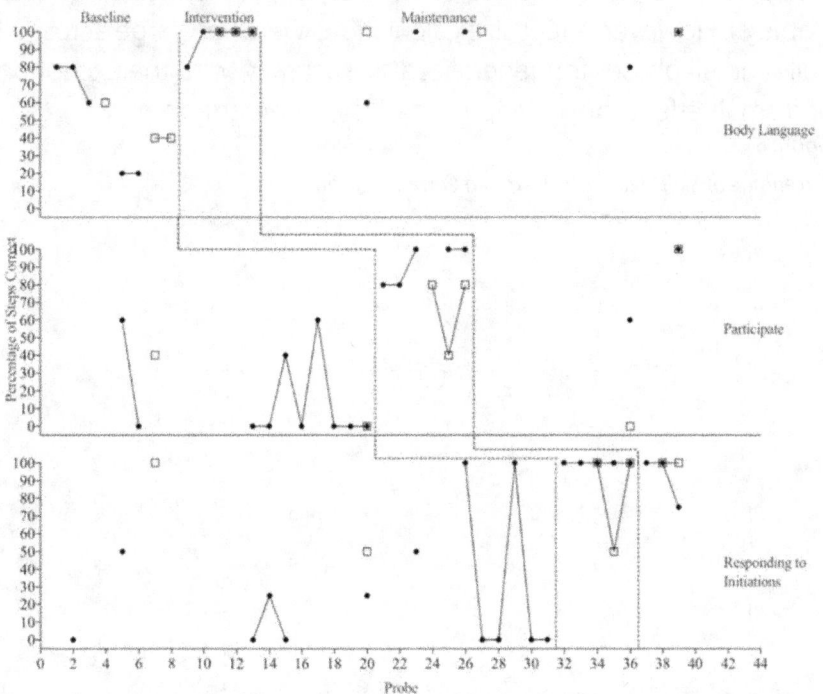

**Note.** Filled circles = training setting; open squares = generalization setting.

## Kevin

During baseline, Kevin demonstrated variable, low to moderate levels of skill accuracy across all skills in both the training and generalization settings (Figure 8). Upon introduction to intervention, levels of skill accuracy for body language remained at low levels for one probe in the training setting and then increased for the remainder of the intervention phase, and skill accuracy was high in the generalization setting. For participation, levels of skill accuracy were initially low before increasing during the last two probes. Levels of skill accuracy were low in the generalization setting. Intervention data for responding to initiations was high in training and generalization settings. Similar levels and patterns of data were observed during the maintenance and follow-up phases across skills and settings. Baseline-corrected tau effect size calculations indicated small to moderate effects for all skills across all phases (Table 1). However, effect size calculations were very large across all skills and all phases for generalized skill acuracy, with the exception of a small effect for participation in the intervention.

**Figure 8**

*Percentage of Skill Steps Demonstrated Correctly, Kevin*

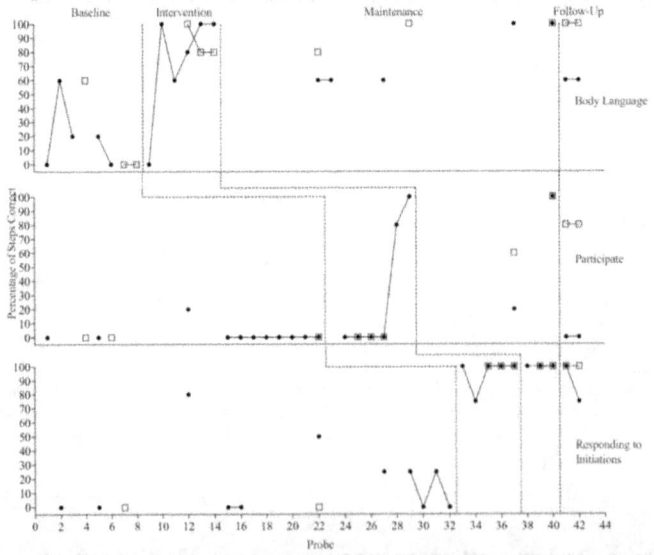

*Table 2*
*Baseline-Corrected Tau Effect Size Calculations*

|  |  | Skill Accuracy | | | Generalized Skill Accuracy | | |
| --- | --- | --- | --- | --- | --- | --- | --- |
|  |  | Body Language | Participate | Responding to Initiations | Body Language | Participate | Responding to Initiations |
| Landon | | | | | | | |
|  | Intervention | 0.76 | 0.49 | 0.58 | 0.91 | 0.00 | 1.00 |
|  | Maintenance | 0.68 | 0.44 | 0.69 | 0.97 | 0.89 | 1.00 |
|  | Follow-up | 0.63 | 0.33 | 0.23 | 0.87 | 0.00 | 0.89 |
| Lance | | | | | | | |
|  | Intervention | 0.85 | 0.82 | 0.63 | 0.37 | 1.00 | 1.00 |
|  | Maintenance | 1.00 | 0.70 | 0.57 | 0.87 | 0.82 | 1.00 |
|  | Follow-up | 0.95 | 0.61 | 0.50 | 0.82 | 1.00 | 0.82 |
| Stephen | | | | | | | |
|  | Intervention | 0.79 | 0.40 | 0.74 | 0.10 | 0.87 | 0.00 |
|  | Maintenance | 0.78 | 0.69 | 0.65 | 0.93 | 0.91 | 0.41 |
|  | Follow-up | 0.77 | 0.61 | 0.58 | 0.87 | 1.00 | 0.89 |
| Jay | | | | | | | |
|  | Intervention | 0.53 | 0.72 | 0.59 | 0.71 | 0.83 | 0.48 |
|  | Maintenance | 0.65 | 0.59 | 0.56 | 0.17 | 0.83 | 0.41 |
|  | Follow-up | 0.59 | 0.56 | 0.49 | 0.29 | 0.82 | 0.62 |
| Bray | | | | | | | |
|  | Intervention | 0.61 | 0.45 | * | 0.87 | * | * |
|  | Maintenance | 0.66 | 0.17 | * | 0.87 | 0.78 | * |
|  | Follow-up | 0.56 | * | 0.11 | 0.82 | 0.82 | 1.00 |
| Joe | | | | | | | |
|  | Intervention | 0.86 | 0.75 | 0.20 | 0.87 | 0.87 | 0.00 |
|  | Maintenance | 0.86 | 0.43 | | 0.87 | 0.89 | * |
|  | Follow-up | 0.73 | 0.82 | 0.32 | 0.82 | 0.89 | 0.00 |
| Matthew | | | | | | | |
|  | Intervention | 0.78 | 0.80 | 0.65 | 0.91 | 0.72 | 0.17 |
|  | Maintenance | 0.59 | 0.62 | 0.52 | 0.91 | 0.22 | 0.58 |
|  | Follow-up | * | * | * | * | * | * |
| Kevin | | | | | | | |
|  | Intervention | 0.56 | 0.33 | 0.73 | 0.83 | 0.00 | 1.00 |
|  | Maintenance | 0.73 | 0.79 | 0.69 | 0.83 | 0.93 | 1.00 |
|  | Follow-up | 0.63 | 0.12 | 0.55 | 0.87 | 1.00 | 1.00 |

*Note. Effect sizes scores below .2 are considered small, between .2 and .6 are considered moderate, between .6 and .8 are considered large, and above .8 are considered very large (Vannest & Ninci, 2015). Very large effect scores are in bold. Asterisk indicates data was not available.*

## Social Validity

Upon completion of the study, the URP-IR and the CIRP were completed by the teacher and seven of the student participants to assess their acceptance of the intervention package. Questions on both the URP-IR and CIRP were based on 6-point Likert scales ranging from 1 (strongly disagree) to 6 (strongly agree). The teacher reported consistently high scores on the URP-IR across all six factors, including acceptability (M = 5.78), understanding (M = 5.67), home-school collaboration (M = 5.33), feasibility (M = 5), system climate (M = 5.8), and system support (M = 4.67). These scores are interpreted as an indication that the teacher found the intervention components acceptable, easy to understand, and feasible to implement with her class. Although she indicated that collaboration with the students' home was important, this was not a component of the intervention. As for the CIRP, all participants' scores indicated that they found the intervention moderately to highly acceptable (M = 4.84; R = 3.67- 6.0). Matthew was absent the day the CIRP was completed.

## Discussion

The current study sought to evaluate the effects of a TIP implemented in a naturalistic setting (i.e., recess) on the acquisition of social skills of students with special education classifications of autism and developmental delays. Overall, increases in percentages of skill acquisition were observed during implementation of TIP across most participants and skills in both training and generalization phases. However, substantial variability was noted across participants related to maintaining skill acquisition during maintenance and follow-up phases in both the training and generalization settings.

As a secondary measure to evaluate TIP effectiveness, baseline-corrected tau was used to calculate effect sizes across phases. Results indicate moderate to very large effect sizes for body language in the training setting, with a range of small to very large effects in the generalization setting. Effect sizes for participation ranged from small to very large effects in both the training and generalization settings. Lastly, effect sizes ranged from small to very large effects in both the training and generalization setting for responding to initiations. Social validity was also assessed, and results suggested that the participants found TIP to be moderately to highly acceptable. Further, the teacher noted consistently high scores across all factors on the URP-IR, suggesting an overall positive perception of the intervention.

Previous research has suggested that social skills interventions should be implemented within more naturalistic contexts (Gresham et al., 2001) as a means to promote generalization of skill acquisition. The current study extends the literature base by evaluating a TIP implemented within a recess setting. Though the results were not as desirable as intended, particularly in relation to maintenance and generalization of skill acquisition, the findings are still meaningful in that they may inform future practice in the context of social skills teaching procedures for students with autism and developmental delays. Specifically, additional procedures may need to be incorporated to ensure maintenance and generalization of social skill acquisition for some students.

Several factors that may have contributed to these findings should be considered. First, the social skills group consisted of a relatively large number of students (i.e., eight), whereas most groups consist of three to five students. The current group was larger because every student in the class participated. The number of students within the group may have impacted students' likelihood to attend during sessions since more opportunities for distractions were available. Additionally, the frequency with which the intervention was implemented may not have been sufficient. Recommendations indicate that social skills interventions should be implemented at a high dosage (Bellini et al., 2007; Gresham et al., 2001); however, the duration of current intervention sessions were relatively short (i.e., approximately 35 minutes). The rationale for the brevity of sessions was a means to promote feasibility of intervention implementation. However, based on lack of maintenance of skill acquisition, more exposure and practice may have been beneficial for these participants. Lastly, the participants demonstrated relatively low levels of cognitive and language abilities which may have contributed to current findings. Previous research has indicated that these factors can impact outcomes of social skills interventions (Kasari et al., 2006).

## Limitations

Limitations must be considered when interpreting current results. First, it is unclear if the target skills were developmentally appropriate for the current participants based on their language abilities. Though some of these skills (e.g., body language) were nonverbal in nature, others (e.g., participation and responding to initiations) may have been too advanced given students' current behavioral repertoires. The current study utilized teacher interview to identify target skills; however, this may have not been a specific enough assessment procedure. Future research should incorporate a multimodal assessment approach that considers the students' cognitive and language abilities to best identify skills that correspond to their developmental level.

Another limitation is the potential impact of carryover effects. Given the nature of skill acquisition and similarity between some of the task analyses, there was likely some previous exposure and learning by participants prior to intervention for the subsequent skill. For instance, body language and participation have two discrete steps that are identical. It is likely that students learned these steps during the body language intervention phase, which then carried over to the participation skill and thus impacted the internal validity of the study. This should also be noted for the first step of responding to initiations and the entirety of the task analysis for body language. The pre-exposure or learning occurring prior to the specific skill intervention may also explain the substantial increase in responding to initiations that was observed for Bray. More specifically, Bray did not receive intervention for responding to initiations, but substantial increases in skill acquisition in both the recess and classroom setting were observed, which may be attributed to carryover effects.

## Conclusion

Social and communication deficits can lead to a plethora of undesirable outcomes (Garrison-Harrell et al., 1997; Locke et al., 2013; McConnell, 2002) therefore, it is important to identify strategies to support social skill development. TIP is an evidence-based strategy that has been shown to increase skill acquisition for students with developmental disabilities. (Leaf et al., 2009; Leaf et al., 2010). The purpose of the current study was to evaluate a TIP implemented in a naturalistic setting (i.e., recess). Overall, the findings suggest a TIP implemented in a naturalistic setting may be an effective way to increase skill acquisition for students with autism and developmental delays. However, future researchers should consider additional strategies to strengthen maintenance and generalization of skill acquisition as well as multimodal assessment procedures to better identify target skills.

## References

American Psychiatric Association. (2013). *Diagnostic and statistical manual of mental disorders* (5th ed.). American Psychiatric Publishing.

Bedlington, M. M., Solnick, J. V., Schumaker, J. B., Braukmann, C. J., Kirigin, K. A., & Wolf, M. M. (1978). Evaluating group homes: The relationship between parenting behaviors and delinquency. In *American Psychological Association Convention, Toronto, Ontario*.

Bellini, S., Peters, J. K., Benner, L. & Hopf, A. (2007). A meta-analysis of school-based social skills interventions for children with autism spectrum disorders. *Remedial and Special Education, 28*, 153-162.

Chafouleas, S. M., Briesch, A. M., Nuegebauer, S. R., & Riley-Tillman, T. C. (2011). *Usage Rating Profile- Intervention (Revised)*. University of Connecticut.

Cooper, J. O., Heron, T. E., Heward, W. L. (2019). *Applied Behavior Analysis 3rd Edition*. Pearson Education.

Dawson, G. (2013). Early intensive behavioral interventions appears beneficial for young children with autism spectrum disorders. *The Journal of Pediatrics, 162*, 1080-1081.

Garrison-Harrell, L., Kamps, d., & Kravits, T. (1997). The effects of peer networks on social-communicative behaviors for students with autism. *Focus on Autism and Other Developmental Disabilities, 12*, 241-255.

Gresham, F. M., Sugai, G., & Horner, R. H. (2001). Interpreting outcomes of social skills training for students with higher-incidence disabilities. *Teaching Exceptional Children, 67*, 331-344. Individuals with Disabilities Education Act, 20 U.S.C. § 300.8 (2004).

Kasari, C., Freeman, S., Paparella, T. (2006). Joint attention and symbolic play in young children with autism: A randomized controlled intervention study. *Journal of Child Psychology and Psychiatry, 47,* 611-620.

Kasari, C., Gulsrud, A. C., Wong, C., Kwon, S., & Locke, J. (2010). Randomized controlled caregiver mediated joint engagement intervention for toddlers with autism. *Journal of Autism and Developmental Disorders, 40*(9), 1045-1056.

Leaf, J. B., Taubman, M., Bloomfield, S., Palos-Refuse, L., Leaf, R., McEachin, J., Oppenheim, M. L. (2009). Increasing social skills and prosocial behavior for three children diagnosed with autism through the use of a teaching package. *Research in Autism Spectrum Disorders, 3,* 275-298.

Leaf, J. B., Dotson, W. H., Oppenheim, M. L., Sheldon, J. B., & Sherman, J. A. (2010). The effectiveness of a group teaching interaction procedure for teaching social skills to young children with pervasive developmental disorder. *Research in Autism Spectrum Disorders, 4,* 186-198.

Leaf, J. B., Townley-Cochran, D., Taubman, M., Cihon, J. H., Oppenheim-Leaf, M. L., Kassardjian, A., Leaf, R., McEachin, J., & Galensky Pentz, T. (2015). The teaching interaction procedure and behavior skills training for individuals diagnosed with autism spectrum disorder: A review and commentary. *Review Journal of Autism and Developmental Disorders, 2,* 402-413.

Locke, J., Kasari, C., Rotheram-Fuller, E., Kretzmann, M., & Jacobs, J. (2013). Social network changes over the school year among elementary school-aged children with and without autism spectrum disorder. *School Mental Health, 5,* 38-47.

McConnell, S. (2002). Interventions to facilitate social interactions for young children with autism: Review of available research and recommendations for educational intervention and future research. *Journal of Autism and Developmental Disorders, 32,* 351-372.

Minkin, N., Braukman, C. J., Minkin, B. L., Timbers, G. D., Timbers, B. J., Fixsen, D. L., et al. (1976). The social validation and training of conversational skills. *Journal of Applied Behavior Analysis, 9,* 127-139.

Neimy, H., Pelaez, M., Carrow, J., Monlux, K., & Tarbox, J. (2017). Infants at risk of autism and developmental disorders: *Establishing early social skills. Behavioral Development Bulletin, 22,* 6-22.

Newborg, J. (2005). *Batelle Developmental Inventory, Second Edition.* Itasca, IL: Riverside Publishing.

Roid, G. H. (2003). *Stanford Binet Intelligence Scales, Fifth Edition,* Technical Manual. Itasca, IL: Riverside Publishing.

Tarlow, K. R. (2017). An improved rank correlation effect size statistic for single-case designs: Baseline corrected *Tau. Behavior Modification, 41,* 427-467.

Witt, J. C., & Elliot, S. N. (1985). Acceptability of classroom intervention strategies. In T. R. Kratochwill (Ed.), *Advances in School Psychology, 4,* 251-288. Erlbaum.

# An Intervention Targeting Academic and Behavioral Skill Deficits in Early Childhood: A Case-Study

*Kayla Bates-Brantley, Mallie Donald, Jasmine Sorrell, Meredith Staggers, Rylee McHenry, and Sarah Wright Harry*

## Abstract

Early literacy skills are considered prerequisites for early learners to eventually become effective readers (Storch & Whitehurst, 2002). Increasing early literacy skills is often the goal of teachers and schools, but skill acquisition can be hindered due to the bidirectional relationship between behavior difficulties and academic skill deficits. To compound this struggle, there is limited research available on the use of behavioral interventions that exist in conjunction with early academic interventions (Volpe et al., 2012). The goal of the current study was to pilot three emerging early literacy interventions: Fluency Letter Wheel; Letter Flash; and I Do, We Do, You Do. All three interventions were pulled from the Florida Center for Reading Research (FCRR), and target letter sound fluency (LSF). The second objective of this study was to examine an early academic intervention in conjunction with behavior management techniques (i.e., reinforcement and differential attention). One 7-year-old student with a history of academic and behavioral difficulties was examined across 13 individual academic sessions. A brief experimental analysis (BEA) was utilized within an alternating treatments design to identify the most effective academic intervention. A changing criterion design was then used after the I do, We do, You do intervention emerged as the most effective academic intervention. Results indicated that this intervention had moderate effects for increasing skill acquisition. In addition, skill acquisition of LSF was noted to increase from a frustrational range to a grade level instructional range during intervention implementation. Limitations, implications, and future directions of this research are discussed.

**Keywords:** *academic intervention, early childhood, early literacy, skill deficit, performance deficit*

## An Early Childhood Intervention Targeting Academic and Behavioral Skill Deficits

Over the past few decades, literature has documented the complicated transactional relationship between students' academic skill deficits and behavioral difficulties (i.e., performance deficits; Hinshaw, 1992; Kuchle et al., 2015; Marguin & Loeber, 1996; Nelson et al., 2004). An individual exhibits a skill deficit when they are unable to complete a given task because they do not possess the necessary skillset. On the other hand, a performance deficit is when an individual possesses the skills needed to complete a task but fails to exhibit these skills due to some internal or external variables (Eckert et. al., 2002). While the etiology of these problems is not always clear, research has suggested that academic and behavior problems occur in tandem for 50-80% of students (Benner et al., 2010).

Research evaluating the correlation between on-task behaviors and skill acquisition has reported a common theme: solely targeting behavioral skill deficits does little to improve academic performance (Daly et al., 2002; Duhon et al., 2004; Gickling & Armstrong, 1978). Other studies have noted that when skill deficits and behavioral problems coincide, skill acquisition is often dramatically slowed or, in severe cases, nonexistent if the behavioral problems are not addressed (Nelson et al., 2004). Gilbertson et al. (2008) demonstrated this concept by comparing the effects of contingent reinforcement of on-task behaviors to contingent reinforcement of on-task behaviors in conjunction with a math fluency intervention. They found that, across four elementary students referred for both academic and behavior problems, contingent reinforcement with the math fluency instruction yielded the highest increases for both math fluency and on-task behaviors. This example emphasizes the importance of incorporating evidence-based interventions that provide both behavior and academic support.

Other examples of successful interventions for students with both behavior and academic concerns have been documented. For example, Cook et al. (2012) examined the relative effectiveness of a behavioral intervention alone and a combined behavioral and academic intervention for increasing reading fluency and decreasing behavioral concerns with six middle school students. Their results indicated that, across all six students, the combined intervention was most effective for increasing reading fluency rate and decreasing behavioral difficulties. More recently, Gettinger et al. (2021) highlighted the need for integrated academic-behavior interventions as the demands on educators increase and resources decrease for most American schools. Gettinger and colleagues' approach entitled Academic and Behavior Combined Support outlined ten steps (i.e., expectations, goal setting, modeling, repeated practice, prompting, feedback, error correction, graphing, rewards, and programmed generalization) that educators should use when elementary students fall below benchmarking standards for reading fluency (Gettinger et al., 2021). Like many other comprehensive approaches, support for Academic and Behavior Combined Support has been documented, but peer-reviewed literature replicating the success of such integrated practices is limited. There is even less documented support for the use of academic-behavioral interventions for early childhood populations.

## Importance of Academic and Behavioral Support in Early Childhood Education

Early childhood education, defined as preschool through third grade, is a critically important period for children's educational trajectory. It is well established that early literacy proficiency is a leading mediating factor linked to positive long-term educational outcomes (Bakken et al., 2017; Gullo, 2013). As a child progresses through school, skills continue to build upon previously taught material, and they are expected to be a proficient reader by the third grade (Musen, 2010). The shift from "learning to read" to "reading to learn" often becomes problematic for children who do not have foundational literacy skills, such as letter-sound blending and reading fluency (Musen, 2010). Research conducted with young children has found that struggles with early literacy skills can be predictors of later reading difficulty (Juel, 1988; Scanlon & Vellutino, 1996; Willson & Hughes, 2009). As such, there is clearly a need for research that examines early literacy interventions. A combination approach that utilizes both an academic intervention and behavioral supports would be ideal practice, especially in early childhood environments. While an argument can be made that a combination approach would be useful for children of all ages, young children's academic deficits are often masked as behavioral difficulties such as noncompliance when presented with instructions to complete academic task demands. Unfortunately, combined academic-behavior interventions that target early literacy are often not utilized for a number of reasons (e.g., time, resources, staff, etc.). Increasing the literature with regard to evidence-based early literacy interventions, specifically those that utilize a combined academic and behavior approach, could potentially remove barriers that are hindering their utilization in schools.

While it is well understood that early literacy skills are cornerstone behaviors for future proficient reading, gaps still exist in evidence-based early literacy interventions (Storch et al., 2002). One resource that has attempted to bridge the gap between academic interventions and evidence-based practices is The Florida Center for Reading Research (FCRR). The FCRR is a free online resource designed to provide educators and other support staff with one-on-one and small-group activities for students who struggle with reading. The website outlines specific skills for each grade level (i.e., prekindergarten through fifth grade) that are associated with the

"The Big Five" reading components. These five skills (i.e., phonemic awareness, phonics, fluency, vocabulary, and comprehension) were identified by the National Reading Panel as the most essential skills required to be a successful reader (National Reading Panel [NRP], 2000). Because the FCRR is organized both by grade level and the Big Five skills, educators can select activities based on students' unique performance levels. Each activity includes a resource guide that describes the objective, materials needed, and instructions. Most activities include printable materials as well as data collection sheets to record student progress. While most of the activities outlined on the FCRR's website are based on and/or use components of evidence-based practices (e.g., direct instruction, repeated practice, visual stimuli, prompts, feedback, etc.), no peer-reviewed studies have specifically demonstrated their effectiveness. It is evident that this free resource provides an abundant amount of guidance to struggling readers; however, the FCRR's early literacy resources require empirical examination and replication.

## Purpose of the Current Study

The current case study sought to combine evidence-based behavioral interventions with an early literacy reading intervention in order to expand the knowledge of this process while addressing the needs of the individual participant. It is well-accepted that early intervention, whether behavioral or academic in nature, is fundamental to long-term student outcomes (e.g., Reinke et al., 2009; National Reading Panel, 2000). By combining academic and behavioral supports, the researchers hypothesized that the participant would perform at a more optimal level across both academic and behavioral domains. The study had two goals: (1) to utilize a brief experimental analysis (BEA) within an alternating treatments design to evaluate three different FCRR letter sound interventions and their effectiveness at increasing phonic fluency, and (2) to implement a token economy with a goal-setting component to address performance deficits identified during baseline.

## Method

**Participant and Setting**

The study included one 7-year-old, African American female who will be referred to as Ann throughout this paper. Ann attended a small private school in a middle-class, rural town in the Southeastern United States. Ann's school had approximately 223 students enrolled in grades pre-kindergarten-12. No demographic data was provided for students enrolled. Ann's parents and teachers reported that Ann was below age/grade level in early literacy and numeracy skills, which prevented her from advancing to higher-order academic skills. These deficits also led to Ann's retention in kindergarten. While Ann was receiving no formal academic support through an individualized educational plan, she did stay after school two days per week for additional tutoring services. In addition to tutoring, her parents sought out additional services through the community, and she received reading interventions twice a week for one hour through a local non-profit agency. The non-profit agency was sponsored through grant funding and utilized an Orton Gillingham-based program designed to teach reading and spelling. Despite receiving services for a year and a half, Ann made little progress beyond identifying letters. Data reported by the local non-profit agency indicated that Ann was fluent in letter identification, but progress monitoring scores were inconsistent due to behavioral challenges. When this study was conducted, Ann was awaiting a clinical comprehensive psychoeducational evaluation to address parental concerns regarding learning and attention difficulties in home and school settings.

Ann was referred for intensive summer academic services provided by a Southeastern university clinic by her parents and the local non-profit agency. The clinic served school-aged children in the local community who presented with academic skill deficits across reading, math, writing, and spelling. All clinical services were implemented by doctoral or specialist-level school psychology students. Services included a comprehensive academic assessment followed by individual intervention sessions. Academic intervention sessions occurred for 1 hour per day Monday-Thursday for four weeks. When Ann began services, she had just completed her second year of kindergarten and had been promoted to first grade, although per parent report, the school did not feel that she had mastered kindergarten material. Ann's evaluation and intervention services occurred across 13 clinic sessions within a 4-week period. Academic intervention sessions were run by a female doctoral school psychology graduate student (i.e., clinician) and supervised by an upper-level graduate student and credentialed faculty member.

**Dependent Variable and Data Collection**

To identify Ann's current level of academic functioning, the clinician administered the AIMSweb curriculum-based measurement early literacy benchmarking probes and focused on letter identification, letter sounds, nonsense words, and word segmentation at the kindergarten and first grade levels. Three probes were administered for letter identification, letter sounds, nonsense words, and word segmentation to identify Ann's current instructional level. Letter sounds correct per minute (LSCPM) was selected as the dependent variable of the current study. To collect LSCPM, 1-minute LSF AIMSweb probes were administered. All probes were administered by a doctoral level school psychology graduate student. To score LSCPM, the number of correct letter sounds identified within a minute was subtracted from the number of incorrect responses (Shinn & Shinn, 2002).

**Interobserver Agreement and Treatment Integrity**

LSCPM data were recorded by a doctoral level school psychology graduate student who received prior training in AIMSweb scoring procedures. The clinician that served as the data collector across benchmarking served as the primary data collector for the intervention procedures. Additional observers (doctoral level graduate students and graduate supervisors) served as independent raters and collected interobserver agreement (IOA) and treatment integrity data.

IOA data were collected across BEA and intervention sessions. The total percentage of observed agreement was calculated by dividing the smaller number of LSCPM into the larger number of LSCPM and multiplying it by 100 (Joslyn & Vollmer, 2020). LSCPM IOA was collected in-session by secondary observers who listened to Ann enunciate each sound and individually scored the answers while the clinician administered each probe. IOA data were collected for 33% of all BEA sessions with 100% agreement. IOA data were collected across 29% of all intervention sessions, with a mean agreement of 97% (range = 90%-100%).

Treatment integrity data were collected to ensure that the clinician followed the FCRR activity, token economy procedures and goal-setting procedures. A checklist for each intervention was formatted based on the FCRR guidelines. See the FCRR website for specific steps included on treatment integrity checklists. To collect treatment integrity, a secondary observer sat-in and observed 33% of all BEA sessions and 23% of intervention phases. Treatment integrity was scored by dividing the scored number of steps completed by the total possible number of steps, which was then multiplied by 100. This number (i.e., steps per intervention) varied with the intervention being implemented. Mean treatment integrity across the BEA and intervention phases was 100%.

**Experimental Design**

BEA procedures within an alternating treatments design were used to identify the most effective intervention for improving LSCPM. The BEA procedures within an alternating treatments design allowed for the rapid assessment of different intervention strategies to determine the best fit for the individual student (Ollendick et al., 1980). A changing criterion design was then utilized to evaluate the effectiveness of the intervention identified via the BEA. A changing criterion design involves approximate increases in the target goal and the offering immediate reinforcement when the goal is met (Hartmann & Hall, 1976).

## Procedures
### Benchmarking and Baseline Data Collection
Baseline data were collected during benchmarking. During the benchmarking process, no intervention was provided. Three benchmarking probes were administered for letter identification, letter sounds, nonsense words, and word segmentation. Benchmarking provided data for clinicians to utilize when selecting a starting point for Ann's instructional skill level. Across benchmarking, Ann scored below the tenth percentile for spring kindergarten norms, indicating she had overall deficits in early literacy skills. According to the AIMSweb manual, when interpreting norms, scores below the 25th percentile (i.e., 1st-24th) are at a "frustrational" level, scores that fall between the 25th-75th percentiles are considered at an "instructional" level, and scores above the 75th percentile (i.e., 76th-100th) are at a "mastery" level. Because Ann's scores fell below the tenth percentile, researchers concluded that she was at frustrational level across all benchmarked skills. When Ann was presented with the probes, her compliance to the task demand significantly decreased and impacted her performance on the probes. Due to behaviors displayed during the benchmarking process, Ann's results were interpreted with caution. Ann's behavioral concerns included work refusal, verbal protests, inattention, and limited effort.

Typical AIMSweb procedural guidelines recommend starting Ann's intervention with the initial skill (i.e., letter identification) due to her low performance. However, it was decided to start the intervention with letter sounds (i.e., Letter Sound Fluency) because records from previous academic interventions at the local non-profit agency indicated that Ann exhibited mastery of letter identification when behavioral concerns did not occur. These records also noted that performance deficits were a consistent barrier for accurate progress monitoring of her true ability. Furthermore, Ehri (2005) stated that students must first learn to map sounds to letters before reading can begin, and Ann's parents were persistent in wanting Ann to read. Therefore, a clinical decision was made in conjunction with Ann's parents to target LSF. More specifically, LSCPM was selected as the dependent variable. Once benchmarking data were complete, the BEA procedures within an alternating treatments design began.

**BEA**

The benefit of utilizing a BEA is that it trials numerous intervention options and ultimately exposes the student to intervention components that the researcher may not have considered. It also eliminates the "guess and hope" mentality behind intervention selection and provides a data-based rationale as to why a given intervention was selected (Wilber & Cushman, 2006). A BEA involves the rapid implementation of multiple interventions across intervention sessions (Eckert et al., 2002). In this study, the rapid nature of the BEA allowed the primary clinician to quickly analyze Ann's performance across three LSF interventions (Letter Flash; I do, We do, You do; and Fluency Letter Wheel) and, ultimately, determine the most effective of the three. Each intervention was presented three times in a randomized order. Randomization occurred by assigning each intervention a number (i.e., 1. Letter Flash; 2. I do, We do, You do; and 3. Fluency Letter Wheel) and then by using a random number generator to determine the order in which they would be presented. A typical clinic visit allowed the clinicians to run four academic sessions. The BEA took three clinic visits to complete. Across BEA interventions, Ann was reminded of the expected behaviors that would be reinforced by a token economy.

**Letter Flash.** This intervention was presented based on guidelines provided by the FCRR. To begin the intervention, the clinician placed a YES and NO card in front of Ann and explained the rules of the intervention. Ann was presented with one letter card at a time and was asked to provide the corresponding letter sound.

All 26 letters across the English language were presented. If Ann answered correctly, the card was placed under YES. If Ann answered incorrectly, the card was placed under NO. All incorrectly answered letters were provided with error correction (i.e. presentation of the correct letter sound) followed by repeated practice until each incorrect letter were answered correctly and placed under YES. Following this intervention, Ann was given a 1-minute LSF probe at the kindergarten level to monitor response to this intervention.

**I do, We do, You do.** This intervention was based on teaching principles outlined by the FCRR. The intervention combined components of scaffold teaching strategies in which the skill was modeled, followed by in-vivo practice with feedback, and ended with independent practice. At the beginning of this intervention, Ann was informed that time would be divided between listening and leading the activity. The clinician first went through each of the 26 letters across the English language while providing Ann with the corresponding letter sound. Then, the clinician and Ann answered each letter sound together. The final phase of this intervention involved Ann saying the letter sounds with feedback provided for any incorrect letter sound. Following this intervention, Ann was given a 1-minute LSF probe at the kindergarten level to determine her current performance.

**Fluency Letter Wheel.** This intervention was presented based on guidelines provided by the FCRR and involved preconstructed letter wheels. Ann was instructed to spin the wheel, wait for the spinner to land on a letter, and then identify the specific letter sound. All 26 letters in the English language were presented on the letter wheel. For each correct answer, Ann received a token that she could place in jar. The clinician offered immediate corrective feedback for incorrect responses. Following this intervention, Ann was given a 1-minute LSF probe at the kindergarten level to determine current performance.

**Token Economy.** To prevent academic performance deficits and disruptive behavior, the clinician implemented a token economy during the BEA. The clinician predetermined that ten tokens were required for Ann to receive access to a designated reinforcer for 2 minutes following the intervention. The token economy would reward Ann for both completing the instructed tasks and for exhibiting expected academic behaviors (i.e., orienting towards clinician, complying with academic task demands, exhibiting active academic engagement). Ann's target behaviors were operationally defined and explained to her prior to beginning the BEA. During the BEA, tokens were given on a fixed ratio (FR1) schedule at the completion of each academic session (i.e., after completing one BEA trial). Following the BEA, the token economy was removed; therefore, Ann was only rewarded for her academic performance for the rest of the study and was no longer rewarded for exhibiting appropriate academic behaviors.

**Goal Setting.** A changing criterion design was utilized to evaluate the effectiveness of I do, We do, You do, identified via the BEA. A goal-setting component was used in conjunction with the academic intervention. The initial criterion was set by increasing mean baseline levels of LSCPM by 5%, and adjustments to the criterion were made when Ann met the goal during three consecutive sessions. Specifically, following the third consecutive trial of meeting the phase's criterion, the subsequent phase's criterion was increased by 5% (Klein et al., 2015). Immediately after each session, Ann's LSCPM was calculated. If Ann met her goal, she received access to a designated reinforcer for 2 minutes following the intervention. These procedures continued until the intervention ended, due to the completion of the intensive summer academic clinic.

**Data Analysis**

Data analysis occurred in two phases. First, BEA data were analyzed by comparing baseline performance to LSCPM across interventions to determine which intervention was the most effective. Second, Ann's LSCPM data were visually analyzed across phases. These data were analyzed to consider changes in the level, trend, variability, immediacy of effect, consistency of data, and overlap of data points (Kratochwill et al., 2013). To determine a quantitative effect of the intervention, data were analyzed using nonoverlap of all pairs (NAP). NAP procedures consider each data point within the research design and calculate the percentage of points that overlap (Parker & Vannest, 2014). The fewer points that overlap, the higher the effect size of the intervention. When evaluating effect sizes using NAP, scores of 0-.65 are considered weak effects, .66-.91 are considered medium effects, and .92-1.00 are considered large effects.

## Results

Visual analysis and NAP effect size analysis were the primary methods for interpreting the effectiveness of each intervention in the BEA and the eventual implementation of I Do, We Do, You Do. Ann's BEA data demonstrated her performance in response to each of the three interventions (Figure 1). A detailed breakdown of the NAP effect sizes across phases indicated a range of .64-.94 (Table 1). Likewise, intervention data following the BEA indicated the effectiveness of I do, We do, You do (Figure 2). Results from the BEA and intervention are described in greater detail below.

**Figure 1**

*Letter Sounds Brief Experimental Analysis Data*

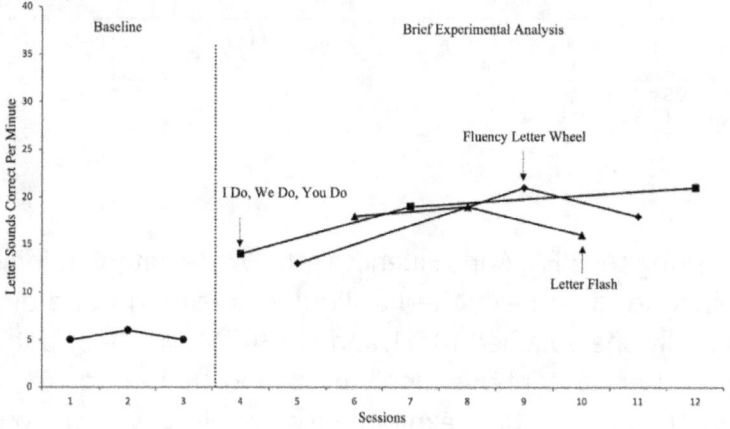

**Figure 2**
*I do, We do, You do: Analysis Data*

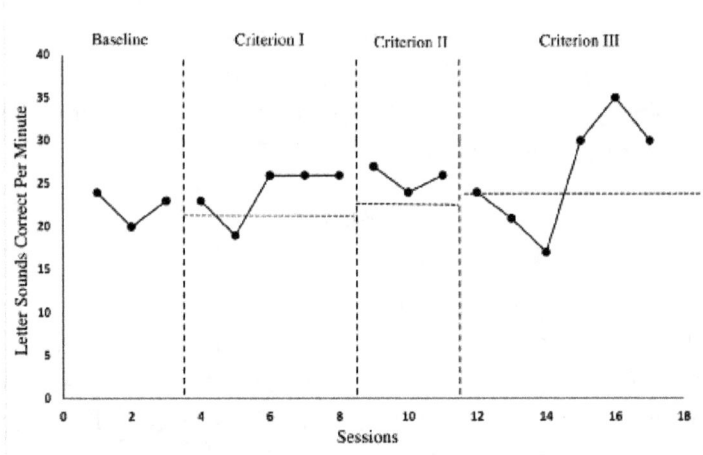

**Table 1**
*Mean Letter Sounds Correct Per Minute and Nonoverlap of All Pairs*

| Baseline Mean of Letter Sounds Correct | First Criterion Intervention Mean of Letter Sounds Correct (NAP) | Second Criterion Mean of Letter Sounds Correct (NAP) | Third Criterion Intervention Mean of Letter Sounds Correct (NAP) |
|---|---|---|---|
| 22.3 | 24.0 (0.700)[b] | 25.67 (0.944)[a] | 26.17 (0.6944)[b] |

[a] Large Effect Size
[b] Medium Effect Size

## BEA

During the BEA, Ann's Fluency Letter Wheel intervention data remained level and exhibited a slightly increasing trend overall. Specifically, she obtained 13, 21, and 18 LSCPM (M = 17.3). Likewise, for the Letter Flash intervention, Ann scored 18, 19, and 16 LSCPM (M = 17.6), and her data exhibited a stable level with an overall increasing trend despite the last data point. Finally, for the I do, We do, You do intervention, Ann obtained an average of 18 LSCPM by identifying 14, 19, and 21 letter sounds correctly for each trial. Based on the data from the BEA, the I do, We do, You do intervention was slightly more effective than the other two interventions. In addition, Ann reported that this intervention was her favorite because it allowed her to assume responsibility and some level of control. Therefore, I do, We do, You do was used for the remainder of the intervention.

**I do, We do, You do Analysis**

During baseline, Ann's scores (M = 22; range = 20 – 24) were at a moderate level, had little variability, and were stable. Once a criterion was set and the intervention began, Ann's first two data points overlapped with baseline but then stabilized to a higher, stable level (M = 24; range = 19 – 26). Her intervention data exhibited a slightly increasing trend at a stable level that was centered around the established criterion. The NAP score for the first criterion was .7 and demonstrated a medium effect size. The second criterion's data exhibited stability at a higher level (M = 25.67; range = 24 – 27) and had a large effect size (NAP = 1.00). Finally, when the third criterion was set, Ann's data initially had a decreasing trend and was lower than in any other phase (M = 26.17; range = 17 – 25). After three data points, however, her data increased to a consistently high level with little variability. Despite its variability, Ann's data had a medium effect for the final criterion when compared with baseline (NAP = .694).

## Discussion

Given that skill acquisition is often hindered by the bidirectional relationship of behavior difficulties and academic skill deficits, the purpose of the current study was two-fold. First, the researchers wanted to evaluate the effectiveness of three emerging early literacy interventions on LSCPM. Second, the current study evaluated the effectiveness of using a goal-setting component in conjunction with an academic intervention to decrease behavioral difficulties that were interfering with academic skill acquisition. More specifically, a token economy followed by a goal-setting component was implemented to address Ann's noncompliance and level of motivation. Researchers hypothesized that if Ann were more compliant, then the academic intervention could more effectively and efficiently target her letter sound identification skill deficits.

Initially, results from AIMSweb benchmarking probes indicated that Ann's LSCPM skills were at a kindergarten frustrational level, and her scores remained low and stable during baseline. During the benchmarking procedures, Ann engaged in work refusal, verbal protests, inattention, and limited effort when presented with letter sound probes. All disruptive behaviors were incompatible with on-task behaviors. A token economy was added to reinforce appropriate academic on-task behaviors before a BEA was implemented. Results from the BEA indicated that, overall, all three interventions were effective at increasing her letter sound identification skills.

While all three interventions resulted in similar levels of LSCPM during the BEA, Ann responded well to interventions that allowed her to assume responsibility and some level of control; thus, the I do, We do, You do intervention was implemented using a changing criterion design and a goal-setting component. The goal-setting component was introduced to increase Ann's motivation to comply with the reading tasks and to increase her performance level to grade level. Contingent upon Ann meeting her goal of LSCPM during each session, she was immediately provided access to her reinforcers (i.e., YouTube videos, games with clinician, or coloring). However, if Ann did not meet her goal, access to reinforcement was not provided. When the changing criterion design was implemented, Ann was consistently engaging in the behaviors required to attend to the reading tasks. Therefore, the token economy was faded out, and reinforcement was only provided contingent upon her academic performance.

Overall, results indicated that Ann's letter sound knowledge increased by 25 sounds. Considering Ann's academic gains across the various intervention phases, the data suggest that providing reinforcement contingent upon meeting performance goals results in a reduction in behavioral challenges. Upon the reduction of her problem behavior, Ann was able to identify letter sounds at a level similar to her same-grade peers by the end of intervention. Since it was implemented with high levels of fidelity, the I do, We do, You do intervention paired with a goal-setting component appeared to be effective for increasing LSCPM and decreasing behavioral difficulties that interfere with academic engagement.

Taken together, these results have important implications regarding interventions aimed at increasing academic and behavioral skills in the educational setting. First, the results of the current study provide further evidence for the efficacy of combining academic and behavioral interventions to enhance student outcomes (Kuchle et al., 2015). While there is evidence that intervening in one area (e.g., reading) will improve the other area (e.g., behavior), the current study used an integrated intervention approach because assessment revealed that Ann exhibited both skill and performance deficits. Additionally, given the evidence of the bidirectional relationship between academic deficits and problem behaviors, a combined intervention approach is likely to be a more efficient method for increasing academic achievement compared to implementing either intervention in isolation (Cook et al., 2012). The current study was conducted over 13 intervention sessions across a 4-week period, and, despite the limited amount of time, gains in Ann's letter sound skill acquisition and fluency were observed. It seems plausible that targeting Ann's behavioral challenges was critical in maximizing the impact of the academic intervention.

## Limitations

While the results indicated positive academic and behavioral outcomes for the participant, several limitations warrant acknowledgement and should be addressed in future research. Perhaps of most significance, the clinician implemented a token economy during the BEA to teach and reinforce appropriate academic behaviors, but no specific data were collected on Ann's behavior. The current study relied on anecdotal data alone regarding the intervention's effectiveness of reducing behavioral difficulties. While it was reported that her appropriate behaviors increased and her academic data indicated gains that were not observed before the addition of the behavioral component, only correlation can be speculated.

It should also be noted that one deviation from standard AIMSweb guidelines was made after the completion of benchmarking. Benchmarking data indicated that Ann was in the frustrational range across all early literacy skills (i.e., letter naming, letter sounds, phoneme segmentation, and nonsense words). Using this data, AIMSweb guidelines would recommend starting with the lowest order skill (letter naming) before processing to high order skills. However, the current study began with letter sounds. This decision was made considering multiple factors, including previous data and anecdotal behavioral data. First, it should be noted that Ann engaged in disruptive behaviors throughout the benchmarking process. These behaviors were incompatible with on-task behaviors and greatly interfered with the implementation of the benchmarking probes. Second, Ann's previous records indicated that performance deficits were a consistent challenge across the 18 months Ann participated in reading interventions with a local community agency. Data were presented that indicated Ann had indeed mastered letter identification. Finally, literature supports that a student must first learn to map sounds to letters before reading can begin and therefore this was a socially valid goal that had the support of Ann's parents and teachers (Ehri, 2005).

While it was hypothesized that Ann presented with a combination of skill and performance deficits, this was not confirmed during the BEA procedures. Specifically, a BEA condition should have been run that directly assessed whether Ann's performance was a skill deficit ("can't do") or performance deficit ("won't do").

It was noted that when the third criterion was implemented, Ann seemed less interested in her previously preferred reinforcers. The clinician offered her an alternative reinforcer to work towards, and there were immediate increases in her academic skill performance. This further confirmed the clinician's hypothesis that Ann presented with a skill deficit in conjunction with performance deficits. Future studies should collect additional behavioral data in conjunction with academic skill acquisition data to evaluate the effectiveness of intervention packages targeting both behavior and academics.

The current study was conducted with one participant in a highly controlled environment where distractions were limited and the student to clinician ratio was one to one. The feasibility of implementing this intervention in the classroom setting where distractions are more frequent and the student to teacher ratio is much higher is unknown. Thus, future research should extend the application of this intervention across a larger sample and in the classroom setting while also examining the feasibility and social validity when it is implemented by teachers.

While these results appear promising in terms of the short-term gains observed in the participant, the emergence of problem behavior may become increasingly apparent when children are presented with increasingly challenging academic tasks. More convincing information on the extent to which the current procedures promote complete acquisition, generalization, and maintenance is warranted, as these components together are likely necessary for sustained benefits and should, therefore, be the focus of future research.

Finally, due to time constraints, the current study took place over a 4-week period in which the I do, We do, You do intervention and the goal-setting component were only implemented over a 2-week period. While the results indicate that the intervention was effective at increasing letter sound acquisition and managing behaviors, data were not collected on the maintenance or generalization of these skills. Therefore, future studies should consider conducting follow-up sessions to assess the extent to which the skills sustain in the absence of intervention. Additionally, future research should assess the extent to which the generalization of skill acquisition and behavioral reductions occur across a range of settings and academic areas.

Overall, the current study demonstrated emergent evidence for the effectiveness of behavioral interventions in conjunction with early academic interventions to increase foundational literacy skills. Considering the lack of peer-reviewed studies examining the effectiveness of integrated intervention approaches for early childhood, future studies should continue to examine the effectiveness and efficiency of a combined approach to target academic and behavioral deficits. Publications that do so would build on the results of the current study. Future research should also examine the effects of a combined approach across a larger, more varied sample to better understand the extent to which results would generalize across various populations, skills, and behavioral profiles.

**References**

Bakken, L., Brown, N., & Downing, B. (2017). Early childhood education: The long-term benefits. *Journal of Research in Childhood Education, 31*(2), 255–269. https://doi.org/10.1080/02568543.2016.1273285

Benner, G. J., Beaudoin, K. M., Chen, P.-Y., Davis, C., & Ralston, N. C. (2010). The impact of intensive positive behavioral supports on the behavioral functioning of students with emotional disturbance: How much does fidelity matter? *Journal of Behavior Assessment and Intervention in Children, 1*(1), 85-100. http://dx.doi.org/10.1037/h0100361

Cook, C., Dart, E., Collins, T., Restori, A., Daikos, C., & Delport, J. (2012). Preliminary study of the confined, collateral, and combined effects of reading and behavioral interventions: Evidence for a transactional relationship. *Behavioral Disorders, 38*(1), 38–56. https://doi.org/10.1177%2F019874291203800104

Daly, E. J. III, Murdoch, A., Lillenstein, L., Webber, L., & Lentz, F. E., Jr. (2002). An examination of methods for testing treatments: Conducting brief experimental analyses of the effects of instructional components on oral reading fluency. *Education and Treatment of Children, 25*, 288–316. http://www.jstor.org/stable/42899707

Duhon, G. J., Noell, G. H., Witt, J. C., Freeland, J. T., Dufrene, B. A., & Gilbertson, D. N. (2004). Identifying academic skill and performance deficits: The experimental analysis of brief assessments of academic skills. *School Psychology Review, 33,* 429 – 443. https://doi.org/10.1080/02796015.2004.12086260

Eckert, T. L., Ardoin, S. P., Daly III, E. J., & Martens, B. K. (2002). Improving oral reading fluency: A brief experimental analysis of combining an antecedent intervention with consequences. *Journal of Applied Behavior Analysis, 35*(3), 271-281. https://doi.org/10.1901/jaba.2002.35-271

Ehri, L. C. (2005). Learning to read words: Theory, findings, and issues. *Scientific Studies of Reading, 9*(2), 167-188. https://doi.org/10.1207/s1532799xssr0902_4

Florida Center for Reading Research. (n.d.). *Kindergarten and first grade*. Retrieved July 9th, 2021, from https://fcrr.org/student-center-activities/kindergarten-and-first-grade

Gettinger, M., Kratochwill, T., Foy, A., & Eubanks, A. (2021). Development and implementation of an integrated academic-behavior intervention. *Intervention in School and Clinic, 0*(0), 1–6. https://doi.org/10.1177%2F10534512211047571

Gilbertson, D., Witt, J. C., Duhon, G., & Dufrene, B. (2008). Using Brief Assessments to Select Math Fluency and On-task Behavior Interventions: An Investigation of Treatment Utility. *Education and Treatment of Children, 31*(2), 167–181. http://www.jstor.org/stable/42899971

Gickling, E. E., & Armstrong, D. L. (1978). Levels of instructional difficulty as related to on-task behavior, task completion, and comprehension. *Journal of Learning Disabilities, 11,* 559–566. https://doi.org/10.1177%2F002221947801100905

Gullo, D.F. (2013). Improving Instructional Practices, Policies, and Student Outcomes for Early Childhood Language and Literacy Through Data-Driven Decision Making. *Early Childhood Education Journal, 41,* 413–421. https://doi.org/10.1007/s10643-013-0581-x

Hartmann, D. P., & Hall, R. V. (1976). The changing criterion design. *Journal of Applied Behavior Analysis, 9*(4), 527-532. https://doi.org/10.1901/jaba.1976.9-527

Hinshaw, S. (1992). Externalizing behavior problems and academic underachievement in childhood and adolescence: Causal relationships and underlying mechanisms. *Psychological Bulletin, 111*(1), 127–155. https://psycnet.apa.org/doi/10.1037/0033-2909.111.1.127

Intervention Central. (n.d.) *Listening passage preview.* Intervention Central. Retrieved July 9, 2021, from https://www.interventioncentral.org/academic-interventions/reading-fluency/listening-passage-preview

Joslyn, P. R., & Vollmer, T. R. (2020). Efficacy of teacher-implemented good behavior game despite low treatment integrity. *Journal of Applied Behavior Analysis, 53*(1), 465-474. https://doi.org/10.1002/jaba.614

Juel, C. (1988). Learning to read and write: A longitudinal study of 54 children from first through fourth grades. *Journal of Educational Psychology, 80*(4), 437-447. https://doi.org/10.1037/0022-0663.80.4.437

Klein, L. A., Houlihan, D., Vincent, J. L., & Panahon, C. J. (2015). Best Practices in Utilizing the Changing Criterion Design. *Behavior analysis in practice, 10*(1), 52–61. https://doi.org/10.1007/s40617-014-0036-x

Kuchle, L., Edmonds, R., Danielson, L., Peterson, A., & Riley-Tillman, T. C. (2015). The next big idea: A framework for integrated academic and behavioral intensive intervention. *Learning Disabilities Research and Practice, 30*(4), 150–158. https://doi.org/10.1111/ldrp.12084

Kratochwill, T. R., Hitchcock, J., Horner, R. H., Levin, J. R., Odom, S. L., Rindskopf, D. M. & Shadish, W. R. (2013). Single-case intervention research design standards. *Remedial and Special Education, 34*(1), 26-38. https://doi.org/10.1177/0741932512452794

Marguin, E., & Loeber, R. (1996). Academic performance and delinquency. *Crime and Justice, 20,* 145–264. https://doi.org/10.1086/449243

Musen, L. (2010). *Early reading proficiency: Leading indicators for education.* Annenberg Institute for School Reform, Brown University. at www.annenberginstitute.org/WeDo/leading_indicators.php.

National Reading Panel (2000). *Teaching children to read: An evidence-based assessment of the scientific research literature on reading and its implications for reading instruction* (National Institute of Health Pub. No. 00-4769). National Institute of Child Health and Human Development.

Nelson, J. R., Benner, G., Lane, K., & Smith, B. (2004). Academic achievement of K-12 students with emotional and behavioral disorders. *Exceptional Children, 71*(1), 59–73. https://doi.org/10.1177%2F001440290407100104

Ollendick, T. H., Matson, J. L., Esveldt-Dawson, K., & Shapiro, E. S. (1980). Increasing spelling achievement: An analysis of treatment procedures utilizing an alternating treatments design. *Journal of Applied Behavior Analysis, 13*(4), 645-654. https://doi.org/10.1901/jaba.1980.13-645

Parker, R. I., & Vannest, K. J. (Eds.). (2014). Non-overlap analysis for single-case research. In T. R. Kratochwill & J. R. Levin (Eds.), *Single-case intervention research: Methodological and statistical advances* (pp. 127–151). American Psychological Association. https://doi.org/10.1037/14376-005

Reinke, W. M., Splett, J. D., Robeson, E. N., & Offutt, C. A. (2009). Combining school and family interventions for the prevention and early intervention of disruptive behavior problems in children: A public health perspective. *Psychology in the Schools, 46*(1), 33-43. https://doi.org/10.1002/pits.20352

*Reviewer Guidance for Use with the Procedures and Standards Handbook*. What Works Clearinghouse. (n.d.). https://ies.ed.gov/ncee/wwc/.

Shinn, M. R., & Shinn, M. M. (2002). *AIMSweb early literacy*. Administration and scoring guide. Pearson.

Scanlon, D. M., & Vellutino, F. R. (1996). Prerequisite Skills, Early Instruction, and Success in First-Grade Reading: Selected Results from a Longitudinal Study. Mental Retardation & *Developmental Disabilities Research Reviews, 2*(1), 54–63. https://doi.org/10.1002/(SICI)1098-2779(1996)2:1<54::AID-MRDD9>3.0.CO;2-X

Storch, S. A., & Whitehurst, G. J. (2002). Oral language and code-related precursors to reading: Evidence from a longitudinal structural model. *Developmental Psychology, 38*(6), 934–947. https://doi.org/10.1037/0012-1649.38.6.934

Volpe, R. J., Young, G. I., Piana, M. G., & Zaslofsky, A. F. (2012). Integrating classwide early literacy intervention and behavioral supports: A pilot investigation. *Journal of positive behavior interventions, 14*(1), 56-64. https://doi.org/10.1177%2F1098300711402591

Wilber, A., & Cushman, T. P. (2006). Selecting effective academic interventions: An example using brief experimental analysis for oral reading. *Psychology in the Schools, 43*(1), 79-84. https://doi.org/10.1002/pits.20131

Willson, V. L., Hughes, J. N. (2009). Who is retained in first grade? A psychosocial perspective. *The Elementary School Journal, 109*(3), 251–266. https://doi.org/10.1086/592306

# Strategies to Promote Positive Mealtime Behavior in Early Childhood

*Hailey E. Ripple, Hallie M. Smith, and Kayla Bates-Brantley*

## Abstract

Picky eating and problem behavior during meals are commonly reported issues among young children, particularly toddlers (Manikam & Perman, 2000). It is estimated that up to 50% of children under the age of 5 experience difficulties during mealtimes (Benjasuwantep et al., 2013). These difficulties may include tantrums when nonpreferred foods are presented, turning their head away from bites, pushing food away, crying, spitting out bites of nonpreferred food, and holding bites in the mouth. Over time, these behaviors can lead to significant limitations in the variety and amount of foods that children consume, thus compromising their growth and development. While there are a variety of reasons a child may engage in these problem behaviors, the food refusal or selectivity often persists after other contributing factors have been resolved (Dobbelsteyn et al., 2005). A behavior analytic approach can be used to address mealtime problem behavior. These interventions are focused on changing aspects of the child's environment and caregiver response in order to change the child's behavior during meals. This approach has been well-evaluated in the literature, and many regard it to be the most effective intervention for treating children's problem behavior during meals (Kerwin, 1999). The scope of this paper was to provide evidence-based behavior analytic recommendations to caregivers, teachers, and other early childhood therapeutic providers. Recommendations provided in this article are applicable to a variety of feeding difficulties that may present in early childhood. While recommendations discussed in this paper have been supported in the literature, research lacks a comprehensive instructional guide of best practices that can be used by providers with limited expertise or experience in feeding concerns.

**Keywords:** *mealtime, early childhood, feeding, behavioral intervention*

## Strategies to Promote Positive Mealtime Behavior in Early Childhood

Picky eating (i.e., food selectivity) and problem behavior during meals are commonly-reported issues among toddlers and young children (Manikam & Perman, 2000). Food selectivity refers to a child being selective about which foods they will eat based on the color, taste, appearance, or texture of the food (Bandini et al., 2010). For example, a child may only eat foods that are orange or brown in color (e.g., cheese, chicken nuggets, macaroni and cheese, Goldfish crackers). Some children may only eat foods that are smoother in texture and do not require chewing (e.g., yogurt, oatmeal, applesauce). Other children may only eat foods if they are prepared a certain way or if they are a certain brand (e.g., only eating chicken nuggets from a specific fast-food restaurant or eating only one brand of frozen pizza). Estimates of the prevalence of picky eating among children are inconsistent. Studies have reported prevalence rates ranging from 5 to 59% (Wolstenholme et al., 2020). A recent review estimated that 22% of children over 2.5 years of age are picky eaters (Cole et al., 2017). Caregivers have reported that their child's food selectivity leads to conflicts during mealtime, frustration, increased stress, and concern about their child's health and growth (Wolstenholme et al., 2020).

When caregivers notice that their child's eating has become more selective, they often try a variety of tactics to get the child to accept food. Examples of this include the parent attempting to convince, negotiate with, or coax their child into eating bites of the foods that they are refusing. A parent may require the child to stay at the table until they eat, or they may offer a reward for eating the food. A caregiver may feed the nonpreferred food to the child directly by bringing the bite up to their mouth. As a result of caregiver efforts, a child may resist and begin to engage in behaviors to avoid or escape taking bites of nonpreferred or lesser-preferred foods. These problem behaviors that occur during meals can be collectively defined as inappropriate mealtime behavior (IMB). IMB can look different for every child, but commonly-reported IMB includes turning one's head away from the food or spoon, pushing the food or the feeder away, crying, screaming, leaving the meal area, throwing food, negotiating, and delaying taking bites of nonpreferred foods (Piazza et al., 2003). Consistent engagement in IMB can result in ongoing food selectivity and may also lead to children eating a limited volume of food (i.e., only eating small portions during mealtimes), taking an extended period of time to eat a meal, or becoming dependent on or developing a preference for high-caloric drinks (e.g., formula, whole milk, Pediasure). The occurrence of IMB can exacerbate caregivers' frustration, stress, and concern about their child's eating.

In this paper, the authors describe the use of a behavior analytic approach to address food selectivity in young children and provide an instructional guide that caregivers and other professionals can utilize to increase a child's appropriate mealtime behaviors. This paper is the first comprehensive instructional guide that can be used by parents and early-childhood educators who have limited expertise or experience in addressing feeding concerns.

## Consideration of Medical Variables and Oral-Motor Skill Development

Before implementing any of the strategies recommended in this paper, it is necessary that a medical provider examine the child to ensure that there are no medical or structural problems that may be contributing to a child's IMB or food selectivity (Silverman, 2015). Since eating and digesting food involves the integration of many body systems and organs, it is critical that caregivers make sure that those systems are functioning properly before they initiate any sort of intervention. This is of particular importance for young children and for children with an intellectual or developmental disability, because they may not be able to effectively communicate pain or discomfort. For example, a child may not be able to notify their caregiver that certain foods cause them to experience pain, and this pain is what leads them to refuse those foods or cry when they are presented (Douglas & Bryon, 1996; Horvath et al., 1999; Wu et al., 2012). Common medical concerns that are associated with food selectivity are reflux, food allergies, eosinophilic esophagitis, and structural anomalies of the digestive system (Goday et al., 2019; Wu et al., 2012). It is important that these medical variables are considered and addressed before any intervention begins.

Additionally, it is important to consider the oral-motor skill development of the child to ensure that they have the skills necessary to appropriately and safely manage foods that are being presented to them. Adults might not think about the many movements and steps that it takes to chew and swallow food. The process is quite complex and requires the use and coordination of several oral-motor skills (Stevenson & Allaire, 1991; Volkert et al., 2014). For example, a child needs to be able to move the bite of food to their molars, chew the bite, recognize how much of the bite they must chew before it is safe to be swallowed, and move the masticated bite to the back of their tongue. Although most children develop these skills naturally and efficiently engage in them by around 15 months of age, some children have oral-motor skill deficits or other delays that may prevent them from being able to chew and swallow a wide variety of foods (Carruth & Skinner, 2002).

When chewing is difficult or effortful, a child may be less likely to chew foods that are dense or firm (e.g., meats, raw vegetables). They may refuse to eat those foods because they do not have the skills to sufficiently chew and swallow them. In some cases, when a child attempts to eat foods that they don't have the skills to safely chew, they may choke or swallow prematurely, which can be an aversive event that further perpetuates the avoidance of those foods (Manno et al., 2005).

Because feeding is a complex behavior, it sometimes requires cross-discipline collaboration to maximize treatment outcomes (Manno et al., 2005). Children with oral-motor skill deficits or perceived deficits should be evaluated by an oral-motor therapist (i.e., speech language pathologist, occupational therapist) and should receive interventions to support oral-motor skill development either before or in conjunction with behavioral services.

## Considerations for a Multi-Disciplinary Approach

As discussed above, feeding concerns often have complex etiologies. Depending on the presentation of the concern, specific providers may be more appropriate to address the feeding problem, or a multi-disciplinary approach may be necessary. For some children, the primary problem may be solely related to oral-motor skill deficits, behavioral contingencies that exist in their environment, or medical concerns; however, some children's feeding problems may stem from a combination of concerns (González et al., 2018). Professionals in applied behavior analysis, occupational therapy, speech language pathology, nutrition, or medicine may be required to effectively target feeding concerns.

While some feeding problems can be effectively addressed by caregivers using strategies discussed in this paper, it is important to acknowledge that feeding problems may be severe enough to warrant more intensive intervention and oversight from professionals trained in the treatment of pediatric feeding disorders. Severe symptoms of pediatric feeding problems include the total refusal to eat or drink, weight loss or failure to gain weight/meet appropriate developmental growth parameters, and dehydration (González et al., 2018). Additional variables to consider when evaluating the severity of a feeding problem include the current volume, variety, and texture of food being consumed; the child's ability to engage in age-appropriate mealtime behaviors (e.g., staying seated at the table, using age-appropriate utensils or cups, etc.); and the severity of IMB they are exhibiting.

## Brief Overview of Functions of IMB

When approaching the treatment of a feeding problem from a behavior analytic standpoint, it is important to consider the function of the child's IMB. A function of problem behavior can be conceptualized as the environmental variable that is maintaining a problem behavior (Piazza et al., 2003). The most common function of IMB is escape (Hodges et al., 2020). In these instances, when a bite of nonpreferred or novel food is presented, the child engages in IMB to have the bite removed or to escape the situation in which the bite is being presented. However, other functions of IMB have been documented, such as access to social attention (Woods et al., 2010). Social attention during meals may present in a variety of ways. Caregivers may engage in coaxing (e.g., "Please take this bite, it will make you big and strong!"), reprimands (e.g., "Do not spit that bite out like that!"), or comfort statements (e.g., "It's all right, you're okay."). Woods et al. (2010) found that parental social attention was commonly followed by brief decreases in IMB and an increased likelihood of food acceptance; however, decreases in IMB were not observed to be maintained over time and often resulted in reoccurrences of IMB at an increased level. This indicates that social attention may have served as a reinforcer for IMB. Children's IMB may be maintained by a single function or by multiple functions. A common combination of functions that maintain IMB is access to social attention and escape from the bite (Borrero et al., 2010; Kirkwood et al., 2020). In these instances, upon the child's engagement in food refusal, a parent may provide a brief comfort statement while simultaneously removing the bite. By providing the child with verbal comfort and the removal of the aversive food, the child's IMB is reinforced, thus making it more likely that they will repeat this in the future. These existing functions are critical to consider when designing treatment for feeding problems in order for the intervention to be functionally relevant. When an intervention matches the function of the IMB, it is more likely to be effective because the child is able to learn socially acceptable and appropriate ways to access the reinforcer without engaging in IMB.

## Antecedent Strategies

Antecedent interventions are used to make changes to the events that precede problem behavior. Antecedent interventions have been widely used to address a variety of problem behaviors (Cooper et al., 2020). This involves the modification of any stimulus in the environment that was present before the problem behavior occurred. In the context of feeding, this largely refers to various stimuli related to the presentation of the food that the child does not want to eat. All of the interventions described below have been shown to be effective at addressing food selectivity and IMB.

**Stimulus Fading**

Stimulus fading is a procedure that involves the gradual increase of the presence of a stimulus (Cooper et al., 2020). More specifically, demand fading is an intervention strategy used to gradually increase the demand required so that, over time, the end goal is achieved (i.e., the terminal demand is delivered). Instead of presenting a demand that the parent knows their child will not complete, they present an easier version of the demand that the child is more likely to comply with. When they are successful with that demand, they can gradually modify the demand until they ultimately present the final, terminal demand. Research has shown that this strategy was effective at increasing the volume and variety of food children consumed both with and without additional reinforcement components (González et al., 2018; Knox et al., 2012; Najdowski et al., 2010).

For example, if a child refuses to eat the serving of broccoli on their plate, caregivers could instead only present a single bite of broccoli at their next meal. Over time, they could gradually increase the number of bites until they present the entire serving to the child. Demand fading can also be used to gradually increase the size of each bite. If a child refuses to eat an age-appropriate bite size of chicken (e.g., quarter-size bite), caregivers could decrease it to a dime-size bite in order to decrease the difficulty of the demand. This decreases the response effort required to complete the demand and, therefore, makes it more likely that the child will eat the bite of chicken.

**Choice**

Another antecedent intervention that can be used to prevent the occurrence of IMB is the use of choice when preparing children's meals. By including choices and considering the child's preferences, caregivers are more likely to be successful with getting their child to consume the presented foods. Previous research has indicated that when a child is allowed to choose between different tasks or stimuli needed to complete the task, they are more likely to comply with the task even when it is nonpreferred. Studies have also shown that utilizing a child's choice decreases and even prevents challenging behavior that is reinforced by escape (Harding et al., 2002; Rispoli & Neely, 2013). This strategy easily applies to IMB since escape is a primary reinforcer in feeding problems. In fact, a study conducted by Fernand and colleagues (2016) found that the consumption of nonpreferred foods increased when the child was given the choice of which nonpreferred food they had to eat.

Implementation of this strategy can be done in a variety of ways depending on the presentation of the feeding problem. If a child gets to the table, looks at the plate, and complains that they don't like the foods, caregivers could give the child three food options from each food group and allow them to create their own meal with the caregivers' guidance and restrictions. On the other hand, if interventionists are working with a child who eats a variety of preferred foods but refuses nonpreferred foods, they could ask the child to choose between three different nonpreferred foods. When utilizing this strategy, it is important that the child's choices are honored and that once the meal is presented, there are no modifications made to the meal or to their choices. While this strategy allows the child to choose their own foods, it still allows the adults to control their choices and ensure that there is an appropriate variety of food from each food group.

## Structured Feeding Schedules

In feeding scenarios, hunger acts as an establishing operation. An establishing operation is a setting or environmental event that temporarily increases the effectiveness of a reinforcer and, as a result, increases the occurrence of the behaviors that facilitate access to that reinforcer (Cooper et al., 2020). Hunger is an establishing operation because it increases the likelihood that someone will eat and engage in appropriate eating behaviors. The hungrier an individual is, the more reinforcing food becomes. If an individual is not hungry, however, satiation serves as an abolishing operation because it makes food less reinforcing and discourages the individual from engaging in eating behaviors.

Hunger and satiation are particularly important to consider when children are picky eaters or do not consistently eat enough during meals. If a child eats very little food during breakfast but then eats several preferred snacks before lunch, they are less likely to eat lunch because they are satiated. This can be avoided by ensuring that the child only eats during mealtimes. Establishing a mealtime schedule that is structured and consistent can maximize a child's hunger and make it more likely that they will eat during meals (Fischer & Silverman, 2007).

A critical component of meal schedules is that food is not provided or allowed between mealtimes. The child must learn that food is available contingently and is offered only during scheduled times. Caregivers should also be mindful of their child's consumption of high-caloric liquids during and between meals, particularly if they are trying to transition their child to consuming only solid foods. For those children, it is recommended that solid food be presented first before they have access to the high-caloric drink (e.g., whole milk, formula).

## Use of Rules During Meals

The development and consistent use of verbal contingencies (i.e., rules) is considered best practice in any context of instruction. Research has indicated that instructional control is a critical part of appropriate behavior maintenance, and it is only established when rules are provided (Falcomata et al., 2008). Applying this concept to mealtimes, the adult would present the rules of the meal when the child receives their plate of food. Rules should be specific and describe the contingencies that are in place. They should also include the behavioral expectations for the meal (e.g., eating a specified amount of food) and what consequences will follow meeting those behavioral expectations (e.g., access to dessert, preferred tangible item, etc.).

By providing these rules at the start of the meal, the caregiver is clearly stating the expectations that they have for the child as well as the consequences of adhering and not adhering to the rules. The use of these contingency-specific rules is only effective if the described contingencies are followed.

**Bite Board Visual Prompt**

Some children who are not consuming an age-appropriate volume of food may engage in IMB because the expectation for how much they need to eat is not clear or consistent across meals. One way to prevent this type of IMB is by utilizing a visual prompt that helps them understand exactly how many bites they are required to eat. It is important to note that volume requirements should be based on age-appropriate expectations and not an arbitrary amount determined by caregivers. These visual prompts have been termed "bite boards." In a study that sought to increase the food consumption of a child with food refusal and a complex medical history, the use of a bite board resulted in increases in food consumption (Williams et al., 2019).

An example of a basic bite board for a young child is five laminated pictures of spoons that are attached to a board via Velcro. At the beginning of a meal, all of the spoon images are attached to the board. When the child takes a bite of food, they get to take off one of the spoons, and the caregiver then reminds them that they have only four bites left. This would continue until all five spoons are removed from the board, and the child could then have access to their reinforcer. This strategy allows the child to have a consistent reminder of the expectations of their meal.

**Sequential Bite Presentation**

When presented with a plate of food, a picky eater commonly chooses to eat all of their most-preferred food before eating any of their less-preferred foods. This makes the demand of eating the nonpreferred foods even more difficult and can often lead to lengthy meals and IMB. One strategy to combat this is to instruct the child to eat their bites in a specific sequence so that they are alternating between bites of preferred and nonpreferred food throughout the meal. For example, one could first present a bite of carrot (i.e., nonpreferred), then present a bite of macaroni and cheese (i.e., preferred), and continue this sequence throughout the meal. The preferred food serves as a built-in reinforcer for eating the nonpreferred bite. Sequential presentation has been found to be an effective strategy for addressing food selectivity and increasing the consumption of nonpreferred and novel foods in preschool-aged children (Weber & Gutierrez, 2015; VanDalen & Penrod, 2010). In one study, children reported that they preferred the sequential bite presentation over other presentation options (VanDalen & Penrod, 2010).

**Noncontingent Escape**

Mealtimes with young children who are picky eaters can last for very long periods of time. Often, caregivers struggle to know when to end the meal, when to stop trying to get their child to keep eating, and when to continue and require them to eat a certain amount before leaving the table. In many cases, caregivers become frustrated, stressed, and tired and ultimately decide to end the meal because their child's IMB has escalated and become intolerable and/or unmanageable. When this happens, the child learns that escape from the meal or nonpreferred foods will be provided if they engage in such IMB. This escape then serves as a reinforcer for their IMB and makes them more likely to repeat this in the future.

A strategy to prevent this continued reinforcement of IMB is to allow the child to escape from the meal after a predetermined amount of time. This escape will happen no matter what the child did or did not eat during that time, so the escape occurs noncontingently. This gives caregivers an exit strategy without inadvertently reinforcing IMB. Noncontingent escape has been recommended to address IMB, as it helps break the cycle of reinforcing IMB by ending meals prematurely (González et al., 2018). To implement this strategy, caregivers must decide on a maximum meal duration (e.g., 20 minutes) and set a timer for that amount of time as soon as they start the meal or present the food to their child. No matter what happens during the meal and regardless of how much food was consumed, the meal must end at that designated time and the remaining food must be removed so that the child is provided escape.

**Noncontingent Reinforcement**

Providing noncontingent reinforcement (i.e., providing access to a reinforcer [e.g., tangible item, attention from caregivers] regardless of the behavior that the individual engages in) has been well-established in the literature as an effective intervention in decreasing a variety of problem behaviors and increasing appropriate behaviors (e.g., Kodak et al., 2003; Smith et al., 2019; Wilder et al., 2005). To implement this strategy during meals, caregivers or teachers should provide the child access to their preferred items (e.g., toys, iPad, videos) throughout the entire meal. No matter what behavior they engage in during the meal, the preferred items should remain present. When reinforcement from alternative sources is freely available, children are less likely to seek reinforcement in the form of escape from their meal. Ultimately, noncontingent reinforcement decreases the likelihood that they will engage in IMB because they automatically receive reinforcement from their preferred item.

## Consequent Strategies

Just as antecedent conditions can be manipulated to improve various feeding problems, consequent strategies can also be used to improve IMB. Consequent strategies that can be implemented by caregivers include the use of prompting sequences, extinction, differential reinforcement of alternative behaviors, and combinations of these strategies such as levels systems and token economies.

**Three-Step Prompting**

A three-step prompting hierarchy can be a useful tool for identifying the amount of support an individual currently requires to complete a task, and for ensuring that the child knows what the desired behavior looks like. Prompting hierarchies are often used to teach new skills (Libby et al., 2008) and include verbal prompts, modeling, and some form of physical prompting. In feeding, the most common physical prompt is called a hand-over-hand (HOH) prompt (Borrero et al., 2013). A HOH prompt involves the caregiver placing their hand over the child's hand and physically guiding them to complete the demand. If a caregiver wanted to use a prompting hierarchy in a meal setting, they would begin by delivering a verbal prompt such as, "Take a bite." After issuing this initial demand, the caregiver should wait a developmentally-appropriate amount of time for the child to respond (i.e., typically between 5-10 seconds). If the child does not take the bite following the verbal demand or waiting period, the caregiver should then model the expected behavior. Specifically, the caregiver should pick up the spoon and bring it to their mouth while saying, "This is how we take a bite." After modeling the behavior, the spoon should be placed back in front of the child to allow them the opportunity to respond with the appropriate behavior. If the child still does not respond, the caregiver should implement the HOH prompt. The caregiver should physically guide their child's hand over the handle of the spoon, help them pick up the spoon, and bring it to their mouth. It is important to remember to only use the demands and phrases associated with the prompting hierarchy when utilizing this strategy; the child should not receive any additional attention or prompts.

**Extinction**

Extinction is a well-documented, consequent-based strategy that can be applied to decrease IMB during meals (LaRue et al., 2011; Piazza et al., 2003; Reed et al., 2004). Specifically, extinction refers to the withholding of reinforcement for engaging in a specific behavior (Cooper et al., 2020). In other words, the consequence -- good or bad -- that typically follows one's engagement in a behavior is no longer provided, rendering the current behavior ineffective. When considering extinction, it is especially important to identify the function of the problem behavior (i.e., what is maintaining or reinforcing the current behavior) so that extinction can be applied appropriately. It is a common misconception that extinction simply means ignoring a problem behavior; however, that would only be the case if social attention was maintaining the problem behavior. When discussing functions of problem behavior, the most-reported function of IMB is escape (Hodges et al., 2020). In order to apply extinction in these scenarios, escape should not be provided upon the engagement in IMB. For example, if the child swipes a nonpreferred bite of food off their plate and the parent picks the food up and places it in the trash, escape would be provided. However, parents could implement extinction by instead placing a new bite of the nonpreferred food on the child's plate following their IMB. Additionally, if the caregiver normally responds to the swiping behavior by providing social attention (e.g., "Oh no! Why would you do that?"), the caregiver would instead ignore the swiping behavior and continue as if nothing happened. It should be noted that when extinction is applied to a behavior, it may become worse for a period of time. This is because the behaviors that previously provided the child with reinforcement are no longer doing so; therefore, the child may try novel exhibitions of the behavior or increase the intensity of those behaviors in an effort to get them to work again. This is referred to as an extinction burst (Cooper et al., 2020). When an extinction burst occurs, it is important to continue implementing extinction instead of giving in and providing reinforcement because this could reinforce the novel, more intense behavior. If extinction is being used to decrease inappropriate behavior, these procedures should not be utilized in isolation. Strategies that provide opportunities for reinforcement should be implemented in conjunction with extinction, because they increase the occurrence of appropriate behavior that will replace the IMB when it is ultimately extinguished.

**Differential Reinforcement**

Differential reinforcement of alternative behavior (DRA) is a common procedure used in applied behavior analysis (MacNaul & Neely, 2018). It is typically embedded within treatment plans, or used in combination with other procedures like extinction (Shirley et al., 1997). Vazquez and colleagues (2019) found in surveying parents that DRA procedures were the most preferred intervention component to treat feeding concerns. Reinforcement refers to a response that will increase the likelihood that a certain behavior will occur in the future. Reinforcement can be delivered in a variety of ways according to the functions of behavior that were discussed previously. For example, social attention, access to tangible items, and escape can all be provided to someone when they engage in previously determined appropriate behaviors. Once the caregiver identifies the behavior(s) they want to increase, they should use reinforcement while applying extinction to any undesired behaviors (Athens & Vollmer, 2010). This combination of reinforcing desired behaviors and extinguishing undesired behaviors constitutes the DRA procedures. A critical consideration when using DRA is to think about how reactions differ when a child engages in appropriate behaviors versus inappropriate behaviors. The purpose of DRA is to make sure that responses to appropriate behavior are heavily emphasized and enthusiastic, and responses to inappropriate behaviors are neutral or do not occur at all. The potency or intensity of negative reactions (e.g., yelling, reprimands, etc.) may influence behavior, so caregivers should do their best to exhibit a neutral reaction. The use of DRA to increase acceptance and decrease IMB is prevalent throughout the literature (e.g., Berth at al., 2019; de los Santos & Silbaugh, 2020; Patel et al., 2002).

If a child's desired mealtime behaviors are increasing bites of food and staying seated during a meal, a caregiver could implement DRA by providing social attention to increase the likelihood of those behaviors. If at any time during the meal the caregiver observed their child taking a bite of food, they might say, "Wow, great job taking your bites!" If the caregiver observed their child staying seated while simultaneously pushing their food around, the caregiver would not acknowledge that they weren't taking bites of their food. Instead, they would say, "You are doing such a good job staying in your seat tonight!" In this scenario, the parents are providing an enthusiastic response for a desired behavior while not reacting to or acknowledging the lack of bite-taking.

If the desired behavior was to take a bite of carrots, one could choose to offer access to a preferred item or activity for a brief amount of time following the child's compliance. Specifically, they could present the child with a preprepared bite of carrots and say, "If you take this bite of carrots, you can play with your tablet for one minute." If the child takes the bite of carrots, praise would be provided immediately and access to the tablet would be allowed. If the demand was delivered and the child began crying before taking the bite of carrots, praise would be provided immediately for taking the bite and the child would be allowed access to their tablet despite the fact that they cried. The important thing to remember in this scenario is to provide behavior-specific praise (e.g., emphasize the behavior being reinforced) and to provide little to no reaction for any undesired behavior (e.g., crying).

## Combination Strategies

While the strategies described above can be implemented in insolation, they can also be combined into an intervention package.

### Levels Systems

A levels system uses a combination of differential reinforcement and response cost to simultaneously increase desired behaviors and decrease undesired behaviors (Bauer et al., 1986; Hagopian et al., 2003). As explained above, differential reinforcement is the reinforcement of desired behaviors while simultaneously placing other responses on extinction. Response cost involves the removal of a reinforcer contingent upon a certain behavior. A levels system is a combination of these two procedures. When using a levels system, a behavioral criterion is determined based on the child's current ability to perform the skill or behavior. Based on their performance and whether they meet the criterion or not, they are assigned a level. Each level is associated with varying degrees of access to preferred items and activities. Ripple and colleagues (2022) used a levels system to increase mealtime consumption in an adolescent who presented with food refusal. Prior to the meal, the child was informed of the rules and the two different levels (i.e., red and green) were described. The child was given a set amount of time to consume a meal that consisted of an age-appropriate volume of both preferred and nonpreferred foods. If the child consumed the entire meal within the specified time, they would be on the green level which allowed them access to all of their preferred activities and items. However, if they did not consume the presented volume, they would be on the red level which allowed them access to their lesser or nonpreferred activities. The child would remain on the earned level until the next meal during which they would have the opportunity to earn a different level. When choosing to use a levels system, it is critical that access to preferred items and activities are restricted when the child has not earned the green level. Failure to follow the behavioral contingencies would render the levels system ineffective.

### Token Economy

Another consequence-based strategy that can be used to target feeding problems is a token economy (Kahng et al., 2003;

Williams et al., 2007). A token economy is another procedure that employs a variety of behavioral principles and strategies. When using a token economy, a target response is identified, and tokens (i.e., conditioned reinforcers) are exchanged for access to preferred items or activities (Hackenberg, 2009; Ivy et al., 2017). The child learns that a previously meaningless item (i.e., the token) is a means of gaining access to what they want (Doll et al., 2013). Tokens are beneficial because they can easily be delivered when access to other preferred items or activities are not readily available. There are several components of token economies that should be carefully considered prior to its implementation: (a) the type of tokens used (e.g., small coins, fake money, hole punches, etc.), (b) the rewards that tokens will be exchanged for, and (c) the type of schedule that will be implemented for the exchange of tokens for reinforcers. When considering which tokens to use, parents should ensure that the tokens cannot be easily counterfeited and ensure that the delivery of tokens remains under the control of the parents (Doll et al., 2013). Additionally, when deciding how frequently tokens can be exchanged, the age of the child and their understanding of delayed reinforcement should be considered (e.g., if they earn tokens all day long, will they understand and still find this reinforcing if they can't exchange them until the end of the week?). It is recommended that when first implementing a token economy, opportunities for exchange be rather frequent (Doll et al., 2013).

Prior to beginning the use of a token economy, it is critical to outline the behaviors that will earn tokens and to ensure that the behavioral expectation for earning tokens is made clear to the child (Doll et al., 2013). The behavioral expectations should always be communicated in a developmentally-appropriate format. Expectations can be communicated orally or through written communication (e.g., a list of rules), or can be modeled for the child. In the context of feeding, target behaviors for earning tokens could include taking bites of new or nonpreferred foods, staying seated at the dinner table, or finishing the food that is on their plate. A specific number of tokens that can be earned for engaging in these behaviors should be identified. For example, one token could be earned for each bite of a new or nonpreferred food, three tokens could be earned for staying seated at the table for the entire meal, and three tokens could be earned for finishing all of the food on their plate. It is important to adjust the reward system appropriately to ensure that it is somewhat difficult to earn rewards but not impossible. Similar to the levels system, in a token economy the initial expectation for these behaviors should be based the child's current level of behavior. It is important that the child has the opportunity to access or earn the reinforcement so that they can learn and understand the contingencies in place.

## Conclusion

Although feeding problems in children can be complex, this paper aimed to provide practical guidance to caregivers and providers (e.g., teachers, other early childhood therapeutic providers) addressing IMB in young children. This paper is the first of its kind to provide a comprehensive review and guidelines in the treatment of feeding problems from a behavior analytic perspective, to individuals who may have limited experience in this approach. It is important to remember that medical concerns and oral-motor skill deficits need to be addressed prior to implementing any of the recommendations provided. Practitioners working with children with feeding concerns should be willing and ready to collaborate with providers across disciplines to provide the most effective services. In addition to the group of interventions discussed in this paper, there are other evidence-based treatment options that were not included due to the level of training and expertise that are required to implement them with integrity. If mealtime behavior does not improve after consistent practice with the interventions described in this paper, it is recommended that more intensive services be provided by a Board Certified Behavior Analyst or Licensed Psychologist with specific training in pediatric feeding disorders.

## References

Athens, E. S. & Vollmer, T. R. (2010). An investigation of differential reinforcement of alternative behavior without extinction. *Journal of Applied Behavior Analysis, 43*(4), 569-589. https://doi.org/10.1901/jaba.2010.43-569

Bandini, L. G., Anderson, S. E., Curtin, C., Cermak, S., Evans, E. W., Scampini, R., Maslin, M., & Must, A. (2010). Food selectivity in children with autism spectrum disorders and typically developing children. *The Journal of Pediatrics, 157*(2), 259-264. https://doi.org/10.1016/j.jpeds.2010.02.013

Bauer, A. M., Shea, T. M., & Keppler, R. (1986). Levels systems: A framework for the individualization of behavior management. *Behavioral Disorders, 12*(1), 28-35. https://doi.org/10.1177/019874298012001

Benjasuwantep, B., Chaithirayanon, S., & Eiamudomkan, M. (2013). Feeding problems in healthy young children: Prevalence, related factors and feeding practices. *Pediatric Reports, 5*(2), 38-42. https://doi.org/ 10.4081/pr.2013.e10

Berth, D. P., Bachmeyer, M. H., Kirkwood, C. A., Mauzy, C. R., Retzlaff, B. J., & Gibson, A. L. (2019). Noncontingent and differential reinforcement in the treatment of pediatric feeding problems. *Journal of Applied Behavior Analysis, 53*(3), 622-641. https://doi.org/10.1002/jaba.562

Borrero, C. S. W., Schlereth, G. J., Rubio, E. K., & Taylor, T. (2013). A comparison of two physical guidance procedures in the treatment of pediatric food refusal. *Behavioral Interventions, 28,* 261-280. https://doi.org/10.1002/bin.1373

Borrero, C. S. W., Woods, J. N., Borrero, J. C., Masler, E. A., & Lesser, A. D. (2010). Descriptive analyses of pediatric food refusal and acceptance. *Journal of Applied Behavior Analysis, 43*(1), 71-88. https://doi.org/10.1901/jaba.2010.43-71

Carruth, B. R. & Skinner, J. D. (2002). Feeding behaviors and other motor development in healthy children (2-24 months). *Journal of the American College of Nutrition, 21*(2), 88-96. https://doi.org/10.1080/07315724.2002.10719199

Cole, N.C., An, Ruopeng, Lee, S.Y., & Donovan, S. (2017). Correlates of picky eating and food neophobia in young children: A systematic review and meta-analysis. *Nutrition Reviews, 75*(7), 516-532. https://doi.org/10.1093/nutrit/nux024

Cooper, J. O., Heron, T. E., & Heward, W. L. (2020). *Applied Behavior Analysis* (3rd Edition). Pearson Education.

de los Santos, M. & Silbaugh, B. C. (2020). Differential reinforcement of acceptance without escape extinction in a boy with developmental delays and food selectivity. *Journal of Developmental and Physical Disabilities, 32*(6), 963-981. http://doi.org/10.1007/s10882-020-09732-2

Dobbelsteyn, C., Marche, D. M., Blake, K., & Rashid, M. (2005). Early oral sensory experiences and feeding development in children with CHARGE syndrome: A report of five cases. *Dysphagia, 20,* 89-100. doi:10.1007/s00455-004-0026-1

Doll, C., McLaughlin, T. F., & Barretto, A. (2013). The token economy: a recent review and evaluation. *International Journal of Basic and Applied Science, 2*(1), 131-149.

Douglas, J. E., & Bryon, M. (1996). Interview data on severe behavioural eating difficulties in young children. *Archives of Disease in Childhood, 75,* 304-308. http://doi.org 10.1136/adc.75.4.304

Falcomata, T. S., Northrup, J. A., Dutt, A., Stricker, J. M., Vinquist, K. M., & Engebretson, B. J. (2008). A preliminary analysis of instructional control in the maintenance of appropriate behavior. *Journal of Applied Behavior Analysis, 41,* 429-434.

Fernand, J. K., Penrod, B., Fu, S. B., Whelan, C. M., & Medved, S. (2016). The effects of choice between nonpreferred foods on the food consumption of individuals with food selectivity. *Behavioral Interventions, 31*(1), 87-101. https://doi.org/10.1002/bin.1423

Fischer, E. & Silverman, A. (2007). Behavioral conceptualization, assessment, and treatment of pediatric feeding disorders. *Seminars in Speech and Language, 28*(3), 223-231. http://dx.doi.org/10.1055/s-2007-984728

Goday, P. S., Huh, S. Y., Silveman, A., Lukens, C. T., Dodrill, P., Cohen, S. S., Delaney, A. L., Feuling, M. B., Noel, R. J., Gisel, E., Kenzer, A., Kessler, D. B., de Camargo, O. K., Browne, J., & Phalen, J. A. (2019). *Journal of Pediatric Gastroenterology and Nutrition, 68*(1), 124-129. https://doi.org/10.1097/MPG.0000000000002188

González, M. L., Mulderink, T. D., & Girolami, P. A. (2018). Avoidant restrictive food intake disorder. In A. Maragakis & W. T. O'Donohue (Eds.), Principle-based stepped care and brief psychotherapy for integrated care settings (pp. 53–64). Springer International Publishing/Springer Nature. https://doi.org/10.1007/978-3-319-70539-2_6

Hackenberg, T. D. (2009). Token reinforcement: a review and analysis. *Journal of Applied Behavior Analysis, 91*(2), 257-286. https://doi.org/10.1901/jeab.2009.91-257

Hagopian, L. P., Rush, K. S., Richman, D. M., Kurtz, P. F., Contrucci, S. A., & Crosland, K. (2003). The development and application of individualized levels systems for the treatment of severe problem behavior. *Behavior Therapy, 33,* 65-86. http://doi:10.1016/S0005-7894(02)80006-5

Harding, J. W., Wacker, D. P., Berg, W. K., Barretto, A., Rankin, B. (2002). Assessment and treatment of severe behavior problems using choice-making procedures. *Education and Treatment of Children, 25*(1), 26-46.

Hodges, A., Davis, T. N., & Kirkpatrick, M. (2020). A review of the literature on the functional analysis of inappropriate mealtime behavior. *Behavior Modification, 44*(1), 137-154. https://doi.org/10.1177/0145445518794368

Horvath, K., Papadimitriou, J., Rabsztyn, A., Drachenberg, C., & Tildon, J. T. (1999). Gastrointestinal abnormalities in children with autistic disorder. *Journal of Pediatrics, 135,* 559-563. https://doi.org/10.1016/s0022-3476(99)70052-1

Ivy, J. W., Meindl, J. N., Overley, E., & Robson, K. M. (2017). Token economy: a systematic review of procedural descriptions, *Behavior Modification, 41*(5), 708-737. https://doi.org/10.1177/0145445517699559

Kahng, S., Boscoe, J. H., & Byrne, S. (2003). The use of an escape contingency and a token economy to increase food acceptance. *Journal of Applied Behavior Analysis, 36*(3), 349-353. https://doi.org/10.1901/jaba.2003.36-349

Kerwin, M. E. (1999). Empirically supported treatments in pediatric psychology: Severe feeding problems. *Journal of Pediatric Psychology, 24*(3), 193-214. https://doi:10.1093/jpepsy/24.3.193

Kirkwood, C. A., Bachmeyer-Lee, M. H., Sheehan, C. M., Mauzy, C. R., & Gibson, L. A. (2021). Further examination of the treatment of multiply controlled inappropriate mealtime behavior. *Journal of Applied Behavior Analysis, 54*(1), 429-450. https://doi.org/10.1002/jaba.738

Knox, M., Rue, J. C., Wildenger, L., Lamb, K., & Luiselli, J. K. (2012). Intervention for food selectivity in a specialized school setting: Teacher implemented prompting, reinforcement, and demand fading for an adolescent students with autism. *Education and Treatment of Children, 35*(3), 407-417.

Kodak, T., Miltenberger, R. G., & Romaniuk, C. (2003). A comparison of differential reinforcement and noncontingent reinforcement for the treatment of a child's multiply controlled problem behavior. *Behavioral Interventions, 18*(4), 267-278. https://doi.org/10.1002/bin.143

LaRue, R. H., Stewart, V., Piazza, C. C., Volkert, V. M., Patel, M. R., & Zeleny, J. (2011). Escape as reinforcement and escape extinction in the treatment of feeding problems. *Journal of Applied Behavior Analysis, 44*(4), 719-735. https://doi.org/10.1901/jaba.2011.44-719

Libby, M. E., Weiss, J. S., Bancroft, S., & Ahearn, W. H. (2008). A comparison of most-to-least and least-to-most prompting on the acquisition of solitary play skills. *Behavior Analysis and Practice, 1*(1), 37-43. https://doilorg/10.1007/BF03391719

MacNaul, H. L. & Neely, L. C. (2018). Systematic review of differential reinforcement of alternative behavior without extinction for individuals with autism. *Behavior Modification, 42*(3), 398-421. https://doi.org/10.1177/0145445517740321

Manikam, R. & Perman, J. A. (2000). Pediatric feeding disorders. *Journal of Clinical Gastroenterology, 30*(1), 34-46. https://doi.org/10.1097/00004836-200001000-00007

Manno, C. J., Fox, C., Eicher, P. S., & Kerwin, M. E. (2005). Early oral-motor interventions for pediatric feeding problems: What, when and how. *Journal of Early and Intensive Behavior Intervention, 2*(3), 145-149. http://dx.doi.org/10.1037/h0100310

Najdowski, A. C., Wallace, M. D., Reagon, K., Penrod, B., Higbee, T. S., & Tarbox, J. (2010). Utilizing a home-based parent training approach in the treatment of food selectivity. *Behavioral Interventions: Theory & Practice in Residential & Community-Based Clinical Programs, 25*(2), 89-107. https://doi.org/10.1002/bin.298

Patel, M. R., Piazza, C. C., Martinez, C. J., Volkert, V. M., & Santana, C. M. (2002). An evaluation of two differential reinforcement procedures with escape extinction to treat food refusal. *Journal of Applied Behavior Analysis, 35*(4), 363-374. https://doi.org/10.1901/jaba.2002.35-363

Piazza, C. C., Fisher, W. W., Brown, K. A., Shore, B. A., Patel, M. R., Katz, R. M., Sevin, B. M., Gulotta, C. S., & Blakely-Smith, A. (2003). Functional analysis of inappropriate mealtime behaviors. *Journal of Applied Behavior Analysis, 36*(2), 187-204. https://doi.org/10.1901/jaba.2003.36-187

Piazza, C. C., Patel, M. R., Gulotta, C. S., Sevin, B. M., & Layer, S. A. (2003). On the relative contributions of positive reinforcement and escape extinction in the treatment of food refusal. *Journal of Applied Behavior Analysis, 36*(3), 309-324. https://doi.org/10.1901/jaba.2003.36-309

Reed, G. K., Piazza, C. C., Patel, M. R., Layer, S. A., Bachmeyer, M. H., Bethke, S. D., & Gutshall, K. A. (2004). On the relative contributions of noncontingent reinforcement and escape extinction in the treatment of food refusal. *Journal of Applied Behavior Analysis, 37*(1). 27-42. https://doi.org/10.1901/jaba.2004.37-27

Ripple, H. E., Smith, H. S., Whipple, H., & Druffner, R. (2022). Evaluation of an individualized levels system to increase consumption for an adolescent with food refusal. *Clinical Case Studies*. https://doi.org/10.1177/15346501211053614

Rispoli, M. Lang, R., & Neely, L. (2013). A comparison of within-and-across-activity choices for reducing challenging behavior in children with autism spectrum disorders. *Journal of Behavioral Education, 22*(1), 66-83. http://dx.doi.org/10.1007/s10864-012-9164-y

Shirley, M. J., Iwata, B. A., Kahng, S., Mazaleski, J. L., & Lerman, D. C. (1997). Does functional communication training compete with ongoing contingencies of reinforcement? An analysis during response acquisition and maintenance. *Journal of Applied Behavior Analysis, 30*(1), 93-104. https://doi.org/10.1901/jaba.1997.30-93

Silverman, A. H. (2015). Behavioral management of feeding disorders of childhood. *Annals of Nutrition and Metabolism, 66*(5), 33-42. https://doi.org/10.1159/000381375

Smith, H. M., Gadke, D. L., Stratton, K. K., Ripple, H., & Reisener, C. D. (2019). Providing noncontingent access to music in addition to escape extinction as a treatment for liquid refusal in a child with autism. *Behavior Analysis: Research and Practice, 19*(1), 94-102. http://dx.doi.org/10.1037/bar0000092

Stevenson, R. D., & Allaire, J. H. (1991). The development of normal feeding and swallowing. *Pediatric Clinics of North America, 38*(6), 1439-1453. https://doi.org/10.1016/S0031-3955(16)38229-3

VanDalen, K. H., & Penrod, B. (2010). A comparison of simultaneous versus sequential presentation of novel foods in the treatment of food selectivity. *Behavioral Interventions, 25*(3), 191–206.

Vazquez, M., Fryling, M. J., & Hernandez, A. (2019). Assessment of parental acceptability and preference for behavioral interventions for feeding problems. *Behavior Modification, 43*(2), 273-287. https://doi.org/10.1177/0145445517751435

Volkert, V. M., Peterson, K. M., Zeleny, J. R., & Piazza, C. C. (2014). A clinical protocol to increase chewing and assess mastication in children with feeding disorders. *Behavior Modification, 38*(5), 705-729. https://doi.org/10.1177/0145445514536575

Weber, J. & Guiterrez, A. (2015). A treatment package without escape extinction to address food selectivity. *Journal of Visualized Experiments, 102.* https://doi.org/10.3791/52898

Wilder, D.A., Normand, M. and Atwell, J. (2005), Noncontingent reinforcement as treatment for food refusal and associated self-injury. *Journal of Applied Behavior Analysis, 38,* 549-553. https://doi.org/10.1901/jaba.2005.132-04

Williams, K., Adams, W., Creek, L. (2019). The combined effects of immediate and delayed reinforcement to increase consumption of solid food: A brief report. *Developmental Neurorehabilitation, 22*(8), 576-580.

Williams, K. E., Riegel, K., Gibbons, B., & Field, D. G. (2007). Intensive behavioral treatment for severe feeding problems: a cost-effective alternative to tube feeding? *Journal of Developmental and Physical Disabilities, 19,* 227-235.

Wolstenholme, H., Kelly, C., Hennessy, M., & Heary, C. et al. (2020). Childhood fussy/picky eating behaviours: A systematic review and synthesis of qualitative studies. *International Journal of Behavioral Nutrition and Physical Activity, 17*(2), 1-22. https://doi.org/10.1186/s12966-019-0899-x

Woods, J. N., Borrero, J. C., Laud, R. B., Borrero, C. S. W. (2010). Descriptive analyses of pediatric food refusal: the structure of parental attention. *Behavior Modification, 34*(1), 35-56. https://doi.org/10.1177/0145445509355646

Wu, Y. P., Franciosi, J. P., Rothenburg, M. E., & Hommel, K. A. (2012). Behavioral feeding problems and parenting stress in eosinophilic gastrointestinal disorders in children. *Pediatric Allergy and Immunology, 23*(8), 730-735. https://doi.org/10.1111/j.1399-3038.2012.01340.x

# The Effect of Token Economies on Student Behavior in the Preschool Classroom: A Meta-Analysis

*Lynda B. Hayes, Brad A. Dufrene, Crystal Taylor, D. Joe Olmi, Leonard Troughton, Evan H. Dart, and Caitlyn M. Weaver*

## Abstract

There has been a recent push in the literature to identify and use more evidence-based practices for positive behavioral supports for challenging student behaviors in the classroom environment. Further, interest in targeting early education environments such as preschool has been growing given the persistence of behavioral difficulties in the absence of early and effective intervention (Campbell & Ewing, 1990; Kazdin, 1987; Powell et al., 2006; Stormont, 2002). Two previous meta-analyses (Maggin et al., 2011; Soares et al., 2016) provided some initial support for effectiveness of token economies with challenging student behavior; however, the inclusion of the preschool setting was limited and both studies used older versions of design standards to evaluate the quality of studies in the literature. The present study served to extend those meta-analyses by targeting preschool classrooms. Further, the current study included the most recent What Works Clearinghouse Design Standards to evaluate whether token economies meet criteria as an evidence-based practice. Ten studies were included in the final analyses. Two sets of effect sizes were calculated: Baseline-Corrected Tau and Hedge's g. An omnibus effect size showed an overall large effect; however, similar to previous meta-analyses, several methodological concerns were identified. Moderator analyses for several variables were conducted; however, no moderator analyses were significant. Limitations and future directions were discussed.

**Keywords:** token economy, preschool student behavior, disruptive behavior, design standards

# The Effect of Token Economies on Student Behavior in the Preschool Classroom: A Meta-Analysis

## Introduction

Researchers and educators are interested in evidence-based universal classroom management procedures for preschool classrooms. Relative to research in K-12 classrooms, far less research has been conducted testing classroom management strategies at the preschool level (Soares et al., 2016). Overall, student risk for emotional and behavior disorders (EBDs) is increasing (Pastor & Reuben, 2015). Further, preschool children's rates of EBDs are similar to rates in older children and may be higher for specific diagnoses (e.g., oppositional defiant disorder, anxiety disorders; Egger & Angold, 2006). Preschool children with EBDs may exhibit a host of symptoms, including both internalizing (e.g., withdrawal, anxiety) and externalizing (e.g., aggression, property destruction). These types of symptoms hinder children's development and success in behavioral and academic domains (Nelson et al., 2004). Further, negative outcomes such as school and social failure occur more often for children that have or are at risk for EBDs when compared to their peers. In fact, research findings indicate that over 30% of children with EBDs may drop out of high school (U.S. Department of Education, 2020), and since the 1990s, dropout rates in this category have been higher than in any other disability category.

Preschool is a critical period for identifying students who are at risk, and providing them with successful supports to increase their chances of success in academic and behavioral domains and their overall school readiness. For example, Bulotsky-Shearer et al. (2011) evaluated predictors of school readiness (e.g., early literacy, early mathematics, social-emotional competence, peer relations) and found that problem behavior (e.g., inattention, poor turn-taking skills with peers) exhibited early in the preschool academic year predicted academic outcome, motivation, attention, and persistence with future tasks. Given these findings, researchers and preschool educators should evaluate universal classroom management systems that support preschool children's behavioral and academic development.

**Token Economies**

Token economies have been implemented as universal and targeted interventions, in isolation and also within larger tiered systems of support (Boerke & Reitman, 2011). Token economies have been studied for several decades and are generally shown to be effective (Doll et al., 2013). Moreover, token economies are based on fundamental principles of learning, such as positive reinforcement, and serve as the foundation for the most widely researched classroom-based interventions, such as the Good Behavior Game (Barrish et al., 1969). A benefit of the token economy is its utility in both the behavior management of an individual child or a group of children (e.g., class wide; Drabman et al., 1974; Filcheck et al., 2004; Klimas, 2007; McGoey & DuPaul, 2000; Reitman et al., 2004). Although there have been a number of variations of the token economy, the key feature is the immediate delivery of a conditioned reinforcer (e.g., token, points, sticker) after an individual (or group) exhibits a particular target behavior or class of behaviors. The token can later be exchanged for a backup reinforcer, typically from a reward menu of items pre-determined as reinforcing for the individual. The key benefit of the token economy is the ability to bridge the delay between a target behavior and the delivery of the terminal reinforcer. Bridging the delay between behavior and reinforcement is important, as delays have been shown to potentially weaken the effects of reinforcers (Boerke & Reitman, 2011; Doll et al., 2013).

Maggin et al. (2011) and Soares et al. (2016) conducted meta-analyses and design standard reviews of the token economy in the school-based literature. These meta-analyses calculated effect sizes to quantitatively synthesize the findings of studies and design standards and evaluated the methodological rigor of studies using standards described by the What Works Clearinghouse (WWC; Kratochwill et al., 2010). Maggin et al. (2011) was the first meta-analysis conducted on token economies in the school literature that evaluated the methodological rigor of the included studies. This analysis included a total of 24 studies of the effects of token economies on student behavior. Effect sizes of the studies indicated overall improvements in student behaviors, and offered some initial support for the effectiveness of token economies implemented in the school setting on either the individual-student or class-wide level. However, the evaluation of the quality of these studies indicated several weaknesses that do not support token economies as an evidence-based practice. For example, many studies failed to meet WWC design standards (Kratochwill et al., 2010) such as insufficient demonstrations of treatment effect or three or fewer data points per phase.

Soares et al.'s (2016) results were similar to those of Maggin et al. (2011) in that token economies produced overall improvements in student behavior across the 28 included studies. In fact, approximately 25% and 68% of studies produced medium and large effect sizes, respectively. Soares et al. (2016) also evaluated the overall quality of the included studies, and results suggested the number of studies in this body of literature demonstrating acceptable standards of quality may be higher than Maggin et al. (2011); however, about 39% of included studies still demonstrated weak quality.

Overall, Maggin et al. (2011) and Soares et al. (2016) found that token economies implemented in school settings show favorable effects on student behavior in the classroom. However, there are notable limitations to both meta-analyses that warrant further investigation. First, there is a limited number of studies that included preschool populations in these meta-analyses. In fact, Maggin et al. (2011) only included K-12 in the inclusion criteria for their meta-analysis, excluding preschool children, and Soares et al. (2016) only included 6 studies with preschool-aged children. Further, both meta-analyses utilized previous versions of WWC design standards (Kratochwill et al., 2010). WWC Version 4.1 (WWC, 2020) is an updated version including design standards that are more stringent than previous versions. Further, meta-analyses that evaluate the degree to which studies meet WWC Design Standards typically use an all-or-nothing approach. That is, studies are typically labeled as "Meets Standards," "Meets with Reservations," or "Does Not Meet" whether it fails to meet only one of the design standards or fails to meet all the standards. It may be important to parse out the degree to which a study meets each standard separately. While all standards are equally important, it may be particularly important for replication studies to know which design standards current token economy studies fail to meet. Further, it may also be the case that studies that meet a higher number of design standards yield a stronger effect size than studies that meet fewer design standards.

Although the above literature review outlined several studies that implemented variations of a token economy resulting in positive effects on student inappropriate or disruptive behavior, there are limitations of the current literature base that warrant further scientific evaluation. First, across individual and class-wide token economy studies, there are fewer studies evaluating effects for preschool-aged children compared with older students (e.g., ages 6 to 15 years; Soares et al., 2016). With the growing emphasis on early intervention strategies (Feil et al., 2016; Fox et al., 2002; Stormont, 2002), studies that evaluate viable strategies in the preschool setting are essential. Second, of the token economy strategies utilized in the preschool setting, many studies used a level system strategy and response cost (a procedure in which tokens are removed following inappropriate behavior; e.g., Filcheck et al., 2004; Reitman et al., 2004), and the effect of other strategies within this setting should be further evaluated.

## Purpose of the Current Study

The current meta-analysis determined the effect size of single-case design token economy studies implemented within the preschool setting. This meta-analysis focused on studies using single subject research designs. Historically, token economy studies have used single subject research designs; and as such, limiting this meta-analysis to single subject research designs allows for a common metric for evaluating intervention effect. Additionally, this study evaluated the methodological rigor of studies included in the meta-analysis. Finally, this study included an evaluation of moderators of the effects of token economies in preschool settings. The following research questions were addressed:

1. *What is the effect of token economies implemented in the preschool classroom setting on child behavior?*
2. *Is the effectiveness of token economies on preschool children's behavior impacted by moderator variables (e.g., number of WWC design standards met, interventionist type, primary dependent variable, design type, and presence of response cost)?*
3. *To what degree do token economies in preschool settings meet current design standards?*

## Method

### Literature Search

A literature review was conducted using a multi-step process, ensuring the included articles were most appropriate to the current research questions. Two relevant, readily available databases were used: APA PsycInfo and Psychology and Behavioral Sciences Collection. Three groups of keywords were searched within the databases using Boolean Operators to target the search to more applicable studies: "preschool" or "early childhood" or "head start" or "prek" or "pre-k" AND "token economy" or "tokens" or "token" or "token system" AND "classroom."

Articles were then examined and included if they met the following inclusion criteria: 1) utilized single-case design, 2) participants were preschool-aged (2 to 5 years old), 3) setting was the preschool classroom, 4) the study evaluated the effect of token reinforcement on student behavior, 5) article was published in a peer-reviewed journal, 6) article was available in English, and 7) publishing year was 1980 or after. The references for the articles were searched to identify any additional articles, and subsequent abstracts or full manuscripts of relevant articles were reviewed for inclusion criteria.

**Article Coding**

Each article was coded for four general categories: WWC Design Standards, participant characteristics, study characteristics, and interventionist characteristics. Based on WWC Design Standards 4.1 (WWC, 2020), each design standard was coded separately as "Meets Without Reservations," "Meets with Reservations," or "Does Not Meet." Two additional variables were added that computed the percentage of design standards met as well as an absolute variable (i.e., coding as "Met" required all standards to be met; coding as "Does Not Meet" required only a single standard not being met). Six separate design standard variables were coded based on WWC Version 4.1 and included the following: data availability (data must be presented visually, either in a graphical or tabular format), systematic manipulation (the experimenter must decide when and how the independent variable is manipulated), interobserver agreement (IOA; at least 20% of the data within each phase must be collected across two separate observers simultaneously and the agreement between the data must be 80% or greater), residual effects (for studies with three or more intervention types, it must be determined that there are no residual treatment effects), attempts at intervention (three attempts must be made to show a treatment effect), and meet the minimum phase length and minimum threshold of data points per phase depending on the intervention type. Although within the WWC Version 4.1 Design Standards, the phase length and minimum data points per phase is grouped into one standard, this standard was separated into two variables for the purpose of this meta-analysis.

For participant characteristics the following variables were coded: whether the study reported participant ethnicity, percentage of participants that were female, percentage of participants that were male, age range of participants, mean age of participants, special education status of participants, and socioeconomic status of participant families. Study characteristic variables included: study setting, geographic location, whether maintenance or generalization data were collected, design type, primary dependent variable and its method, and intervention components (e.g., presence of response cost, exchange schedule). Additional variables included whether the study included data on treatment integrity and social validity. Interventionist characteristics included the primary interventionist's status (e.g., teacher/staff, experimenter). Several variables were used in moderator analyses to determine whether specific variables moderate or impact the effectiveness of token economies on the behavior of preschool students. Moderator variables included: Design type, setting, components, interventionist status, percentage of WWC design standards met, overall WWC design standards, and primary dependent variable. Of note, a total of 32 variables were originally coded; however, several variables were not retained for descriptive or statistical analyses due to lack of reporting across all studies (e.g., interventionist age, interventionist years of experience); however, all original variables were coded for intercoder agreement.

## Data Extraction

DigitizeIt Version 2.5 (Bormann, 2012; Rakap et al., 2016) was used to extract each numerical data point from an image of the graphs for each article to calculate effect sizes. Steps of extracting data for each article included the following: 1) taking a screen shot of each graph, 2) pasting the screenshot into the DigitizeIt software, 3) clicking on the minimum and maximum values for both the X and Y axes, and 4) clicking the center of each data point. Values for each data point were then retrieved from the software and entered into Excel for analyses. Prior to final analyses, negative values (determined to result from extraction errors) were changed to 0.

**Interrater Agreement**

Agreement between the primary author and trained graduate students was calculated on several variables. Independent literature searches were conducted and discrepancies in article inclusion were discussed until 100% agreement was reached. For variable coding, the primary author trained a secondary coder on the coding scheme until 100% agreement in coding was met on a practice article. Label codes were created for the 10 articles included in the current study, label codes were randomized, and the first 3 were chosen for secondary coding (i.e., 30% of articles). Coding agreement used an extract agreement method across variables. Agreement percentage was calculated by dividing the number of variables agreed by the total number of variables and multiplied by 100. Average agreement was 84.38% across all variables (range = 0% - 100%). If agreement for a single variable fell below 80%, the raters discussed the codes until 100% agreement was reached.

The secondary coder also extracted data with Digitize It for 30% of the articles. Agreement on datum to the nearest whole number was calculated using the exact agreement method, as well as a calculation of proportional agreement in which the smaller number was divided by the larger number and multiplied by 100. Exact agreement was within an acceptable range ($M = 85.28\%$, range = 88.79% - 98.27%). Proportional agreement was also calculated and found to also be within an acceptable range ($M = 92.61\%$, range = 88.79% - 98.27%).

**Effect Sizes**

Baseline-corrected Tau (Tarlow, 2017) was utilized, which is an effect size statistic appropriate for single case design studies and incorporates both overlap of data points between phases as well as any present baseline trend. Categorical qualifiers outlined by Vannest and Ninci (2015) are used to determine the extent to which the effect size is small (< 0.2), moderate (0.2 – 0.6), large (0.6 – 0.8), or very large (> 0.8). A free calculator available online (Tarlow, 2016) was used to calculate baseline-corrected Tau using A-B contrasts where A was a baseline phase and B was an adjacent treatment phase (Parker & Brossart, 2006). Of note, maintenance or follow up data were not included in phase contrasts for the current meta-analysis as the aim of the current analysis was on initial treatment effects. If trends in the baseline data were found, the calculator applied the baseline correction prior to calculating the final effect size. If trends in the baseline data were not found, Tau (without baseline correction) was used to calculate the final effect size.

Given the lack of consensus regarding the best effect size calculation for single case designs and to increase confidence in results, Hedge's g was also calculated for each study and across studies to produce an omnibus effect size. Interpreting Hedge's g uses the same rules of thumb as Cohen's d: 0.2 is interpreted as a small effect, 0.5 is interpreted as a medium effect, and 0.8 is interpreted as a large effect (Cohen, 1992). For analysis, means and standard deviations for each phase of each study were calculated using Microsoft Excel and entered into R (Harrer et al., 2019a; R Core Team, 2013) using the same phase contrasts as baseline-corrected Tau. Within R, the dmetar package was utilized (Harrer et al., 2019b). Due to differences in sampling across studies, a random effects model was used to calculate the omnibus effect of token economies on preschool students' behavior.

## Results
### Literature Search

The initial phase of the literature search with the included Boolean operators yielded 42 articles across both the APA PsycInfo and Psychology and Behavioral Sciences databases. Initially, abstracts were reviewed and studies were excluded if they failed to meet any of the 6 inclusion criteria. For the remaining articles, the manuscripts were reviewed in full to determine if each study met inclusion criteria. Based on these inclusion criteria, 10 articles were retained for the meta-analysis. The author included one additional study following the ancestral search (i.e., Wolfe et al., 1983); however, the study was ultimately excluded due to graphical representation of the data that could not be extracted using the current methods. In total, 10 articles were determined to meet inclusion criteria for the current meta-analysis.

## Descriptive Statistics

### WWC Design Standards

None of the included studies fully met WWC Version 4.1 (WWC, 2020) design standards, as each study failed to "Meet without Reservations" on at least one design standard variable and only 20% of articles met all criteria with reservations (see Table 1).

Table 1
WWC Design Standards

|  | DS1 | DS2 | DS3 | DS4 | DS5 | DS6 | Percentage of Standards Met |
|---|---|---|---|---|---|---|---|
| Tiano et al. (2005) | MS | MS | MS | NA | MS | DNM | 80% |
| McGoey & DuPaul (2000) | MS | MS | DNM | NA | MS | MWR | 60% (80%*) |
| Filcheck et al., 2004 | MS | MS | DNM | NA | DNM | MWR | 40% (60%*) |
| Plavnick et al., 2010 | MS | MS | DNM | NA | DNM | DNM | 40% |
| Reitman et al., 2004 | MS | MS | MS | MS | MS | MWR | 83.33% (100%*) |
| Sran & Borrero, 2010 | MS | MS | DNM | NA | MS | MS | 80% |
| Swiezy et al., 1993 | MS | MS | DNM | NA | MS | MWR | 60% (80%*) |
| Miller et al., 1981 | MS | MS | DNM | DNM | MS | MS | 66.67% |
| Conyers et al., 2004 | MS | MS | MS | MS | MS | MWR | 83.33% (100%*) |
| Conyers et al., 2003 | MS | MS | DNM | NA | MS | DNM | 60% |

**Note.** DS1 = Data availability, DS2 = Systematic manipulation, DS3 = Interobserver agreement, DS4 = Residual effects, DS5 = Attempts at intervention effect, DS6 = Data points per phase, MS = Meets standard without reservation, MWR = Meets standard with reservation, DNM = Does not meet standard, NA = Not applicable. An asterisk (*) indicates percentages of standards met without or with reservations.

All of the included studies met design standards for data availability and systematic manipulation. Only 30% of the studies met the design standard regarding IOA. The design standard related to residual effects was met by 66.67% of studies of which this design standard was applicable (i.e., 2 of 3 studies). Eighty percent of the studies met the attempts at intervention effects design standard. Twenty percent of the studies met the design standards for minimum data points per phase without reservations, and 50% of the studies met the design standards for minimum data points per phase with reservations.

### *Participant, Interventionist, and Study Characteristics*

Overall, there were limited data provided for participant and interventionist characteristics across studies. For example, 70% of studies failed to report race or ethnicity data for participants. Studies that did report these data show that most participants were white or Caucasian and male (64.74%). Although all the included studies took place in a preschool classroom setting, location types varied across the set of studies: 60% took place in a regular, public preschool classroom while 20%, 10%, and 10% of studies took place in Head Start classrooms, special education classrooms, and parochial preschool classrooms, respectively. Interventionists in 60% of the studies were preschool classroom teachers or staff and the remaining were experimenters. Of note, one study did not report status of the interventionist (Conyers et al., 2003).

The majority (40%) of studies utilized an alternating treatments or multielement design. The remaining studies used a reversal (20%), withdrawal (20%), or multiple baseline (20%) design. Each study's primary dependent variable was coded into two general categories: inappropriate student behavior or appropriate student behavior with most studies using inappropriate student behavior as the primary dependent variable. Examples of inappropriate student behavior included off-task behavior and breaking classroom rules (e.g., keep hands to self). Examples of appropriate student behavior included appropriate sitting behavior, responding to the target task, and appropriate rest-time behavior. Half of the included studies included a response cost. Of those studies, the response cost procedure was either incorporated within the components of the token economy (60%) or directly compared to token reinforcement and response cost (40%). The exchange rate of tokens also varied across the included studies: 50% exchanged tokens once daily, 30% multiple times per day, and 20% failing to report the exchange rate.

Treatment integrity data were reported in five studies. Tiano et al. (2005) reported treatment integrity was above 85% and no retraining was necessary throughout the study. McGoey and DuPaul (2000) reported treatment integrity remained at 100% across all phases of the study; however, the researchers only checked treatment integrity once per week. Across all phases in Filcheck et al. (2004), average treatment integrity was reported to be 67.8% and a total of seven retrainings were required across the duration of the study. Plavnick et al. (2010) reported an average treatment integrity of 84% across the teacher participants. Finally, although Swiezy et al. (1993) reported they collected data on treatment integrity, the authors did not provide the data within the article.

Social validity data were reported in 4 studies (Filcheck et al., 2004; McGoey & DuPaul, 2000; Reitman et al, 2004; Tiano et al., 2005). However, two of those studies failed to report specific outcomes (Filcheck et al., 2004; Tiano et al., 2005. Both studies that did report outcomes used teacher-rated treatment acceptability as the measure of social validity based on the Intervention Rating Profile-15 (IRP-15; Martens et al., 1985). The IRP-15 consists of 15 items rated on a Likert scale ranging from 1 (not acceptable) to 6 (very acceptable). Total scores on the IRP-15 range from 15 to 90 and higher scores represent higher acceptability. McGoey and DuPaul (2000) reported a per-item average rating of 5.1 representing high acceptability. Reitman et al. (2004) reported varied acceptability across all 3 participants: poor (IRP-15 = 20), moderate (IRP-15 = 61), and high (IRP-15 = 83).

Forty percent of the included studies reported a maintenance or follow up phase. Of those studies, one study reported the maintenance phase began immediately after the final intervention phase (Miller et al., 1981), one study reported the maintenance phase began within 1 month of the final intervention phase (McGoey & DuPaul, 2000), and two studies reported the maintenance phase began at or more than one month after the final intervention phase (Filcheck et al., 2004; Tiano et al. 2005). Swiezy et al. (1993) evaluated the degree to which their treatment effects in the classroom generalized to the school playground and was the only study that reported generalization data.

## Effect Size Calculations

### *Baseline-Corrected Tau*

A total of 63 phase contrasts across studies were analyzed to calculate Baseline-Corrected Tau effect sizes. No baseline corrections were necessary and the final effect size was calculated using Tau (without baseline correction). Overall, effect sizes across studies ranged from 0 to 0.745 with a mean of 0.499. See Table 2 for Baseline-Corrected Tau effect sizes across phase contrast within each study.

## Table 2

*Baseline-Corrected Tau Across Studies*

| Study | Participant | Phase Contrast | Baseline-Corrected Tau | Effect Size |
|---|---|---|---|---|
| Tiano et al. (2005) | Ruby | BL1-RC | 0.745 | Large |
|  |  | BL2-TE$^R$ | 0.215 | Moderate |
|  | Damon | BL1-RC | 0.537 | Moderate |
|  |  | BL2-TE$^R$ | 0.000 | Small |
|  | Mitch | BL1-RC | 0.566 | Moderate |
|  |  | BL2-TE$^R$ | 0.336 | Moderate |
| McGoey & DuPaul (2000) | Derek | BL1-TE1 | 0.728 | Large |
|  |  | BL2-RC1 | 0.252 | Moderate |
|  |  | BL3-TE2 | 0.775 | Large |
|  |  | BL4-RC2 | 0.378 | Moderate |
|  | Douglas | BL1-TE1 | 0.542 | Moderate |
|  |  | BL2-RC1 | 0.478 | Moderate |
|  |  | BL3-TE2 | 0.775 | Large |
|  |  | BL4-RC2 | 0.258 | Moderate |
|  | Monica | BL1-RC1 | 0.726 | Large |
|  |  | BL2-TE1 | 0.630 | Large |
|  |  | BL3-RC2 | 0.258 | Moderate |
|  |  | BL4-TE2 | 0.756 | Large |
|  | Rebecca | BL1-RC1 | 0.189 | Small |
|  |  | BL2-TE1 | 0.629 | Large |
|  |  | BL3-RC2 | 0.602 | Large |
|  |  | BL4-TE2 | 0.775 | Large |
| Filcheck et al. (2004) | Classwide | BL1-TE$^R$ | 0.411 | Moderate |
|  |  | BL2-CDI | 0.463 | Moderate |
|  |  | BL2-PDI | 0.693 | Large |
| Plavnick et al. (2010) | Toby | BL-TE | 0.399 | Moderate |
|  | Kendra | BL-TE | 0.213 | Moderate |
| Conyers et al. (2004) | Classwide | BL1-RC1 | 0.622 | Large |
|  |  | BL2-TE | 0.639 | Large |
|  |  | BL2-RC2 | 0.510 | Moderate |
| Conyers et al. (2003) | Classwide | BL1-TE1 | 0.603 | Large |
|  |  | BL2-TE2 | 0.366 | Moderate |
| Reitman et al. (2004) | Simon | BL1-GR1$^R$ | 0.539 | Moderate |
|  |  | BL1-IN1$^R$ | 0.346 | Moderate |
|  |  | BL2-GR2$^R$ | 0.679 | Large |
|  |  | BL2-IN2$^R$ | 0.680 | Large |
|  | Xavier | BL1-GR1$^R$ | 0.396 | Moderate |
|  |  | BL1-IN1$^R$ | 0.693 | Large |
|  |  | BL2-GR2$^R$ | 0.658 | Large |
|  |  | BL2-IN2$^R$ | 0.756 | Large |
|  | Tom | BL1-GR1$^R$ | 0.587 | Moderate |
|  |  | BL1-IN1$^R$ | 0.702 | Large |
|  |  | BL2-GR2$^R$ | 0.648 | Large |
|  |  | BL2-IN2$^R$ | 0.770 | Large |
| Sran & Borrero (2010) | Dylan | BL-NO | 0.065 | Small |
|  |  | BL-SI | 0.287 | Moderate |
|  |  | BL-VA | 0.348 | Moderate |
|  | Mira | BL-NO | 0.367 | Moderate |
|  |  | BL-SI | 0.472 | Moderate |
|  |  | BL-VA | 0.472 | Moderate |
|  | Milo | BL-NO | 0.147 | Small |
|  |  | BL-SI | 0.219 | Moderate |
|  |  | BL-VA | 0.219 | Moderate |
|  | Luke | BL-NO | 0.339 | Moderate |
|  |  | BL-SI | 0.139 | Small |
|  |  | BL-VA | 0.261 | Moderate |
| Swiezy et al. (1993) | Pair A | BL1-TE1 | 0.518 | Moderate |
|  |  | BL2-TE2 | 0.518 | Moderate |
|  | Pair B | BL1-TE1 | 0.724 | Large |
|  |  | BL2-TE2 | 0.655 | Large |
| Miller et al. (1981) | Classwide | BL1-TE1 | 0.716 | Large |
|  |  | BL2-TE2 | 0.730 | Large |
|  |  | BL2-TE3 | 0.745 | Large |

*Note.* BL = Baseline, TE = Token Economy, RC = Response Cost, CDI = Child Directed Interaction, PDI = Parent Directed Interaction, GR = Group Token Economy, IN = Individual Token Economy, NO = No Choice, SI = Single Choice, VA = Varied Choice. Superscript R denotes token economies that also included a response cost component.

## Hedge's g

Hedge's g was computed for each of the 10 included studies (see Table 3). The majority of studies produced a large effect size based on the rule of thumb (i.e., 0.8 threshold; Cohen, 1992). Filcheck et al. (2004)'s effect size was small (0.4425). Plavnick et al. (2010) and Sran and Borrero (2010) reported medium effect sizes. See Table 4 for Hedge's g effect sizes, confidence intervals, and standard errors for all studies. See Figure 1 for a forest plot of effect sizes for each study.

**Figure 1**
*Forest Plot of Effect Sizes by Study*

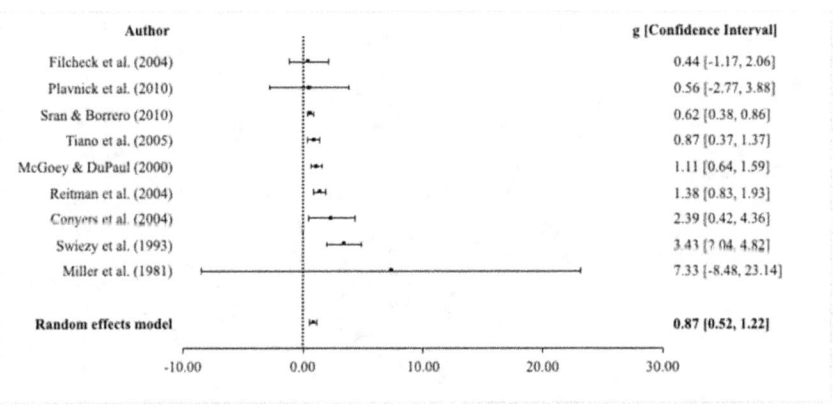

*Note.* Conyers et al. (2003) was removed from the final forest plot due to inability to interpret the forest plot with it included (due to its wide confidence interval [-66.16 to 81.68]).

Hedge's g was also calculated across all included studies to produce an omnibus effect size. The omnibus effect size using Hedge's g was 0.8704, $p = 0.003$ and is considered a large effect size. The included studies were analyzed to determine whether there were outliers present. The find.outliers function within the dmetar package detected an outlier based on a significant test of heterogeneity ($p = 0.0033$). The outlier (Swiezy et al., 1993) was removed from analysis and the test of heterogeneity was not significant ($p = 0.1762$) for the final omnibus effect size calculation.

With the outlier removed, Hedge's g was 0.8257, p < 0.0001 and is also considered a large effect size (Cohen, 1992).

**Table 3**
*Effect Size by Study*

| Study | Number of Contrasts | Hedge's g | Confidence Intervals | | Standard Error |
|---|---|---|---|---|---|
| | | | Lower | Upper | |
| Tiano et al. (2005) | 6 | 0.8694$^L$ | 0.3686 | 1.3701 | 0.25548469 |
| McGoey & DuPaul (2000) | 16 | 1.1138$^L$ | 0.6352 | 1.5924 | 0.24418367 |
| Filcheck et al. (2004) | 3 | 0.4425$^S$ | -1.1727 | 2.0576 | 0.82405612 |
| Plavnick et al. (2010) | 2 | 0.5574$^M$ | -2.7681 | 3.883 | 1.69670918 |
| Conyers et al. (2004) | 3 | 2.3889$^L$ | 0.4186 | 4.3592 | 1.0052551 |
| Conyers et al. (2003) | 2 | 7.7557$^L$ | -66.1653 | 81.6766 | 37.7147704 |
| Reitman et al. (2004) | 12 | 1.3796$^L$ | 0.8318 | 1.9274 | 0.2794898 |
| Sran & Borrero (2010) | 12 | 0.6208$^M$ | 0.38 | 0.8615 | 0.12283163 |
| Swiezy et al. (1993) | 4 | 3.4279$^L$ | 2.0383 | 4.8174 | 0.70895408 |
| Miller et al. (1981) | 2 | 7.3282$^L$ | -8.4839 | 23.1403 | 8.06739796 |

**Note.** *The superscript S denotes a small effect, the superscript M denotes a medium effect, and superscript L denotes a large effect.*

## *Moderator Analyses*

Moderator analyses were conducted for seven variables to determine their effects on the impact of token economies on preschool student behavior: Design Type, Setting, Inclusion of Response Cost, Interventionist Status, Number of WWC Standards Met, Overall WWC, and Primary Dependent Variable. Although medium to large effects were found, none of the analyses produced significant results on student behavior outcomes (see Table 4).

*Table 4*
*Effect Sizes for Moderator Variables*

| Moderator | Category | K (studies) | Hedge's g | 95% Confidence Interval | |
|---|---|---|---|---|---|
| | | | | Lower | Higher |
| Design Type | Withdrawal/Reversal | 4 | 0.9729$^L$ | 0.6648 | 1.281 |
| | Alternating Treatments | 2 | 0.7652$^M$ | 0.1329 | 1.3976 |
| | Multiple Baseline | 4 | 2.4066$^L$ | -15.0553 | 19.8684 |
| Setting | Head Start | 2 | 1.1119$^L$ | -2.1255 | 4.3493 |
| | Public Preschool | 6 | 0.7361$^M$ | 0.4118 | 1.0604 |
| | Special Education Preschool | 1 | 0.5574$^M$ | -2.7681 | 3.883 |
| | Church Preschool | 1 | 3.4279$^L$ | 2.0383 | 4.8174 |
| Components | With Response Cost | 5 | 1.1342$^L$ | 0.5781 | 1.6904 |
| | Without Response Cost | 5 | 0.734$^M$ | 0.0345 | 1.3724 |
| Interventionist Status | Teacher | 6 | 1.0832$^L$ | 0.7852 | 1.3813 |
| | Experimenter | 3 | 1.9733$^L$ | -1.7495 | 5.6961 |
| Percent of WWC Standards Met | 66.67% | 3 | 0.8576$^L$ | -3.3891 | 5.1042 |
| | 83.33% | 5 | 1.2291$^L$ | -0.1725 | 2.6308 |
| | 100% | 2 | 1.452$^L$ | -1.8577 | 4.7617 |
| Overall WWC | Met | 2 | 1.452$^L$ | -1.8577 | 4.7617 |
| | Does Not Meet | 8 | 0.7919$^M$ | 0.4118 | 1.172 |
| Primary DV | Appropriate | 4 | 0.7034$^M$ | -0.1811 | 1.5878 |
| | Inappropriate | 6 | 1.1125$^L$ | 0.7732 | 1.4517 |

*Note.* The superscript S denotes a small effect, the superscript M denotes a medium effect, and superscript L denotes a large effect.

# Discussion

Although two recent meta-analyses were conducted evaluating the effect of token economies in classrooms, (Maggin et al., 2011; Soares et al., 2016), the current meta-analysis attempted to expand on those results by targeting the preschool setting and including the latest WWC Version 4.1 Design Standards (WWC, 2020). Similar to the results of Maggin et al. (2011) and Soares et al. (2016), results of the current meta-analysis showed that token economies generally produce favorable and large effects on increasing appropriate behavior and decreasing inappropriate behavior in the preschool classrooms. In the Maggin et al. (2011) and Soares et al. (2016) meta-analyses, the overall effect was large.

However, the preschool setting was not evaluated in Maggin et al. (2011). Soares et al. (2016) did include the preschool setting, and their moderator analysis showed a statistically lower effect size for ages 3 to 5 compared to 6 to 15. The number of articles included in the current meta-analysis represented approximately a 67% increase from the number of preschool articles included in Soares et al. (2016). There was some considerable overlap in the preschool articles included in both studies; specifically, five articles were included in the current meta-analysis and Soares et al. (2016). The inclusion criteria used by Soares and colleagues was limited to public preschool classrooms whereas the current meta-analysis expanded this to other settings (e.g., special education classrooms, parochial classroom); thus, the results of the current meta-analysis may be more generalizable than the results of Soares et al. (2016).

Maggin et al. (2011) and Soares et al. (2016) also evaluated methodological rigor of token economy studies; however, both studies used older WWC standards (Kratochwill et al., 2010). The current meta-analysis reviewed studies utilizing the most recent design standards (WWC, 2020), which are more rigorous than previous WWC standards. Soares et al. (2016) found that token economy studies in preschool settings did not meet design standards; in fact, 50% of the preschool studies included in the meta-analysis were weak (i.e., did not meet standards). Results from this study are consistent with those findings. None of the 10 studies included in this meta-analysis met design standards without reservations based on the most recent standards (WWC, 2020). Moreover, eight studies did not meet standards with reservations. These results indicate that researchers and practitioners must be cautious with regard to interpreting findings from this meta-analysis and from individual studies that have tested token economies in preschool classrooms. Poor research design and execution undermines internal and external validity. For example, if a single case design study includes less than five data points per phase and IOA data for the dependent measures were not adequately sampled, then researchers and practitioners cannot be confident that changes in behavior are due to the intervention. It may be that changes in behavior are due to instrumentation shift or an unreliable, inadequate sample of behavior. Similarly, if treatment integrity data are not provided, then changes in behavior cannot be attributed to the independent variable. Therefore, future research testing token economies in preschool classrooms must be designed and executed with more rigorous designs and procedures.

This study also conducted moderator analyses of several variables, and results indicated no significant moderators of token economy effects. However, it is important to note that this meta-analysis only included 10 studies; results of the moderator analyses should be interpreted with caution given that the inclusion of fewer studies may significantly affect the statistical power necessary to detect differences between groups (Borenstein et al., 2009). Relatively few token economy studies have been conducted in preschool settings. As more studies accumulate, another meta-analysis may be conducted and moderator analyses may yield important moderators of token economy effects in preschool classrooms.

## Limitations

Several limitations of the current meta-analysis should be considered when interpreting its results. First, the initial literature search used only two databases relevant to the social and behavioral sciences. It may be the case that expanding the search to other databases would have yielded a higher number of articles. However, an ancestral search was used to include articles not otherwise available in the initial search. Therefore, this meta-analysis may adequately sample published research testing token economies in preschool classrooms. Relatedly, a second limitation includes the limited number of total articles included in the current meta-analysis. Although it has been suggested that only two studies are needed to conduct a meta-analysis (Valentine et al., 2010) and at least five are needed for sufficient power (Jackson & Turner, 2017), it is likely that overall conclusions of the effectiveness of token economies within the preschool classroom will change as more studies are included in future analyses and statistical power is increased. Further, it may be the case that different sets of inclusion criteria would yield a higher number of articles to include. In this meta-analysis, for example, the author only included articles that were published in peer-reviewed journals, which may be subject to publication bias (i.e., favoring publication of studies with stronger effects; Tincani & Travers, 2019). Future meta-analyses should include grey literature to increase the score of the analysis as well as increase power. Third, the author coded the dependent variables into two general categories (appropriate and inappropriate student behavior). However, specific definitions of behaviors differed across the included studies. It may be the case that token economies have a different effect on different types of student behaviors (e.g., more disruptive externalizing behaviors such as tantrumming versus more passive behaviors such as off-task). In addition, token economies have also been evaluated to improve outcomes other than student appropriate or inappropriate behaviors (e.g., academic achievement; Ayllon et al., 1972) and a meta-analysis that includes a greater variety of outcome variables may produce different effects. Finally, some studies included intervention components outside of the standard procedures of token economies, and the degree to which their presence altered the effectiveness of treatment is unknown. For example, Sran and Borrero (2010) included different variations of token economy exchanges to include a no choice condition (i.e., children exchanged tokens for only one reinforcer), single choice condition (i.e., children exchanged tokens for one of five identical reinforcers), and varied choice condition (i.e., children exchanged tokens for one of five different reinforcers).

In addition to the limitations of the current meta-analysis, limitations of the included studies should also be noted. The majority of studies did not report data for a number of different areas, including specific treatment components, participant characteristics, and interventionist characteristics. Absence of these data limits the extent to which future researchers can attempt to replicate these studies, as well as the degree to which the studies' findings can translate from sample to population. Many studies also did not report sufficient data related to treatment integrity and social validity. Measuring and reporting treatment integrity data are crucial in regard to internal validity. If the degree to which treatment was implemented with integrity is unknown, treatment outcomes cannot be properly assessed or correlated with the treatment. Further, information regarding treatment integrity is important for external validity and the extent to which treatment may be implemented in real-world settings. Relatedly, measures or procedures to calculate treatment integrity and social validity varied across the studies that included those data. Finally, maintenance and generalization data were not collected for most studies; thus, it is unknown if treatment effects maintained over time and generalized to other settings.

**Future Directions**

Although this meta-analysis yielded results in favor of the overall effectiveness token economies have on children's behavior in the preschool classroom, future studies should attend to aforementioned limitations. In particular, researchers should include treatment integrity data due to its importance to internal and external validity. Researchers should provide more information in regard to interventionist characteristics, since treatment integrity may vary based on professional background and training (e.g., researchers, teacher assistants), and variations in treatment integrity may impact treatment outcomes. Moreover, IOA data are needed to strengthen the rigor of the research, and thus increase the believability of findings. Overall, major methodological changes are needed for future studies, including meeting WWC Version 4.1 Design Standards (WWC, 2020), inclusion of treatment integrity data, and inclusion of social validity data to measure the degree to which token economies produce meaningful and sustainable changes to the classroom environment.

## References

*Note: Asterisk (\*) denotes articles included in the current meta-analysis*

Ayllon, T. & Kelly, K. (1972). Effects of reinforcement on standardized test performance. *Journal of Applied Behavior Analysis, 5*(4), 477-484. https://doi.org/10.1901/jaba.1972.5-477

Barrish, H. H., Saunders, M., & Wolf, M. M. (1969). Good behavior game: Effects of individual contingencies for group consequences on disruptive behavior in a classroom. *Journal of Applied Behavior Analysis, 2*(2), 119-124. https://doi.org/10.1901/jaba.1969.2-119

Boerke, K. W., & Reitman, D. (2011). Token economies. In W. W. Fisher, C. C. Piazza, & H. S. Roane (Eds.), Handbook of applied behavior analysis (pp. 370-382). The Guilford Press.

Borenstein, M.R., Hedges, L.V., Higgins, J.P.T., & Rothstein, H.R. (2009). Introduction to meta-analysis. John Wiley & Sons.

Bormann, (2012) DigitizeIt (version 2.0) http://www.digitizeit.de/

Bulotsky-Shearer, R. J., Fernandez, V., Dominguez, X., & Rouse, H. L. (2011). Behavior problems in learning activities and social interactions in Head Start classrooms and early reading, mathematics, and approaches to learning. *School Psychology Review, 40*, 39-56. https://doi.org/10.1080.02796015.2011.12087727

Campbell, S. B. & Ewing, L. J. (1990). Follow-up of hard-to-manage preschoolers: Adjustment at age 9 and predictors of continuing symptoms. *Journal of Child Psychology and Psychiatry, 6*, 871-889. https://doi.org/10.1111/j.1469-7610.1990.tb00831.x

Cohen, J. (1992). Statistical power analysis. *Current Directions in Psychological Science, 1*(3), 98-101. https://doi.org/10.1111/1467-8721.ep10768783

\*Conyers, C., Miltenberger, R., Maki, A., Barenz, R., Jurgens, M., Sailer, A., Haugen, M., & Kopp, B. (2004). A comparison of response cost and differential reinforcement of other behavior to reduce disruptive behavior in a preschool classroom. *Journal of Applied Behavior Analysis, 37*(3), 411-415. https://doi.org/10.1901/jaba.2004.37-411

\*Conyers, C., Miltenberger, R., Romaniuk, C., Kopp, B., & Himle, M. (2003). Evaluation of DRO schedules to reduce disruptive behavior in a preschool classroom. *Child & Family Behavior Therapy, 25*(3). 1-6. https://doi.org/10.1300/J019v25n03_01

Drabman, R. S. & Lahey, B. B. (1974). Feedback in classroom behavior modification: Effects on the target and her classmates. *Journal of Applied Behavior Analysis, 7*(4), 591-598. https://doi.org/10.1901/jaba.1974.7-591

Doll, C., McLaughlin, T. F., Barretto, A. (2013). The token economy: A recent review and evaluation. *International Journal of Basic and Applied Science, 02*(01), 131-149.

Egger, H. L. & Angold, A. (2006). Common emotional and behavioral disorders in preschool children: Presentation, nosology, and epidemiology. *Journal of Child Psychology and Psychiatry, 47*(3/4), 313-337. https://doi.org/10.1111/j.1469-7610.2006.01618.x

Feil, E. G., Small, J. W., Seeley, J. R., Walker, H. M., Golly, A., Frey, A., & Forness, S. R. (2016). Early intervention for preschoolers at risk for Attention-Deficit/Hyperactivity Disorder: Preschool First Step to Success. *Behavioral Disorders, 41*(2), 95–106. https://doi.org/10.17988/0198-7429-41.2.95

*Filcheck, H. A., McNeil, C. B., Greco, L. A., & Bernard, R. S. (2004). Using a whole-class token economy and coaching of teacher skills in a preschool classroom to manage disruptive behavior. *Psychology in the Schools, 41*(3), 351-361. https://doi.org/10.1002/pits.10168

Fox, L., Dunlap, G., Cushing, L. (2002). Early intervention, positive behavior support, and transition to school. *Journal of Emotional and Behavioral Disorders, 10*(3), 149-157. https://doi.org/10.1177/10634266020100030301

Harrer, M., Cuijpers, P., Furukawa, T.A, & Ebert, D. D. (2019a). Doing Meta-Analysis in R: A Hands-on Guide. https://bookdown.org/MathiasHarrer/Doing_Meta_Analysis_in_R/

Harrer, M., Cuijpers, P., Furukawa, T. & Ebert, D. D. (2019b). dmetar: Companion R package for the guide 'Doing Meta-Analysis in R'. R package version 0.0.9000. http://dmetar.protectlab.org/

Jackson, D. & Turner, R. (2017). Power analysis for random-effects meta-analysis. *Research Synthesis Methods, 8,* 290-302. https://doi.org/10.1002/jrsm.1240

Kazdin, A. E. (1987). Treatment of antisocial behavior in children: Current status and future directions. *Psychological Bulletin, 102*(2), 187-203. https://doi.org/10.1037/0033-2909.102.2.187

Klimas, A. & McLaughlin, T. F. (2007). The effects of token economy system to improve social and academic behavior with a rural primary and child with disabilities. *International Journal of Special Education, 22*(3).

Kratochwill, T. R., Hitchock, J., Horner, R. H., Levin, J. R., Odom, S. L., Rindskopf, D.M. & Shadish, W.R. (2010). *Single-Case Designs Technical Documentation.* Retrieved from What Works Clearinghouse website: http://ies.ed.gov/ncee/wwc/pdf/wwc_scd.pdf.

Maggin, D., M., Chafouleas, S. M., Goddard, K. M., & Johnson, A. H. (2011). A systematic evaluation of token economies as a classroom management tool for students with challenging behavior. *Journal of School Psychology, 49,* 529-554. https://doi.org/10.1016/j.jsp.2011.05.001

Martens, B. K., Witt, J. C., Elliott, S. N., & Darveaux, D. X. (1985). Teacher judgments concerning the acceptability of school-based interventions. *Professional Psychology: Research and Practice, 16*(2), 191-198. https://doi.org/10.1037/0735-7028.16.2.191

*McGoey, K. E. & DuPaul, G. J. (2000). Token reinforcement and response cost procedures: Reducing the disruptive behavior of preschool children with attention-deficit/hyperactivity disorder. *School Psychology Quarterly, 15*(3), 330-343. https://doi.org/10.1037/h0088790

*Miller, M. A., McCullough, C. S., & Ulman, J. D. (1981). Carryover effects of multielement manipulations: Enhancement of preschoolers' appropriate rest-time behavior. *Educational Psychology: An International Journal of Experimental Educational Psychology, 1*(4), 341-346. https://doi.org/10.1080/0144341810010405

Nelson, J. G., Benner, G. J., Lane, K., & Smith, B. W. (2004). Academic achievement of K-12 students with emotional and behavioral disorders. *Exceptional Children, 71,* 59-73. https://doi.org/10.1177/001440290407100104

Parker, R. I. & Brossart, D. F. (2006). Phase contrasts for multiphase single case intervention designs. *School Psychology Quarterly, 21*(1), 46-61. https://doi.org/10.1521/scpq.2006.21.1.46

Pastor, P. N. & Reuben, C. A. (2015). Trends in parent-reported emotional and behavioral problems among children using special education services. *Psychiatric Services, 66*(6), 656-659. https://doi.org/10.1176/appi.ps.201400254

*Plavnick, J. B., Ferreri, S. J., & Maupin, A. N. (2010). The effects of self-monitoring on the procedural integrity of a behavioral intervention for young children with developmental disabilities. *Journal of Applied Behavior Analysis, 43*(2), 315-320. https://doi.org/jaba.2010.43-315

Powell, D., Dunlap, G., & Fox, L. (2006). Prevention and intervention for the challenging behaviors of toddlers and preschoolers. *Infants & Young Children, 19,* 25-35. https://doi.org/10.1097/00001163-200601000-00004

R Core Team (2013). R: A language and environment for statistical computing. R Foundation for Statistical Computing, http://www.R-project.org/

Rakap, S., Rakap, S., Evran, D., & Cig, O. (2016). Comparative evaluation of the reliability and validity of three data extraction programs: UnGraph, GraphClick, and DigitizeIt. *Computers in Human Behavior, 55,* 159–166. https://doi.org/10.1016/j.chb.2015.09.008

*Reitman, D., Murphy, M. A., Hup, S. D. A., & O'Callaghan, P. M. (2004). Behavior change and perceptions of change: Evaluating the effectiveness of a token economy. *Child & Family Behavior Therapy, 26*(2), 17-36. https://doi.org/10.1300/J019v26n02_02

Soares, D. A., Harrison, J. D., Vannest, K., & McClelland, S. S. (2016). Effect size for token economy use in contemporary classroom settings: A meta-analysis and moderator analysis of single case research. *School Psychology Review, 45*(4), 379-399. https://doi.org/10.17105/SPR45-4.379-399

*Sran, S. K. & Borreo, J. C. (2010). Assessing the value of choice in a token economy. *Journal of Applied Behavior Analysis, 43*(3), 553-557. https://doi.org/10.1901/jaba.2010.43-553

Stormont, M. (2002). Externalizing behavior problems in young children: Contributing factors and early intervention. *Psychology in the Schools, 39*(2), 127-138. doi: 10.1002/pits.10025

*Swiezy, N. B., Matson, J. L., & Box, P. (1993). The good behavior game. *Child & Family Behavior Therapy, 14*(3), 21-32. https://doi.org/10.1300/J019v14n03_02

Tarlow, K. R. (2016). Baseline corrected tau calculator. http://ktarlow.com/stats/tau/

Tarlow, K. R. (2017). An improved rank correlation effect size statistic for single-case designs: Baseline corrected tau. *Behavior Modification, 41*(4), 427-467. https://doi.org/10.1177/0145445516676750

*Tiano, J. D., Fortson, B. L., McNeil, C. B., & Humphreys, L. A. (2005). Managing classroom behavior of Head Start children using response cost and token economy procedures. *Journal of Early and Intensive Behavior Intervention, 2*(1), 28-39. https://doi.org/10.1037/h0100298

Tincani, M. & Travers, J. (2019). Replication research, publication bias, and applied behavior analysis. *Perspectives on Behavior Science, 42*(1), 59-75. https://doi.org/10.1007/s40614-019-00191-5

U.S. Department of Education. (2020). *Forty-second annual report to Congress on the implementation of the Individuals with Disabilities Education Act.* Author.

Valentine, J. C., Pigott, T. D., & Rothstein, H. R. (2010). How many studies do you need?: A primer on statistical power for meta-analysis. *Journal of Educational and Behavioral Statistics, 35*(2), 215-247. https://doi.org/10.3102/1076998609346961

Vannest, K. J. & Ninci, J. (2015). Evaluating intervention effects in single-case research designs. Journal of Counseling & Development, 93(4), 403.411. https://doi.org/10.1002/jcad.12038

What Works Clearinghouse. (2020). *What Works Clearinghouse Standards Handbook, Version 4.1.* U.S. Department of Education, Institute of Education Sciences, National Center for Education Evaluation and Regional Assistance.

Wolfe, V. V., Boyd, L. A., & Wolfe, D. A. (1983). Teaching cooperative play to behavior-problem preschool children. *Education and Treatment of Children, 6*(1), 1-9.

# Universal Screening in Early Childhood Populations: A Systematic Review

*Mikayla Drymond, Alexis Sanchez, Nathaniel von der Embse, Gabrielle Francis, Dorie Ross, and Samin Khallaghi*

## Abstract

Early childhood is an important period for the development of social, emotional and behavioral (SEB) skills. Deficits in these skills often lead to negative outcomes; thus, early identification is essential for the provision of services. Unfortunately, only a fraction of students with deficits are identified and receive services. One cause of this is the methods used to identify students, such as teacher nominations which do not identify all students in need (Dowdy et al., 2013). Proactive practices, such as universal screening, are a more systematic way of identification. The purpose of this review was to examine commonly used early childhood screeners and their evidence base, effectiveness, and the feasibility and accessibility of their use in early childhood settings. This critical review analysed 18 screeners using Southam-Gerow & Prinstein's (2014) review criteria for evidence-based treatments and a technical adequacy rubric based on Glover and Albers' (2007) considerations for evaluating universal screening assessments. Of the 18 screening tools reviewed, four screeners are highly recommended based on their technical adequacy and usability within early childhood settings. These results highlight the need for further research in the evaluation of early childhood universal screeners.

**Keywords:** *early childhood, social-emotional challenges, universal screening, early intervention*

## Universal Screening in Early Childhood Populations: A Systematic Review

Social, emotional, and behavioral (SEB) knowledge and skills begin developing at a young age (Shonkoff & Phillips, 2000). These skills are crucial for life-span development as they assist in the communication of needs and wants and in forming positive relationships. (Denham et al., 2014). Young children who can clearly express and regulate their emotions are increasingly likely to develop and maintain positive educator and peer relationships (Wu et al., 2018), have greater self-confidence (Zakaria et al., 2020), have more positive feelings about learning (Bulotsky-Shearer et al., 2012), and achieve greater academic success in their early school years (Ramsook et al., 2020). Conversely, young children who enter preschool with lower social-emotional competence are more likely to develop fewer and less supportive educator and peer relationships, have lower self-confidence, have more negative attitudes towards school, and be at risk for social-emotional and academic difficulties (Denham et al., 2016).

It is estimated between 8 to 10% of children under the age of 5 years demonstrate clinically significant SEB problems, including difficulties with social interactions with parents and peers, delayed school readiness, and school-related problems (Gleason et al., 2016). The majority of children who receive SEB interventions receive them in the educational setting (Rones & Hoagwood, 2000). This places great responsibility on early childhood programs to promote SEB competence in young children and to make a systematic effort to identify children who may need additional supports in the social-emotional arena (Dvorsky et al., 2014).

### Relationship Between SEB Challenges in Early Childhood on Future Schooling/Outcomes

SEB development, such as recognizing emotions and communication skills, are important for children to be able to effectively recognize and communicate their needs. Without these skills, children will lack the social skills and emotional capacity needed to advocate for themselves and receive efficient social emotional support in later school years (Bridgeland et al., 2013; Raver, 2002). Negative attention as a result of low perception of school belongingness and conflict between educators and/or peers can lead to a rise in disciplinary actions, feelings of isolation during early development, and a lack of school support (Hamre & Pianta, 2001; Pianta & Stuhlman, 2004). About 8,700 children are expelled from state-funded preschool or prekindergarten classrooms each year and are expelled at three times the rate as K-12 students (Stegelin, 2018). Expulsion also disproportionately affects males with 79% of children expelled being males yet they only represent 54% of preschool children (Graves & Howes, 2011).

**Importance of Early Identification and Intervention**

Limited resources have prevented many children from receiving the requisite intervention support, despite the increasing prevalence of SEB problems during early childhood (Lane et al., 2012). Previous studies have demonstrated the strong relationship between early exposure to negative environmental factors (e.g., poverty, violence, parental substance abuse, and neglect) and the eventual development of SEB difficulties (Cappella et al., 2008). Furthermore, there is a clear link between the behaviors demonstrated by children throughout early childhood and those observed by educators of school-aged children and adolescents (Conroy & Brown, 2004).

These negative outcomes are even more worrying for students of color who are suspended and expelled at rates that exceed three times the rate of their White peers in early childhood programs (Gilliam, 2016). In 2011, the U.S. Department of Education Office for Civil Rights reported that African American children comprise 18% of all students in preschool; however, these students comprise 48% of students receiving more than one out-of-school suspension (U.S. Department of Education, 2014). This trend continues beyond preschool into elementary school and middle school (Skiba et al., 2011), further highlighting the value of early identification of SEB problems in early childhood education. Across the literature, research in three areas supports the need for early identification of SEB concerns. First, while uncommon, indicators of SEB disorders may be present in children beginning at 2 years of age (Egger & Angold, 2006). Second, behavioral and emotional concerns have been demonstrated to persist over time (Lavigne et al., 1998). Third, early identification and intervention have demonstrated promising outcomes for improving the problem behaviors demonstrated throughout early childhood (Bagner et al., 2012). One promising measure for identifying individuals from a prevention framework is universal screening (Essex et al., 2009).

**Common Methods of Identifying Children in Need of Supports**

Three common ways that children are identified for SEB support include: (a) educator nominations, (b) parent referrals and, (c) universal screening. Educator nomination refers to the process whereby educators notice issues and refer students for services (Green et al., 2017). Many educators do not feel confident in their ability to identify students with emotional and behavioral issues (Askell-Williams & Lawson, 2013). In addition, many enter the profession with little to no training in early childhood development which can lead educators to under-identify internalizing behaviors and over-identify externalizing behaviors (Dowdy et al., 2013). Educator nominations may also be influenced by attitudes and beliefs that can lead to over- or under-identifying certain children above others (Loades & Mastroyannopoulou, 2010; Maniadaki et al., 2006). Parents and caregivers are also important sources of information, because parents observe behaviors in the home environment (Heyman et al., 2018) and often initiate mental health services for their children, but many parents and caregivers lack the knowledge or skills to identify children at risk for SEB problems (Jeong et al., 2017).

Early childhood programs can utilize universal screening tools to identify risk in children. Universal screening systematically assesses all students and identifies those in need of further support. This is different from educator and parent nominations, which rely on educators and parents to notice and report signs of risk based upon their subjective understanding of mental health. Universal screeners can be developed using scientific theory and examined for their accuracy. Thus, universal screening also has the potential to be a more accurate method of identifying students because it may reduce the impact of biases on student referrals (Raines et al., 2012). Multi-tiered systems of support models like the pyramid model (Fox et al., 2003) encourage the use of universal screeners. The pyramid model is a tiered model developed to promote SEB development, skills development, and effective intervention in early childhood (National Center for Pyramid Model Innovations, n.d.). Utilization of the pyramid model in early childhood education has led to increases in children's social skills and decreases in challenging behaviors (Hemmeter et al., 2016) and has been implemented in Head Start, childcare classrooms, and university-affiliated early childhood centers. The endorsement of universal screening by this and similar models highlights its usefulness in identifying and addressing mental health needs. Universal screening is a valuable tool because it allows schools to engage in prevention and early intervention, which is especially important in early childhood settings as it can prevent the development of more severe behaviors later in life (Severson et al., 2007). To encourage the use for universal screening, reviews like this one are needed to outline the evidence base of different universal screeners.

## Current Study

The present study examined the characteristics of commonly used early childhood assessments and their effectiveness for identifying preschool students who needed SEB support. Therefore, early childhood assessments were evaluated based on their bibliographies, their respective research literature, and corresponding psychometric evidence. The research questions for this study were twofold. First, do commonly-used early childhood assessments have adequate evidence-based research to support decision-making? Many early childhood screeners, such as the Preschool and Kindergarten Behavior Scales (Merrell, 2002) were created decades ago and may not have recent research to support their continued use. Second, based on a review of the recent research, are the selected early childhood assessments effective at identifying SEB risk for preschoolers, and to what extent?

## Method

Universal screening measures were reviewed for a number of inclusion criteria (i.e., must be peer reviewed studies, must be articles written in English, articles must have studies on SEB screening measures for the preschool age, and there must be at least one study on the screening measure within the past 10 years). Each measure was identified through a systematic search of electronic databases, including PsycINFO, Google Scholar, and ScienceDirect. The researchers used two key phrases in the search: early childhood social-emotional screening measure and preschool social-emotional screening measure. The manual for each tool, if available, was then reviewed to obtain information about the content and use of the tool, the scores and interpretations that each tool was designed to yield, and the psychometric properties of each tool. The psychometric properties of the identified measures were then evaluated, including: (a) reliability evidence, such as internal consistency, inter-rater reliability, test–retest reliability; (b) validity information including construct, content, concurrent, and predictive validity, and (c) sample adequacy such as the size and diversity of the validation sample. In addition, data were collected included: training required for administration, who can complete the measure, social-emotional domains targeted by each tool, length of time to administer, cost of the measure, and the age range for which each tool was designed. The screening measures included in the review were chosen by the soundness of their psychometric properties and usability within early childhood settings.

## Measures

### Review and Evaluation Criteria of Evidence-based Treatments

A modified version of the review criteria of evidence-based treatments presented by Southam-Gerow and Prinstein (2014) was used specifically to evaluate early childhood assessments for the purposes of this study. The criteria listed in Southam-Gerow and Prinstein, 2014 was adapted Adapted from Silverman and Hinshaw (2008), Division 12 Task Force on Psychological Interventions' reports (Chambless et al., 1998; Chambless et al., 1996), Chambless and Hollon (1998), Chambless and Ollendick (2001), and Chorpita et al. (2011). Chambless and Hollon (1998) described criteria for methodology. Critical aspects of universal screeners such as appropriateness for intended use, technical adequacy, and usability, described by Glover and Albers (2007) were also considered in the creation of the assessment evaluation rubric (see Table 1). Methods criteria were considered first to determine whether an assessment could at least be classified as a "possibly efficacious assessment." Methods criteria included study design (power and sample size), an identified independent variable, a clearly defined population, the assessed outcomes, and the appropriateness of the analyses used (i.e., appropriate sample size for detection of effects, and type of analysis makes sense for purpose of the study). Evidence criteria were determined at five different levels of effectiveness, with level one being the evidence-based gold standard and level five being an assessment that requires more evidence in order to determine effectiveness. Evidence criteria levels were: Well-Established Assessments (i.e., level one), Probably Efficacious Assessments (i.e., level two), Possibly Efficacious Assessments (i.e., level three), Experimental Assessments (i.e., level four), and Assessments of Questionable Efficacy (i.e., level five). If studies met all the methods criteria, then they automatically passed level five and were considered at least as an experimental assessment. The original form of this rubric was designed for the evaluation of psychological treatments and interventions (Southam-Gerow & Prinstein, 2014). The authors chose to adapt this rubric for the use of evaluating the early childhood screening tools to create consistency across the selection of universal screening tools and the later selection of interventions and SEB curriculum.

**Assessment Evaluation Rubric**

The assessment evaluation rubric was created by the research team based on the critical aspects of universal screeners (e.g., normality, reliability, and validity results; Glover & Albers, 2007) which provide a more in-depth description of an assessment's efficacy (see Table 1). It is important for evaluative studies to provide evidence to determine if an assessment is applicable, accurate, and consistent for the population that it intends to serve. Assessing for reliability and validity helps rule out measurement biases and potentially misleading results (Karras, 1997). An assessment being adequately normed (i.e., "Is the normative sample representative, recent, and sufficiently large?"; Glover & Albers, 2007, p. 120) can indicate that it is standardized based on relevant demographic information. Since assessments can have adequate norms and standardization and still not be found reliable and/or valid (Cicchetti, 1994), it is important to consider each of these evaluation criteria when considering assessment effectiveness.

**Sample and Procedures**

The initial search for articles on early childhood SEB screeners across databases yielded 825 articles. This was followed by a title and abstract screening which narrowed the results to 155 articles. The research team then completed a full article screening to ensure that articles met criteria (was published within the last ten years, was an early childhood screener, and the primary purpose of study was to examine psychometric properties) resulting in a final 18 screening tools included in this review. In addition to research articles, the research team also reviewed five compendium reports on early childhood screeners for supplemental information (Denham et al., 2010; Moodie et al., 2014; Halle et al., 2011; Ringwalt, 2008; Sosna

& Mastergeorge, 2005). For the final articles included, the research team extracted data regarding the assessments' methodology, effectiveness, and applicability. For each of the 18 assessments discussed, an assessment bibliography was created that comprising the assessment manual and the related empirical studies.

*Table 1*

*Assessment Evaluation Rubric*

| Considerations | Inadequate | Adequate | Strong |
|---|---|---|---|
| Adequacy of norms | Normative sample is lacking in two or more of the following dimensions of representativeness, recency and sample size. | Normative sample is lacking in one of the following dimensions of representativeness, recency and sample size. | Normative sample is representative, recent, and sufficiently large |
| Internal consistency reliability | Items may not measure the same construct and alternate forms are not comparable. Internal consistency coefficients are weak. | Items measure the same construct and alternate forms are comparable. Internal consistency coefficients are moderate. | Items measure the same construct and alternate forms are comparable. Internal consistency coefficients are large. |
| Test–retest reliability | Measurement is inconsistent over time. | Measurement is somewhat inconsistent over time. | Measurement is consistent over time. |
| Interscorer reliability | Scoring is inconsistent across scorers. | Scoring is consistent across scorers. | Scoring is consistent across scorers. |
| Predictive validity: Sensitivity | Of those *at* risk, less than 75% are correctly identified. | Of those *at* risk, between 75% - 80% are correctly identified. | Of those *at* risk, more than 80% are correctly identified. |
| Predictive validity: Specificity | Of those *not* at risk, less than 75% are correctly identified. | Of those *not* at risk, between 75% - 80% are correctly identified. | Of those *not* at risk, more than 80% are correctly identified. |
| Predictive validity: Positive predictive value | Of those *identified* as at risk, less than 75% are correctly identified. | Of those *identified* as at risk, between 75% - 80% are correctly identified. | Of those *identified* as at risk, more than 80% are correctly identified. |
| Predictive validity: Negative predictive value | Of those *identified* as not at risk, an inadequate amount are correctly identified. | Of those *identified* as not at risk a moderate amount are correctly identified. | Of those *identified* as not at risk, most are correctly identified. |
| Concurrent validity | The assessment outcome is not consistent with a criterion measure. | The assessment outcome is somewhat consistent with a criterion measure | The assessment outcome is consistent with a criterion measure. |
| Construct validity | Inadequate support is given that the assessment measures the construct for which it is designed (i.e. the assessment has a weak correlation with another comparable instrument or a strong correlation with an instrument designed to measure different skills). | Adequate support is given that the assessment measures the construct for which it is designed (i.e. the assessment has a moderate correlation with another comparable instrument). | Strong support is given that the assessment measures the construct for which it is designed (i.e. the assessment has a strong correlation with another comparable instrument or a weak correlation with an instrument designed to measure different skills). |
| Content validity | Weak evidence or explanation given for the appropriateness of the assessment format and items (e.g. item-discrimination coefficients, item difficulty indices and differential item functioning). | Sufficient evidence or explanation given for the appropriateness of the assessment format and items (e.g. item-discrimination coefficients, item difficulty indices and differential item functioning). | Strong evidence or explanation given for the appropriateness of the assessment format and items (e.g. item-discrimination coefficients, item difficulty indices and differential item functioning). |

Assessments that were not developed or updated within the past ten years, but had empirical support in the past ten years were still included in the final review with a note that they should be used with caution since they had not been updated considering current cultural and diversity considerations. In this study, 17 assessments had empirical support within the past ten years and one assessment lacked recent empirical support. Next, reviews of empirical studies for each measure were completed based on the evidence-based criteria adapted from Southam-Gerow and Prinstein (2014). Team members were familiarized with the assessment evaluation rubric process through a didactic training led by the lead author. The lead author completed an individual rating and reviewed the steps with all team members to model the process of evaluating an assessment. After the didactic training, team members completed one individual assessment rating and had individual meetings with the lead author on any questions to complete the rating efficiently. Each rating was then reviewed to reach group consensus for an inter-rater reliability of 100% on completing the assessment's evaluation rubric. Following the first rating, each team member was assigned five assessments and added individual ratings to an Excel spreadsheet which were also reviewed for group consensus for inter-rater reliability. Any disagreements between the research team were reviewed by the lead author and then brought to the research team for final agreement. Table 2 represents the characteristics and psychometric properties of assessments classified as Level 1 and 2.

## Table 2

*Elements of Reviewed Screeners (Levels 1 and 2)*

| | PKBS-2 | BASC-3 BESS | CBCL 1.5-5 | DECA-P2 |
|---|---|---|---|---|
| Age | 3–6 years | 3-5 years | 1.5-5 years | 3-5 years |
| Forms | Parent & Teacher | Parent & Teacher | Parent & Teacher | Parent & Teacher |
| # of Items | 76 | 25 | 99 | 38 |
| Time | 12 mins | 5 mins | 10-20 mins | 3-10 mins |
| Topics Assessed | Social cooperation, social interaction, social independence, externalizing and internalizing behaviors | Used to indicate the level of behavioral and emotional functioning of individual children | Emotionally Reactive, Anxious/Depressed, Somatic Complaints, Withdrawn, Sleep Problems, Attention Problems, Aggressive Behavior | Initiative, Self-Regulation, Attachment/Relationships, Behavioral Concerns |
| Languages | English Spanish | English Spanish | 75 Languages | English Spanish |
| Scoring | Hand | Hand/Software/Online | Hand/Software | Hand/Online |
| Cost | $151 (Manual and 50 forms) | $84 - $452 (Manual and 10 Q-global BESS screeners) | $160-$350 (Hand-scoring kit or computer-scoring kit, ADM module, 50 CBCL 1.5-5 and C-TRF forms, manual, and multicultural supplement) | $229.95 for kit (Manual and set of 40 paper record forms); $299.95 for annual online license |
| Scale | 4-point Likert Scale | 4-point Likert Scale | 3-point Likert Scale | 5-point Likert Scale |
| Reliability | Adequate | Adequate | Strong | Strong |
| Validity | Adequate | Adequate | Strong | Strong |
| Normality | Strong | Strong | Strong | Strong |
| Level of Efficacy | 2 | 2 | 1 | 1 |

## Results

### Assessments of Questionable Efficacy (Level Five)

There were two assessments judged to have questionable efficacy and, therefore, are not recommended to be implemented in their current version. The Vineland SEEC (Sparrow et al., 1998) was supported only by a literature review from 2014 using data from the initial psychometric properties (Gokiert et al., 2014). Due to a lack of empirical articles, the Vineland SEEC was not shown to have psychometric properties indicating its effectiveness with current early childhood populations. While the Creative Curriculum Development Profile assessment did have some recent research (Kim & Smith, 2010), results indicate negative and inconsistent outcomes (i.e., false positive and false negative results) between educators and parents.

### Experimental Assessments (Level Four)

Seven assessment tools were found to require further evaluation of psychometric properties, due to insufficient technical adequacy data. The assessments rated as experimental include the Work Sampling System (WSS; Meisels et al., 1994); Denham's Affect Knowledge Test (AKT; Denham, 1986); Sutter-Eyberg Student Behavior Inventory-Revised (SESBI-R; Eyberg & Pincus, 1999); Battelle Developmental Inventory (BDI) Screening Test (Newborg, 2005); SSIS™ Social-Emotional Learning Edition (SSIS SEL; Elliott & Gresham, 2008); Parent's Evaluation of Developmental Status: Developmental Milestones (PEDS:DM; Glascoe & Robertshaw, 2007); and the Preschool Behavioral and Emotional Rating Scale (PreBERS; Epstein & Synhorst, 2008). Assessments evaluated at Level Four included little to no consideration of content validity (WSS, AKT, SESBI-R, BDI Screening Test, SSIS SEL, PEDS:DM), construct validity (WSS, PEDS:DM), and no empirical evidence found related to comparisons with other validated measures (AKT, PreBERS).

## Possibly Efficacious Assessments (Level Three)

Five assessments were rated as possibly efficacious but need additional empirical support for the validity and comparableness to other well-established assessment tools. The assessments included the Preschool Learning Behaviors Scale (PLBS; McDermott et al., 2002), the Social Competence and Behavior Evaluation Scale (SCBE; LaFreniere & Dumas, 1995), the Carey Temperament Scales (CTS; Carey & McDevitt, 1995), the Strengths and Difficulties Questionnaires(SDQ; Goodman, 1997) , and The Children's Behavior Questionnaires (CBQ; Rothbart et al., 1994). Among these assessments, no consideration of content validity for four of the measures was found (PLBS, SCBE, CTS & CBQ). Finally, the SDQ was rated as a Level Three assessment because the majority of studies examining the psychometric properties of the tool were completed with adolescent populations rather than preschool-age children.

## Probably Efficacious Assessments (Level Two)

### *Preschool and Kindergarten Behavior Scales (PKBS-2)*

The PKBS-2 is a behavior rating scale designed for use with children ages 3 to 6 and is specifically designed to assist with intervention planning for children in preschool through kindergarten (Merrell, 2002). For additional information about the PKBS-2, see Table 2. The PKBS-2 received a Level 2, (probably efficacious assessment) using Southam-Gerow & Prinstein's (2014) review criteria because it met all methods criteria and was statistically similar to a well-established assessment (Wang et al., 2011). The evidence base of the PKBS-2 utilized sample sizes with sufficient power (Fernández et al., 2010; Merrell, 2002), had evidence of content and construct validity (Merrell, 2002; Tersi & Matsouka, 2020; Wang et al., 2011), provided adequate data analyses, and completed assessment of validity and reliability (Fernández et al., 2010; Wang et al., 2011). Additionally, the PKBS-2 was evaluated using an assessment evaluation rubric (See Table 1) and was reviewed on different screening elements for educators to consider (See Table 2). Based on this rubric, the PKBS-2 was found to have strong internal consistency (Benítez-Muñoz et al., 2011; Fernández et al., 2010; Major et al., 2017; Merrell, 2002; Tersi & Matsouka, 2020; Wang et al., 2011), adequate test-retest reliability (Merrell, 2002), and adequate interscorer reliability (Merrell, 2002). In addition, the PKBS-2 was found to have strong concurrent validity (Wang et al., 2011), construct validity (Tersi & Matsouka, 2020; Wang et al., 2011), and content validity (Fernández et al., 2010).

### Behavioral and Emotional Screening System (BASC-3 BESS)

The BASC-3 BESS (Reynolds & Kamphaus, 2004) preschool form is intended to assess children between 3 to 5 years old. For additional information about the BASC-3 BESS, see Table 2. The BASC-3 BESS received a Level Two rating using Southam-Gerow & Prinstein's (2014) review criteria because it met all method criteria and was statistically similar to a well-established assessment based on a single empirical study (Dowdy et al., 2013). Following a review of the screener (see Table 2) using the assessment evaluation rubric (see Table 1), the BASC-3 BESS was found to be adequate in the following areas: test-retest reliability (Greer et al., 2015; Dever et al., 2018), interscorer reliability (Greer et al., 2015), internal consistency (Greer et al., 2015), specificity (Dever et al., 2018), positive predictive value (Dever et al., 2018), negative predictive value (Dever et al., 2018), concurrent validity (Dowdy et al., 2013), construct validity (Dowdy et al., 2013; Dever et al., 2018; Greer et al., 2015 & DiStefano et al., 2016), and content validity (Greer et al., 2015). However, this screener also had inadequate sensitivity (Dever et al., 2018).

## Well-Established Assessments (Level One)
### Child Behavior Checklist for Ages 1.5-5 (CBCL 1.5-5)

The CBCL 1.5-5 (Achenbach et al., 2001) preschool form was developed for use with children ages 1.5 to 5 years of age. See Table 2 for additional information regarding the CBCL 1.5-5. The CBCL 1.5-5 received a Level One rating using Southam-Gerow & Prinstein's (2014) review criteria because it met all methods criteria and was statistically similar to well-established assessments, including the BASC-2 Parent Rating Scale Preschool, as indicated by at least two independent research studies and by two independent researcher teams (Aebi et al., 2010; Myers et al., 2010). Based on the technical adequacy rubric, the CBCL 1.5-5 displayed significant adequacy of norms (Cai et al., 2004; Ha et al., 2011; Ivanova et al., 2010; Tan et al., 2006), strong internal consistency (Dias et al., 2012; Pandolfi et al., 2009; Tan et al., 2006), construct validity (Ivanova et al., 2010; Pandolfi et al., 2009), positive predictive validity (Aebi et al., 2010) and content validity (Aebi et al., 2010; Myers et al., 2010).

***Devereaux Early Childhood Assessment Preschool (DECA-P2)***

The DECA-P2 (LeBuffe & Naglieri, 2012) is a measure of SEB strengths and deficits developed for use with preschool children from 3 to 5 years old. For additional details related to the DECA-P2 refer to Table 2. Based on the evaluation rubric adapted from Southam-Gerow & Prinstein (2014), the DECA-P2 was identified as a Level One assessment tool after meeting all methods criteria and was found to be statistically similar to other well-established assessments including the Conners Early Childhood scale (Conners, 2009) and the Preschool Behavioral and Emotional Rating Scale (Epstein & Synhorst, 2009). In addition, the DECA-P2 demonstrates significant adequacy of norms (Bulotsky-Shearer et al., 2013; LeBuffe & Naglieri, 2012), strong internal consistency with parent raters (alpha=.92) and educator raters (alpha=.95; Crane et al., 2011), strong construct validity (Bulotsky-Shearer et al., 2013; Conners, 2009; Epstein & Synhorst, 2009; Lien & Carlson, 2009), and strong content validity (Barbu et al., 2015).

## Discussion

SEB skills are needed for young children to develop future relationships with peers and educators (Denham et al., 2016). Additionally, SEB skills are also associated with grades and academic performance as well as self-confidence and feelings toward school (Denham et al., 2016). Thus, it is important for schools to support the development of these skills and to identify and intervene with students who have SEB difficulties. Universal screeners can be used to identify children who may need additional SEB supports at school. Early childhood programs have a range of screeners to choose from, but may not be aware of the screeners that are supported by current research. The current study addressed this need by reviewing current early childhood screeners, and identifying those screening tools which are supported by current research as well as those which need further research before they can be considered evidence-based.

This study reviewed 18 early childhood screeners for SEB problems based on peer-reviewed and published studies on the assessments over the last ten years and assessed the technical adequacy, effectiveness, and accessibility of each. The authors used both the adapted Southam-Gerow and Prinstein's (2014) review criteria for evidence-based treatments and a technical adequacy rubric adapted from Glover and Alber's (2007) considerations for evaluating universal screening assessments. Based on these criteria, four of the 18 screeners are strongly recommended for use in early childhood SEB screening, specifically within educational settings: Child Behavior Checklist for Ages 1.5-5, Devereaux Early Childhood Assessment Preschool, Behavioral and Emotional Screening System, and Preschool and Kindergarten Behavior Scales.

According to the current review, there are a limited number of early childhood universal screeners with adequate research support which are, therefore, advisable for use in schools. In addition, there is a need for further research into the psychometrics of early childhood SEB screeners. The authors had difficulty finding studies on the technical adequacy of early childhood screeners conducted by independent researchers in the last 10 years, but the tools which received ratings as Level One or Level Two screeners did show high levels of validity and reliability in identifying young children who may need additional SEB supports. A lack of diversity in the normative sample was a common theme throughout the literature and tools reviewed. The Level One and Level Two screeners identified in this review were found to have nationally representative normative samples in terms of ethnic and racial composition, or contained peer reviewed studies published within the last decade that cited their effectiveness with diverse populations. For example, the first edition of the PKBS was criticized for its non-representative normative sample, but further data were collected to create a more representative sample to validate and refine the PBKS-2. Furthermore, there is a need for the development of more cost-effective screening tools. The prices of the most highly rated screeners in this review ranged from $100 - $1,084. Many early childhood programs, including Head Start programs, may not be able to afford either the screener or the necessary training. Easily accessible or free SEB screening tools are needed to ensure that all students at SEB risk are identified early to facilitate early intervention.

## Limitations

Limitations of this review included its criteria for inclusion and exclusion, limiting the number of admissible studies. Studies written in languages other than English or those that were not peer reviewed (e.g., dissertations) were not included, which limited the number of articles used to review the assessments. However, these additional sources of information could have provided additional evidence related to currently available early childhood screeners. Additionally, the authors focused on 18 early childhood universal screeners rather than an exhaustive review of all available SEB screening tools available for this age group. Lastly, the rubrics used were adapted by the researchers. Other rubrics from the universal screening literature could have been utilized to examine the screeners, and these alternative rubrics may have highlighted different strengths and weaknesses that would also be helpful for schools and researchers.

## References

Achenbach, T. M., Dumenci, L., & Rescorla, L. A. (2001). Ratings of relations between DSM- IV diagnostic categories and items. University of Vermont, Research Center for Children, Youth, & Families.

Aebi, M., Winkler Metzke, C., & Steinhausen, H.-C. (2010). Accuracy of the DSM-Oriented Attention Problem Scale of the Child Behavior Checklist in Diagnosing Attention-Deficit Hyperactivity Disorder. *Journal of Attention Disorders, 13*(5), 454–463.

Askell-Williams, H., & Lawson, M. (2013). Teachers' knowledge and confidence for promoting positive mental health in primary school communities. *Asia-Pacific Journal of Teacher Education, 41*(2), 126–143.

Bagner, D. M., Rodríguez, G. M., Blake, C. A., Linares, D., & Carter, A. S. (2012). Assessment of behavioral and emotional problems in infancy: A systematic review *Clinical Child and Family Psychology Review, 15*(2), 113-128.

Barbu, O. C., Yaden Jr, D. B., Levine-Donnerstein, D., & Marx, R. W. (2015). Assessing approaches to learning in school readiness: Comparing the Devereux Early Childhood Assessment to an early learning standards-based measure. *AERA Open, 1*(3), 2332858415593923.

Bridgeland, J., Bruce, M., & Hariharan, A. (2013). The Missing Piece: A National Teacher Survey on How Social and Emotional Learning Can Empower Children and Transform Schools. A Report for CASEL. *Civic Enterprises.*

Bulotsky-Shearer, R. J., Fernandez, V. A., & Rainelli, S. (2013). The validity of the Devereux Early Childhood Assessment for culturally and linguistically diverse Head Start children. *Early Childhood Research Quarterly, 28*(4), 794-807.

Bulotsky-Shearer, R. J., Manz, P. H., Mendez, J. L., McWayne, C. M., Sekino, Y., & Fantuzzo, J. W. (2012). Peer play interactions and readiness to learn: A protective influence for African American preschool children from low-income households. *Child Development Perspectives, 6*(3), 225-231. https://doi.org/10.1111/j.1750-8606.2011.00221.x

Cai, X., Kaiser, A. P., & Hancock, T. B. (2004). Parent and teacher agreement on child behavior checklist items in a sample of preschoolers from low-income and predominantly African American families. Journal of Clinical Child and Adolescent Psychology, 33(2), 303-312.

Cappella, E., Frazier, S., Atkins, M., Schoenwald, S., & Glisson, C. (2008). Enhancing schools' capacity to support children in poverty: An ecological model of school-based mental health services. *Administration and Policy in Mental Health and Mental Health Services Research, 35*, 395–409. https://doi.org/10.1007/s10488-008-0182-y

Carey, W. B., & McDevitt, S. C. (1995). The carey temperament scales. Scottsdale, AZ: *Behavioral-Developmental Initiatives.*

Chambless, D. L., Baker, M. J., Baucom, D. H., Beutler, L. E., Calhoun, K. S., Crits-Christoph, P., ...Woody, S. R. (1998). Update on empirically validated therapies, II. Clinical Psychologist, 51, 3-16. Retrieved from http://iacp.asu.edu/~horan/ced522readings/div12/ chambless98.pdf

Chambless, D. L., & Ollendick, T. H. (2001). Empirically supported psychological interventions: Controversies and evidence. Annual Review of Psychology, 52, 685-716. doi:10.1146=annurev.psych. 52.1.685

Chambless, D. L., Sanderson, W. C., Shoham, V., Johnson, S. B., Pope, K. S., Crits-Christoph, P.,... McCurry, S. (1996). An update on empirically validated therapies. The Clinical Psychologist, 9(2), 5-18. doi:10.1037=e555332011-003

Chorpita, B. F., Daleiden, E. L., Ebesutani, C., Young, J., Becker, K. D., Nakamura, B. J., ... Starace, N. (2011). Evidence-based treatments for children and adolescents: An updated review of indicators of efficacy and effectiveness. Clinical Psychology: Science and Practice, 18, 154-172. doi:10.1111=j.1468-2850.2011.01247.x

Cicchetti, D. V. (1994). Guidelines, criteria, and rules of thumb for evaluating normed and standardized assessment instruments in psychology. *Psychological Assessment,* 6(4), 284. https://doi.org/10.1037/1040-3590.6.4.284

Conners, C.K. (2009). Conners early childhood manual. Toronto, Canada: Multi-Health Systems.

Conroy, M. A., & Brown, W. H. (2004). Early identification, prevention, and early intervention with young children at risk for emotional or behavioral disorders: Issues, trends, and a call for action. *Behavioral Disorders, 29*(3), 224-236. https://doi.org/10.1177/019874290402900303

Crane, J., Mincic, M. S., & Winsler, A. (2011). Parent-teacher agreement and reliability on the Devereux Early Childhood Assessment (DECA) in English and Spanish for ethnically diverse children living in poverty. *Early Education & Development,* 22(3), 520-547.

Denham, S. A., Bassett, H. H., Zinsser, K., & Wyatt, T. M. (2014). How preschoolers' social-emotional learning predicts their early school success: Developing theory-promoting, competency-based assessments. *Infant and Child Development, 23*(4), 426-454. https://doi.org/10.1002/icd.1840

Denham, S. A., Ferrier, D. E., Howarth, G. Z., Herndon, K. J., & Bassett, H. H. (2016). Key considerations in assessing young children's emotional competence. *Cambridge Journal of Education, 46*(3), 299-317. https://doi.org/10.1080/0305764X.2016.1146659

Denham, S. A., Ji, P., & Hamre, B. (2010). Compendium of preschool through elementary school social-emotional learning and associated assessment measures. *Collaborative for Academic, Social, and Emotional Learning.*

Dever, B. V., Dowdy, E., & DiStefano, C. (2018). Examining the stability, accuracy, andpredictive validity of behavioral–emotional screening scores across time to inform repeated screening procedures. *School Psychology Review, 47*(4), 360-371. https://doi.org/10.17105/SPR-2017-0092.V47-4

Dias, P., Carneiro, A., Lima, V. S., Machado, B. C., Veríssimo, L., & Xavier, M. (2012). Assessment of psychopathology in preschool children with the ASEBA battery: preliminary psychometric data from the Portuguese population. *Infant Mental Health Journal, 33*(3), 56-57.

Dowdy, E., Doane, K., Eklund, K., & Dever, B. V. (2013). A comparison of teacher nomination and screening to identify behavioral and emotional risk within a sample of underrepresented students. *Journal of Emotional and Behavioral Disorders, 21*(2), 127- 137. https://doi.org/10.1177/1063426611417627

Dvorsky, M. R., Girio-Herrera, E., & Owens, J. S. (2014). School-based screening for mental health in early childhood. In *Handbook of school mental health* (pp. 297-310). Springer, Boston, MA.

Egger, H. L., & Angold, A. (2006). Common emotional and behavioral disorders in preschool children: Presentation, nosology, and epidemiology. *Journal of Child Psychology and Psychiatry, 47*, 313–337. https://doi.org/10.1111/j.1469-7610.2006.01618.x.

Elliott, S., & Gresham, F. (2008). SSIS Intervention Guide. *Pearson.*

Epstein, M., & Synhorst, L. (2009). Preschool behavioral and emotional rating scale, examiner's manual. Austin, TX: Pro-Ed.

Epstein, M., & Synhorst, L. (2008). Preschool Behavioral and Emotional Rating Scale (PreBERS): Test–Retest Reliability and Inter-Rater Reliability. *Journal of Child and Family Studies, 17*, 853–862. https://doi.org/10.1007/s10826-008-9194-1

Essex, M. J., Kraemer, H. C., Slattery, M. J., Burk, L. R., Thomas Boyce, W., Woodward, H. R., & Kupfer, D. J. (2009). Screening for childhood mental health problems: Outcomes and early identification. *Journal of Child Psychology and Psychiatry, 50*(5), 562-570. https://doi.org/10.1111/j.1469-7610.2008.02015.x

Eyberg, S. M., & Pincus, D. (1999). ECBI & SESBI-R: Eyberg child behavior inventory and Sutter-Eyberg student behavior inventory-revised: Professional manual. Psychological Assessment Resources.

Fernández, M., Benitez Muñoz, J. L., Pichardo Martínez, M. C., Fernández, E., Justicia Justicia, F., García, T., & Alba, G. (2010). Confirmatory factor analysis of the PKBS-2 subscales for assessing social skills and behavioral problems in preschool education.

Fox, L., Dunlap, G., Hemmeter, M. L., Joseph, G. E., & Strain, P. S. (2003). The teaching pyramid: a model for supporting social competence and preventing challenging behavior in young children. Young Children, 58(4), 48-52. doi: 10.1002/cbl.20134

Gilliam, W. S. (2016). Early Childhood Expulsions and Suspensions Undermine Our Nation's Most Promising Agent of Opportunity and Social Justice. *Moriah Group*.

Glascoe F.P. & Robertshaw, N.S. (2007). PEDS: *Developmental Milestones*. Ellsworth & Vandermeer Press.

Gleason, M. M., Goldson, E., Yogman, M. W., & Committee on Psychosocial Aspects of Child and Family Health. (2016). Addressing early childhood emotional and behavioral problems. *Pediatrics, 138*(6). https://doi.org/10.1542/peds.2016-3025

Glover, T. A., & Albers, C. A. (2007). Considerations for evaluating universal screening assessments. *Journal of School Psychology, 45*(2), 117-135. https://doi.org/10.1016/j.jsp.2006.05.005

Gokiert, R. J., Georgis, R., Tremblay, M., Krishnan, V., Vandenberghe, C., & Lee, C. (2014). Evaluating the Adequacy of Social-Emotional Measures in Early Childhood. *Journal of Psychoeducational Assessment, 32*(5), 441–454. https://doi.org/10.1177/0734282913516718

Goodman, R. (1997). The strengths and difficulties questionnaire: a research note. *Journal of Child Psychology, Psychiatry, and Allied Disciplines, 38*(5), 581–586. doi:10.1111/j.1469-7610.1997.tb01545.x.

Graves Jr, S. L., & Howes, C. (2011). Ethnic differences in social-emotional development in preschool: The impact of teacher child relationships and classroom quality. *School Psychology Quarterly, 26*(3), 202. https://doi.org/10.1037/a0024117

Green, J. G., Keenan, J. K., Guzmán, J., Vinnes, S., Holt, M., & Comer, J. S. (2017). Teacher perspectives on indicators of adolescent social and emotional problems. *Evidence-Based Practice in Child and Adolescent Mental Health, 26*(4), 96-101. https://doi.org/10.1080/23794925.2017.1313099

Greer, F. W., DiStefano, C. A., Liu, J., & Cain, L. K. (2015). Preliminary Psychometric Evidence of the Behavioral and Emotional Screening System Teacher Rating Scale–Preschool. Assessment for Effective Intervention, 40(4), 240–246.

Ha, E.H., Kim, S.Y., Song, D.H., Kwak, E.H., & Eom S.Y. (2011). Discriminant Validity of the CBLC 1.5-5 in Diagnosis of Developmental Delayed Infants. *Journal of Korean Academic Child Adolescent Psychiatry, 22*(2): 120-127.

Halle, T., Zaslow, M., Wessel, J., Moodie, S., & Darling-Churchill, K. (2011). Understanding and Choosing Assessments and Developmental Screeners for Young Children Ages 3-5: Profiles of Selected Measures. OPRE Report# 2011-23. *Administration for Children & Families*.

Hamre, B. K., & Pianta, R. C. (2001). Early teacher–child relationships and the trajectory of children's school outcomes through eighth grade. *Child Development, 72*(2), 625-638. https://doi.org/10.1111/1467-8624.00301

Hemmeter, M. L., Snyder, P. A., Fox, L., & Algina, J. (2016). Evaluating the implementation of the pyramid model for promoting social-emotional competence in early childhood classrooms. *Topics in Early Childhood Special Education, 36*(3), 133–146. https://doi.org/10.1177/0271121416653386

Heyman, M., Poulakos, A., Upshur, C., & Wenz-Gross, M. (2018). Discrepancies in parent and teacher ratings of low-income preschooler's social skills. *Early Child Development and Care, 188*(6), 759-773. https://doi.org/10.1080/03004430.2016.1236257

Ivanova, M. Y., Achenbach, T. M., Rescorla, L. A., Harder, V. S., Ang, R. P., Bilenberg, N., Verhulst, F. C. (2010). Preschool psychopathology reported by parents in 23 societies: Testing the seven-syndrome model of the Child Behavior Checklist for ages 1.5-5. *Journal of the American Academy of Child and Adolescent Psychiatry, 49*(12), 1215-1224.

Jenkins, L. N., Demaray, M. K., Wren, N. S., Secord, S. M., Lyell, K. M., Magers, A. M., Setmeyer, A. J., Rodelo, C., Newcomb-McNeal, E., & Tennant, J. (2014). A Critical Review of Five Commonly Used Social-Emotional and Behavioral Screeners for Elementary or Secondary Schools. *Contemporary School Psychology, 18*(4), 241-254.

Jeong, Y. M., McCreary, L. L., & Hughes, T. L. (2017). Qualitative study of depression literacy among Korean American parents of adolescents. *Journal of Psychosocial Nursing and Mental Health Services, 56*(1), 48–56. https://doi.org/10.3928/02793695-20172909-03

Kamphaus, R. W. (2012). Screening for behavioral and emotional risk: Constructs and practicalities. *School Psychology Forum, 6*(4), 89–97.

Karras. (1997). Statistical Methodology: II. Reliability and Validity Assessment in Study Design, Part A. *Academic Emergency Medicine, 4*(1), 64–71. https://doi.org/10.1111/j.1553-2712.1997.tb03646.x

LaFreniere, P. J., & Dumas, J. E.(1995).Social competence and behavior evaluation: Preschool edition (SCBE), Los Angeles, CA: *Western Psychological Services*.

Lane, K.L., Menzies, H.M., Oakes, W.P. and Kalberg, J.R. (2012). *Systematic Screenings of Behavior to Support Instruction from Preschool to High School*. The Guilford Press, New York, NY.

Lavigne, J. V., Arend, R., Rosenbaum, D., Binns, H. J., Christoffel, K. K., & Gibbons, R. D. (1998). Psychiatric disorders with onset in the preschool years: I. Stability of diagnoses. *Journal of the American Academy of Child & Adolescent Psychiatry, 37*(12), 1246-1254. https://doi.org/10.1097/00004583-199812000-00007

LeBuffe, P. A., Naglieri, J. A. (2012). Devereux Early Childhood Assessments for Preschool, second edition (Technical manual). Lewisville, NC: Kaplan Early Learning Company.

Lien, M. T., & Carlson, J. S. (2009). Psychometric properties of the Devereux early childhood assessment in a head start sample. *Journal of Psychoeducational Assessment, 27*(5), 386-396.

Loades, M. E., & Mastroyannopoulou, K. (2010). Teachers' recognition of children's mental health problems. *Child and Adolescent Mental Health, 15,* 150–156. https://doi.org/10.1111/j.1475-3588.2009.00551.x

Major, S., Seabra-Santos, M. J., & Albuquerque, C. P. (2017). Validating the preschool and kindergarten behavior scales-2: Preschoolers with autism spectrum disorders. *Research in developmental disabilities, 65,* 86-96.

Maniadaki, K., Sonuga-Barke, E., & Kakouros, E. (2006). Adults' self-efficacy beliefs and referral attitudes for boys and girls with ADHD. *European Child & Adolescent Psychiatry, 15,* 132–140. https://doi.org/10.1007/s00787-005-0514-3

McDermott, P. A., Leigh, N. M., & Perry, M. A. (2002). Development and validation of the preschool learning behaviors scale. *Psychology in the Schools, 39*(4), 353-365.

Meisels, S. J., Dichtelmiller, M. L., Jablon, J. R., Dorfman, A. B., & Marsden, D. B. (1994). *The work sampling system: An overview (3rd ed.).* Ann Arbor, MI: Rebus Planning Associates.

Merrell, K. W. (2002). Preschool and Kindergarten Behaviour Rating Scales (PKBS-2). Austin, TX: PRO-ED.

Moodie, S., Daneri, P., Goldhagen, S., Halle, T., Green, K., & LaMonte, L. (2014). Early Childhood Developmental Screening: A Compendium of Measures for Children Ages Birth to Five. OPRE Report 2014-11. *US Department of Health and Human Services.*

Myers, C. L., Bour, J. L., Sidebottom, K. J., Murphy, S. B., & Hakman, M. (2010). Same constructs, different results: Examining the consistency of two behavior-rating scales with referred preschoolers. *Psychology in the Schools, 47*(3), 205-216.

National Center for Pyramid Model Innovations. (n.d.). Evidence-Based Practices. https://challengingbehavior.cbcs.usf.edu/Pyramid/practices.html

Newborg, J. (2005). Battelle Developmental Inventory, 2nd Edition: Examiner's manual. Itasca, IL: Riverside.

Pandolfi, V., Magyar, C. I., & Dill, C. A. (2009). Confirmatory factor analysis of the Child Behavior Checklist 1.5-5 in a sample of children with autism spectrum disorders. *Journal of Autism Developmental Disorders, 39,* 986-995.

Pianta, R. C., & Stuhlman, M. W. (2004). Teacher-child relationships and children's success in the first years of school. *School Psychology Review, 33*(3), 444-458.

Raines, T. C., Dever, B. V., Kamphaus, R. W., & Roach, A. T. (2012). Universal screening for behavioral and emotional risk: A promising method for reducing disproportionate placement in special education. *The Journal of Negro Education, 81*(3), 283-296. https://doi.org/10.7709/jnegroeducation.81.3.0283

Ramsook, K. A., Welsh, J. A., & Bierman, K. L. (2020). What you say, and how you say it: Preschoolers' growth in vocabulary and communication skills differentially predict kindergarten academic achievement and self-regulation. *Social Development, 29*(3), 783-800. https://doi.org/10.1111/sode.12425

Raver, C., (2002). Emotions matter: Making the case for the role of young children's emotional development for early school readiness. *Social Policy Report, 16*(3), 1-20. https://doi.org/10.1002/j.2379-3988.2002.tb00041.x

Reynolds, C. R., & Kamphaus, R. W. (2004). *Behavior assessment system for children* (2nd ed.). Bloomington, MN: Pearson Assessments.

Ringwalt, S. (2008). Developmental Screening and Assessment Instruments with an Emphasis on Social and Emotional Development for Young Children Ages Birth through Five. *National Early Childhood Technical Assistance Center (NECTAC)*.

Rones, M., & Hoagwood, K. (2000). School-based mental health services: A research review. *Clinical, Child and Family Psychology Review, 3*, 223-41.

Rothbart, M. K., Ahadi, S. A., & Hershey, K. L. (1994). Temperament and social behavior in childhood. *Merrill-Palmer Quarterly, 21*-39.

Severson, H. H., Walker, H. M., Hope-Doolittle, J., Kratochwill, T. R., & Gresham, F. M. (2007). Proactive, early screening to detect behavior-ally at-risk students: Issues, approaches, emerging innovations, and professional practices. *Journal of School Psychology, 45*,193–223. https://doi.org/10.1016/j.jsp.2006.11.003

Shonkoff, J. P., & Phillips, D. A. (Eds.). (2000). *From neurons to neighborhoods: The science of early childhood development*. National Academies Press.

Silverman, W. K., & Hinshaw, S. P. (2008). The second special issue on evidence-based psychosocial treatments for children and adolescents: A 10-year update. *Journal of Clinical Child and Adolescent Psychology, 37*, 1–7. doi:10.1080=15374410701817725

Skiba, R. J., Horner, R. H., Chung, C. G., Rausch, M. K., May, S. L., & Tobin, T. (2011). Race is not neutral: A national investigation of African American and Latino disproportionality in school discipline. School Psychology Review, 40(1), 85-107. https://doi.org/10.1080/02796015.2011.12087730

Sosna, T., & Mastergeorge, A. (2005). *Compendium of screening tools for early childhood social-emotional development*. Sacramento, CA: California Institute for Mental Health.

Southam-Gerow, M. A., & Prinstein, M. J. (2014). Evidence base updates: The evolution of the evaluation of psychological treatments for children and adolescents. *Journal of Clinical Child & Adolescent Psychology, 43*(1), 1-6. https://doi.org/10.1080/15374416.2013.855128

Sparrow, S., Balla, D. & Cicchetti, D. (1998). The Vineland Social-Emotional Early Childhood Scales. Circle Pines. American Guidance Services, Inc, MN (1998)

Stegelin, D. A. (2018). Preschool suspension and expulsion: defining the issues. *Institute for Child Success.*

Tan, T. X., Dedrick, R. F., & Marfo, K. (2006). Factor structure and clinical implications of Child Behavior Checklist/1.5–5 ratings in a sample of girls adopted from China. *Journal of Pediatric Psychology, 32*(7), 807-818.

Tersi, M., & Matsouka, O. (2020). Improving Social Skills through Structured Playfulness Program in Preschool Children. *International Journal of Instruction, 13*(3), 259-274. https://doi.org/10.29333/iji.2020.13318a

US Dept of Education. (2014). Civil Rights Data Collection: Data Snapshot School Discipline-Issue Brief March 2014.

Wang, H. T., Sandall, S. R., Davis, C. A., & Thomas, C. J. (2011). Social skills assessment in young children with autism: A comparison evaluation of the SSRS and PKBS. *Journal of Autism and Developmental Disorders, 41*(11), 1487-1495.

Wu, Z., Hu, B. Y., Fan, X., Zhang, X., & Zhang, J. (2018). The associations between social skills and teacher-child relationships: A longitudinal study among Chinese preschool children. *Children and Youth Services Review, 88,* 582-590. https://doi.org/10.1016/j.childyouth.2018.03.052

Zakaria, M. Z., Yunus, F., & Mohamed, S. (2020). Examining self-awareness through drawing activity among preschoolers with high socio emotional development *Southeast Asia Early Childhood Journal, 9*(2), 73-81.

# Social-Emotional Interventions for Young Children in Rural Areas: A Single-Case Design Meta-Analysis

*Tyler E. Smith, Melissa Stormont, Marina Antonova, Emily Singell, Wendy M. Reinke*

## Abstract

For young children with early social-emotional difficulties, early intervention is imperative. A number of interventions are available for young children to promote social-emotional competencies. Yet, little is known regarding the impact of early childhood interventions among rural children. Rural communities have several barriers which impede access to early intervention, and rural children often are at increased risk for social-emotional difficulties. Thus, the purpose of this article is to conduct a meta-analysis of single case design studies of social-emotional interventions that have been implemented within rural settings with young children, in an effort to determine the effects and types of early interventions specific to young children in rural areas. A total of 7 studies with 26 participants and 53 effects comprised the final sample. Findings indicated that all interventions, representing three different component types (i.e., teacher/parent behavior management training, social-emotional competency training, parent involvement/ enhancement), produced positive social-emotional outcomes (i.e., improved prosocial behavior and decreased disruptive behavior). Moderating variables (e.g., child characteristics, intervention implementer) that may impact intervention effectiveness were also studied and one variable was significant; specifically, studies published in journals had more impact on outcomes than those which were not published. Implications for future research and policy are provided.

**Keywords:** *rural settings; early childhood; social-emotional interventions; single-case design*

## Introduction

Research consistently demonstrates that social-emotional development is a critical predictor of school success (e.g., Denham, 2006; Stormont, 2021). Specifically, social-emotional skills during preschool predict an array of critical short- and long-term child outcomes (Curby et al., 2015; Raver, 2004). The need to develop specific social-emotional skills and competencies in early childhood is also reflected in kindergarten readiness research and skills needed for success in elementary school (Stormont, 2021). Unfortunately, many children struggle in their social-emotional development for a variety of reasons and need support to learn and use social-emotional skills (Sheridan et al., 2019). For young children with early social-emotional difficulties, early intervention is imperative to support the development of key competencies and skills (Robinson et al., 2017).

Fortunately, a wide range of interventions are available for young children to promote social-emotional competencies (Blewitt et al., 2018; Smith et al., 2020). However, the effectiveness of specific interventions with specific groups is an understudied area. One factor that may affect the availability and use of social emotional interventions and supports is the geographical area where children live (Miller et al., 2013). The impact of where children reside is important, as children may be at greater risk for both needing and not having access to social emotional services due to their geographic location. When compared to urban areas, rural children are more likely to exhibit school-based adjustment problems (Rimm-Kaufman et al., 2000) and to be diagnosed with a behavioral or developmental disorder (Robinson et al., 2017). In addition, young children with social-emotional needs who live in rural areas often face additional challenges (e.g., lack of qualified providers, poverty) that also impact development (Morales et al., 2020; Robinson et al., 2017). To address these issues, the purpose of this article is to conduct a meta-analysis of social-emotional interventions that have been implemented within rural settings with young children.

In the following sections, systemic issues and barriers within rural communities are presented, followed by evidence of the need to systematically review and utilize data from single-case designs.

## Barriers to Rural Early Intervention

There are multiple systemic issues that affect the provision of early childhood interventions and services at the community, family, and professional level (Bailey et al., 2018; Morales et al., 2020; Robinson et al., 2017). Young children acquire social-emotional skills and competencies through their interactions with others, including their caregivers, who can seek support on behalf of their children if they struggle in their development of specific competencies and skills. However, caregivers within rural communities often have less access to resources to address their own mental health, and may also face significant issues related to food insecurity and poverty. In fact, approximately one in four rural children in the U.S. live in poverty, as compared to one in five children nationally (Farrigan & Hertz, 2016). These factors contribute to parents' ability to support their children's development and need for services (Morales et al., 2020). Furthermore, when families are willing to seek and participate in interventions, the lack of qualified professionals can present another barrier. In some communities, qualified professionals are scarce or nonexistent compared to urban areas, which leads to gaps between needs and interventions (Sheridan et al., 2019). Finally, within rural communities there may be logistical barriers (e.g., lack of transportation) or an underutilization of available services due to stigma.

Given the inequity and vulnerability that exists in rural communities, and the impact it has on young children's social emotional development, it is imperative that the professionals who do deliver intervention in rural communities understand cultural factors and barriers to seeking and sustaining services and interventions (Morales et al., 2020). According to research with professionals who work in rural communities, it is essential that professionals implementing services and targeted interventions consider and understand the cultural aspects of such communities (Morales et al., 2020). This understanding is important given that these aspects may contribute to stigmas related to seeking services (e.g., the belief that "I should be able to handle this independently").

**Addressing Barriers in Rural Areas with Effective Intervention**

In order to address barriers and target increased risk for young children with social-emotional needs in rural areas, research must continue to uncover and assess the effects of interventions for rural samples. Available intervention literature has provided key findings concerning the impact of social-emotional interventions on developmental outcomes in early childhood. For instance, large-scale reviews and meta-analyses have broadly demonstrated the importance of early childhood interventions in promoting children's behavioral and social-emotional development (e.g., Blewitt et al., 2018; Luo et al., 2020; Yang et al., 2019). These findings indicate promise for addressing barriers within rural communities; however, these results are inclusive of studies across all geographical regions. More work which focuses on assessing effects for rural early childhood populations is necessary.

Beyond determining intervention effects, it is important to recognize and consider the varying practices and approaches used within early childhood interventions. Schindler and colleagues (2015), for instance, found that early childhood programs with a clear and intensive focus on social-emotional development included child social-emotional skill training (e.g., teaching basic cognitive skills necessary for social problem-solving) as well as parent and/or teacher behavior management training (e.g., teaching effective reward/discipline strategies, limit setting). The importance of parent involvement in supporting children's behavior and social-emotional competencies across all levels of development has also been consistently highlighted across the literature (e.g., Reinke et al., 2019; Smith et al., 2019; Smith & Sheridan, 2019). Within early childhood, in particular, targeted parent involvement interventions have been shown to improve child social-emotional competencies (Sheridan et al., 2010; Smith et al., 2021). Social-emotional interventions within rural areas are also likely to demonstrate varying practices, and uncovering the core components that contribute to intervention effects may yield highly relevant information that is essential to addressing barriers and informing future research and practice.

The body of empirical literature to date showcasing the effects of early childhood interventions and highlighting key intervention components has been vital for the field of early childhood education. That said, these findings are based solely on meta-analyses or large-scale studies of group-design research, and may not be entirely representative of high-quality experimental research conducted in this area. Synthesizing single-case design (SCD) studies may provide further support for group-design findings, and offer unique insights into important systematic factors, intervention characteristics, and child or study-level variables that influence social-emotional interventions for young children in rural areas.

## The Need for SCD Meta-Analyses

SCDs make up a substantial and important part of the literature base in the fields of education and psychology. Given their feasibility and small number of needed participants, SCDs play prominent roles in clinical and applied intervention research. This may be especially true for research on social-emotional interventions used for students with emotional and behavioral disorders (Lane et al., 2009) and other low-incidence disabilities (Pustejovsky & Ferron, 2017). For instance, one comprehensive review of interventions for children with autism found that 89% of the 456 included studies used SCDs (Wong et al., 2015). Another review of positive behavior interventions for children with behavior problems located 62 SCD studies and only one group-design study (Conroy et al., 2005). The size and breadth of research employing SCDs appears to have increased over the past three decades, as evidenced by increased frequency of publications in prominent special education journals (Hammond & Gast, 2010). Given this increase, it is also likely that SCD studies specifically focused on social-emotional interventions in rural areas comprise a significant portion of research in this area. However, to our knowledge, no meta-analyses or large-scale reviews to date have focused on this population.

The prominence of SCD studies in particular fields, their feasibility in applied settings, and their increased prevalence in reported research underscore the need for syntheses and systematic reviews. Visual analysis methods typically used to evaluate findings from SCDs do not create a single summary measure or numerical index to quantify magnitude of behavior change (Pustejovsky, 2018). This makes it difficult to compare outcomes quantitatively across multiple SCD studies. In contrast, meta-analysis procedures allow the average magnitude and distribution of effects to be estimated via combined results (Borenstein et al., 2009). Within group-design research, meta-analyses are often considered to be the highest standard of evaluating intervention effectiveness (Hoffman et al., 2013). Meta-analytic approaches for SCD research, however, have not yet reached the same degree of consensus. Thankfully, recent methodological advances over the last 15 years continue to expand upon the ways in which meta-analyses of SCDs are conducted. Especially in areas of significant need for evidence given a gap in the literature, SCD studies represent a resource that could be utilized to inform intervention and practice.

## Study Purpose

Effectively supporting children during early childhood is critical to a myriad of child outcomes, as social-emotional competencies are predictive of both short- and long-term child success. Unfortunately, many children, families, and schools in rural communities face barriers to accessing social-emotional interventions (e.g., lack of qualified professionals, existing stigma towards services, food insecurity and poverty). Research to date has demonstrated the

# Social-Emotional Interventions for Young Children 141

positive effects of interventions on children's behavioral and social-emotional development. Components of social-emotional interventions have varied widely. Unfortunately, much of the current knowledge regarding intervention effects and specific intervention components is based solely on group-design research that is inclusive of contexts beyond rural settings. More research specific to the types and effects of early childhood intervention specific to rural areas is needed. Given the prominence of SCD studies and recent methodological advancements in SCD meta-analytic practices, a meta-analysis of SCD studies may further support group-design work and provide unique insights regarding the context, usage, and effects of social-emotional interventions in early childhood settings in rural areas. Thus, the current study presents findings of a comprehensive SCD meta-analysis to address these issues and extend research in this area. The following questions guided the current study:

*1. What are the effects of Pre-K social-emotional interventions used in rural areas on children's social-emotional functioning (overall), challenging behavior, and prosocial behavior?*

*2. What components within Pre-K social-emotional interventions used in rural areas are the most effective at improving children's social-emotional functioning?*

*3. To what degree do characteristics of the child (i.e., race/ethnicity, gender), study (i.e., study type), and intervention (i.e., intervention implementer) moderate the effects of interventions on children's social-emotional functioning?*

## Method

The present study is part of a larger, comprehensive meta-analysis focused on the effects of early childhood interventions on children's academic, behavioral, and social-emotional development in rural areas. For purposes of the current study, we were particularly interested in studies which employed SCD methodology in rural settings and examined the effects of early childhood interventions on children's social-emotional and behavioral outcomes. Thus, the following section first describes methods and procedures from our larger, comprehensive meta-analysis, followed by details on the selection, coding, and analyses of studies that met criteria for the current study. Construction of the larger, comprehensive meta-analysis involved two processes: (1) literature search and (2) study identification.

**Literature Search**

Efforts to locate relevant studies involved three central approaches. First, five electronic databases (i.e., Academic Search Premier, APA PsycINFO, APA PsycARTICLES, ERIC, and MEDLINE) were searched using multiple search term parameters and combinations (e.g., "rural," "pre-k," "intervention," "social-emotional," etc.) to identify relevant literature from the years 2000 to 2020. Second, in an attempt to capture grey literature, we conducted searches through Google Scholar and through the online database ProQuest: Dissertation & Theses. Third, we conducted hand searches of nine relevant journals focused on rural education and/or mental health (e.g., Rural Special Education Quarterly, Journal of Rural Mental Health) and early education (e.g., Early Childhood Research Quarterly, Early Education and Development). Search procedures resulted in 1,946 potential studies. See Figure 1 for an overview of search and screening processes at each stage of the study.

Social-Emotional Interventions for Young Children 143

FIGURE 1 – Flowchart of Search and Screening Processes

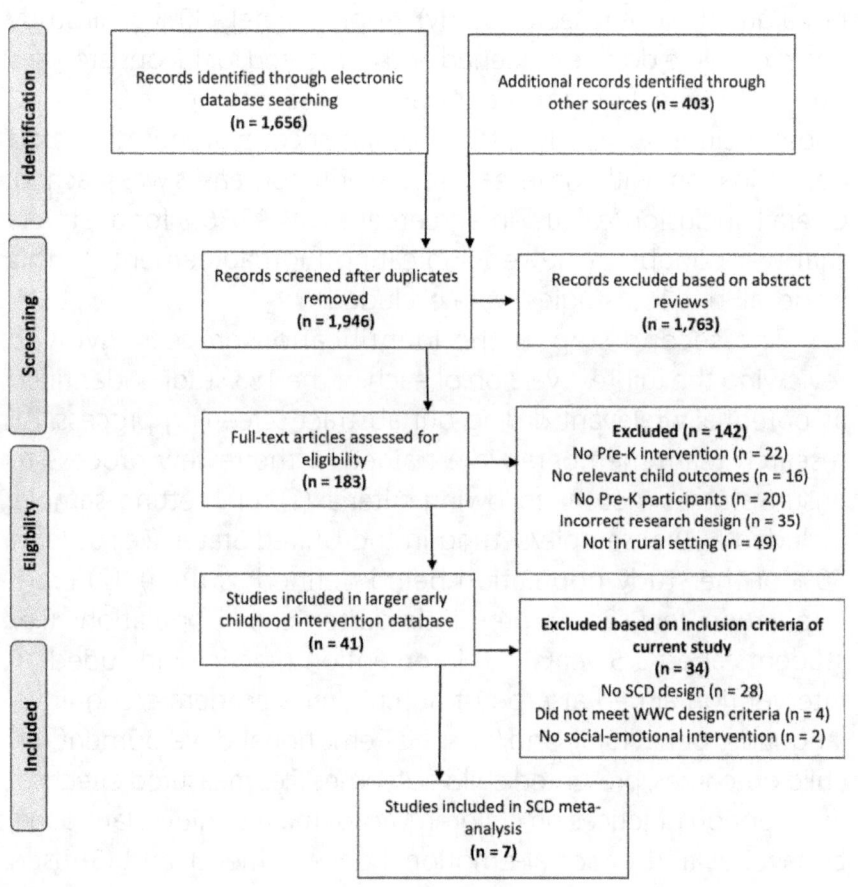

## Study Identification

After search procedures were completed, identification of relevant studies involved a two-step process – abstract screening and full-text article reviews. First, our research team initially screened abstracts in an attempt to exclude any studies that were clearly irrelevant (e.g., did not focus on Pre-K populations, was not a quantitative research study). Approximately 30% of all study abstracts were double-screened and compared for inconsistencies during bi-weekly team meetings. As disagreements occurred about inclusion/exclusion, the first and second author discussed determinations with the research team until consensus was reached. Overall, inclusion/exclusion agreement was 92.76% for abstracts that were double-reviewed, indicating high agreement. At this stage, all but 163 studies were excluded.

The second step of the identification process involved reviewing the full-text version of each of the 183 studies identified as potentially relevant during our abstract screening process. All research team members were trained in the review process to ensure studies met the following criteria: (1) rural setting/sample: included a rural sample/setting in the United States (i.e., at least 50% of the study population being defined as rural), (2) Pre-K population: focused on pre-Kindergarten child populations (i.e., students aged 3-5 years), (3) intervention practices: included an intervention aimed at promoting children's academic/cognitive, language, behavioral, and/or social-emotional development, (4) child outcomes: presented child outcomes (i.e., measured effects of intervention practices on children's academic/cognitive, language, behavioral, and/or social-emotional development), and (5) used any of the following research designs: [a] an experimental or quasi-experimental design that compared groups receiving one or more interventions promoting Pre-K child development with one or more control groups, or [b]: a single case design (SCD) that utilized repeated measurement on at least one direct assessment of a qualifying child outcome measure assessed before (baseline phase) and during the intervention. Based on abstract screening followed by full-text article reviews, 41 total Pre-K intervention studies were included in the final sample of the larger database.

**Final Inclusion Criteria and Coding for the Current Study**

The current study specifically focused on SCD studies that assessed the impacts of Pre-K interventions on children's behavioral and/or social-emotional outcomes. Final inclusion criteria for SCD studies were guided by the Institute of Education Sciences What Works Clearinghouse (IES-WWC) design standards (WWC, 2014). These standards were chosen as an aid in ruling out threats to internal validity. The IES-WWC standards include the following: (a) the independent variable (IV) is systematically manipulated, with the researcher determining when and how IV conditions change, (b) each study variable is measured systematically over time by more than one assessor, with at least 20% of data points in each condition measured, and inter-rater agreement meeting minimal thresholds, (c) the study includes at least three phases to demonstrate an intervention effect at different points in time, and (d) each phase must have an adequate number of data points. Studies that did not meet evidence standards or meet evidence standards with reservations were excluded.

After review of SCD studies based on IES-WWC standards, 7 studies with 26 participants and 53 effects were chosen for the final sample. Included studies were then coded using a codebook developed by the research team. This codebook includes multiple sections designed to focus on a number of study-, participant-, and outcome-level variables. The codebook was developed using an iterative process in which we created initial codes, tested initial codes through pilot coding, and then revised codes as necessary based on piloting. For purposes of the current study, we coded articles based on iteratively developed codes that included social-emotional intervention components (i.e., parent involvement/enhancement, teacher/parent behavior management training, social-emotional competency training), children's social-emotional functioning outcomes (i.e., disruptive behavior or prosocial behavior), study type (i.e., published/unpublished), and intervention implementer (i.e., teacher, parent, interventionist/researcher). We additionally coded articles for child characteristics, including child race/ethnicity (i.e., White, African-American, Latinx, Multi-racial, American Indian, Asian/Asian-American, Native Hawaiian/Pacific Islander, or Other) and gender (i.e., male or female). All seven articles were double-coded to assess reliability. Overall percent agreement was 90.47% indicating high agreement for study codes among coders.

## Data Analysis

*Effect size calculation.* A recently developed effect size index, the log response ratio (LRR; Pustejovsky, 2018), was used in the current study. The LRR accounts for issues in frequently used effect size indices (e.g., Tau-U, Percentage of Non-overlapping Data) that have unknown sampling distributions and are difficult to compare across studies using different measurement procedures. LRR effect sizes were calculated based on extracting raw data from digitized versions of graphs using the data extraction tool WebPlotDigitizer (Rohatgi, 2014), which has previously yielded high reliability and a high degree of usability (Moeyaert et al., 2016). LRR indices were then calculated using an online single-case effect size calculator (i.e., Pustejovsky & Swan, 2018). We calculated the LRR-increasing form of the LRR (i.e., the LRRi), to consistently report results in a single direction (i.e., positive values of effects correspond to both improvement in prosocial behaviors and reductions in disruptive behaviors).

*Meta-analysis.* We followed guidelines recommended by Pustejovsky (2018) based on a proposed three-level, hierarchical model to synthesize and analyze LRRi indices from included studies. This approach allowed us to account for potential issues with multiple cases/effects per study and within study dependence. In particular, for each three-level model synthesizing effects, Robust

Variance Estimation (RVE) techniques (Hedges et al., 2010) were used to account for potentially inaccurate sampling variances. For moderation analyses, meta-regression models for each moderator were conducted. All meta-analysis and RVE procedures were analyzed in R using the metafor (Viechtbauer, 2010) and clubSandwich packages (Pustejovsky, 2021).

## Results

### Characteristics of Included Studies

In total, 7 studies with 26 participants and 53 outcomes were included in the final sample. Of the seven included articles, four (57%) were journal articles and three (43%) were dissertations/theses. Of studies reporting specific information about rural location, three (50%) were located in the Southeastern U.S., followed by two (33%) in the Western U.S., and one (17%) in the Midwest. Regarding the total included child population, 47% were White, followed by 21% Black/African-American, 16% Latinx, 11% multiracial, and 5% American Indian/Native American. Child participants were overwhelmingly male (i.e., 74%); 26% were female. Regarding specific child participant characteristics, 27% of participants had a developmental delay, 23% had a speech or language impairment, 15% had typical development, 12% had autism spectrum disorder, and 23% were considered "at risk" based on other study-specific categorizations (e.g., low SES, significant behavioral problems).

The studies focused on three types of intervention strategies to support child behavior and social-emotional development. The first type of intervention component was teacher and/or parent behavior management training. Dufrene and colleagues (2007), for instance, focused on training teachers in different behavior management strategies for target students based on functional behavioral assessments (FBA); for example, providing differential reinforcement through praise of appropriate behavior while ignoring unwanted behaviors). The second intervention type included efforts aimed at training students to develop specific social-emotional competencies (e.g., social skills, emotion regulation). Stanton-Chapman and colleagues (2012) taught and modeled social communication strategies in order to improve verbal and nonverbal interactions between children (e.g., initiating play with a peer). Finally, parent involvement/enhancement activities were used in three studies, and varied in intensity and specific methods. That is, Wood et al. (2011) interviewed parents as part of FBA procedures used to inform interventions, Beale (2009) shared information and procedures with parents in hopes of generalizing intervention practices to the home setting, and Hoffman et al. (2013) taught parents strategies to support children's critical communication skills at home.

**Intervention Effects on Social-Emotional Functioning**

We synthesized 53 effects across 7 studies to estimate the overall effects of social-emotional interventions on children's social-emotional functioning. Additionally, we synthesized 34 prosocial behavior effects across 3 studies and 19 disruptive behavior effects across 4 studies. Table 1 contains the results of each of the three multi-level meta-analysis models summarizing the pooled effects (i.e., LRRi), robust standard errors, 95% confidence intervals, corresponding percentage change, between-study variance (i.e., study-level SD), and within-study (participant-level SD) variance.

Pooled effects for each of the three models were significantly different from zero. The average LRRi estimate was 0.93 (95% CI [0.45,1.41]) across all social-emotional functioning outcomes, which corresponds to a 153% increase from baseline levels (see Table 1). For prosocial behaviors, the average LRRi estimate was 0.94 (95% CI [0.24, 1.65]), which corresponds to an increase of 155% from baseline levels (95% CI [34%, 177%]). Regarding disruptive behaviors, the average LRRi estimate was 0.91 (95% CI [0.51, 1.39]), which corresponds to a decrease of 148% from baseline levels. Results of all three models of social-emotional functioning outcomes indicate more between-study variability than within-study variability in terms of effect sizes. Between-study SDs were all 0.35 or higher, whereas all within-study variability ranged from 0.02 to 0.28. This indicates that effects were more likely to vary across studies than within studies.

Table 1
Social-Emotional Intervention Effects (LRRi) on Child Outcomes

| | k | n | LRRi (SE) | CIs | % change | t | Study-level SD | Case-level SD |
|---|---|---|---|---|---|---|---|---|
| Social-emotional functioning (overall) | 7 | 53 | 0.93 (0.24) | 0.45, 1.41 | 153.45 | 3.79** | 0.38 | 0.15 |
| Prosocial behavior | 3 | 34 | 0.94 (0.36) | 0.24, 1.65 | 155.99 | 2.63** | 0.35 | 0.28 |
| Disruptive behavior | 4 | 19 | 0.91 (0.27) | 0.51, 1.39 | 148.43 | 2.49* | 0.46 | 0.02 |

*Note:* n = number of effect sizes; k = number of studies; SE = standard error; CIs = 95% confidence intervals; * = p<0.05; ** = p<0.01; *** = p <0.001

## Intervention Component Analyses

The effects of social-emotional interventions on children's social-emotional functioning (overall) were also analyzed based on intervention components used within social-emotional interventions (see Table 2). Results for our three models organized by each intervention component also revealed that all models were significantly different from zero. For studies utilizing teacher and/or parent behavior management training, the average LRRi estimate was 0.99 (0.55,1.32), which corresponds to a 169% increase from baseline levels. Studies using social-emotional competency training had an average LRRi estimate of 1.35 (0.77, 1.93) with a 285% change from baseline, and studies incorporating parent involvement/enhancement had an average LRRi estimate of 1.25 (0.51, 1.99) with a 249% change from baseline. Studies using teacher/parent behavior management training had substantially higher between-study variability, whereas within-study variability was greater across studies using social-emotional competency training and parent involvement/enhancement.

**Table 2**
*Social-Emotional Intervention Effects by Intervention Component*

|  | k | n | LRRi (SE) | CIs | % change | t | Study-level SD | Case-level SD |
|---|---|---|---|---|---|---|---|---|
| Teacher/parent behavior management training | 5 | 33 | 0.99 (0.22) | 0.55, 1.32 | 169.12 | 3.59** | 0.61 | 0.06 |
| Social-emotional competency training | 4 | 35 | 1.35 (0.29) | 0.77, 1.93 | 285.74 | 4.57*** | 0.28 | 0.31 |
| Parent involvement/ Enhancement | 3 | 23 | 1.25 (0.37) | 0.51, 1.99 | 249.03 | 3.29*** | 0.34 | 0.37 |

**Note:** n = number of effect sizes; k = number of studies; SE = standard error; CIs = 95% confidence intervals; * = $p<0.05$; ** = $p<0.01$; *** = $p<0.001$

## Moderation Effects Based on Child, Intervention, and Study Characteristics

Moderator analyses were also undertaken to determine if variability in social-emotional effects was due to child, intervention, or study characteristics (see Table 3). We investigated two child characteristics (i.e., race/ethnicity and gender), neither of which were found to explain a significant degree of variation in effect size estimates. Regarding study/intervention characteristics, we compared studies based on study type (i.e., published journal articles compared to unpublished dissertations/theses), and also explored whether results varied based on who was implementing the intervention (i.e., teacher/parent compared to researcher/ interventionist). No moderation effects were revealed based on intervention implementer; however, study type was found to significantly moderate effects. In particular, the effects of social-emotional interventions were more pronounced in published compared to unpublished studies (F = 7.61, p = 0.01).

*Table 3*
*Moderation Analyses for Child Social-Emotional Outcomes*

| | k | n | LRRi (SE) | CIs | Study-level SD | Case-level SD | Test of between-group differences |
|---|---|---|---|---|---|---|---|
| **Child Characteristics** | | | | | | | |
| *Race/Ethnicity* | | | | | | | $F = 1.02, p = 0.41$ |
| African-Am. | 3 | 4 | 0.92 (0.54) | 0.13, 1.96 | 0.81 | 0.02 | |
| White | 3 | 17 | 1.30 (0.45) | 0.43, 2.17 | 0.53 | 0.13 | |
| Latinx | 3 | 8 | 1.13 (0.42) | 0.33, 1.85 | 0.40 | 0.10 | |
| Other | 2 | 11 | 0.71 (0.25) | 0.21, 1.20 | 0.00 | 0.67 | |
| *Gender* | | | | | | | |
| Female | 3 | 14 | 0.91 (0.18) | 0.55, 1.27 | 0.00 | 0.41 | $F = 0.04, p = 0.94$ |
| Male | 6 | 30 | 1.06 (0.29) | 0.48, 1.63 | 0.46 | 0.13 | |
| **Study/Intervention Characteristics** | | | | | | | |
| *Intervention Implementer* | | | | | | | $F = 1.30, p = 0.28$ |
| Teacher/Parent | 5 | 25 | 0.87 (0.30) | 0.14, 1.13 | 0.44 | 0.04 | |
| Researcher/Interventionist | 2 | 28 | 1.13 (0.42) | 0.39, 1.81 | 0.32 | 0.12 | |
| *Study Type* | | | | | | | $F = 7.61, p = 0.01*$ |
| Journal Article | 4 | 18 | 1.30 (0.32) | 0.85, 1.75 | 0.40 | 0.14 | |
| Dissertation/Thesis | 3 | 35 | 0.46 (0.08) | 0.29, 0.62 | 0.00 | 0.14 | |

**Note:** n = number of effect sizes; k = number of studies; SE = standard error; CIs = 95% confidence intervals; * = $p<0.05$; ** = $p<0.01$; *** = $p <0.001$; Race/ethnicity Other = Multi-racial or American-Indian/Native American

## Discussion

Young children with social emotional problems need access to evidence-based interventions. Nearly one in five children live in rural areas (U.S. Census Bureau, 2016), with many at risk for service gaps and less trained professionals. Understanding the type and effects of early childhood interventions being utilized in rural areas is important because rural settings have specific cultural contexts that are not present in suburban and urban areas (Morales et al., 2020). Thus, given the unique needs of young children in rural areas, the purpose of this study was to conduct a meta-analysis of SCD studies of social-emotional interventions that have been implemented within rural settings with young children. This purpose reflects an effort to determine the effects and types of early interventions specific to young children in rural areas. Three research questions were addressed.

**Research Question 1**

First, the meta-analysis investigated the effects of early childhood interventions on children's overall social-emotional functioning as well as their impacts on prosocial behaviors and disruptive behaviors. Overall, results indicate that Pre-K interventions implemented in rural areas are an effective means for improving children's social-emotional development. Significant and positive findings were consistently revealed across social-emotional functioning (overall) and for both prosocial behavior and disruptive behavior child outcomes. The greatest area of improvement was found for prosocial behavior, where a 156% increase in prosocial behavior was estimated between baseline and intervention phases. This is promising because teaching young children prosocial behaviors (e.g., social skills, problem-solving skills) will likely improve outcomes over time. Young children with prosocial skills enter kindergarten with greater school readiness and ability to meet teacher expectations at this early point in their academic careers (Stormont, 2021). Results for disruptive behaviors are also very promising, given that these behaviors can be harmful to everyone in schools – including students exhibiting disruptive behaviors, their peers, and their teachers (Smith et al., 2022).

**Research Question 2**

Secondly, social-emotional intervention effects were analyzed based on the type of intervention components used. Of the seven SCD studies that met inclusion criteria, three types of components emerged including interventions aimed at supporting teacher and parent behavior management practices, interventions incorporating child skill training, and interventions directed at increasing parent involvement. Overall, all of these intervention practices yielded positive and significant benefits for rural children's social-emotional functioning. The largest impact on child overall social-emotional outcomes came from skill-based child training, meaning that children were taught specific social-emotional skills (e.g., effective communication, understanding emotions). Although adult-based behavior management interventions are evidence-based and highly recommended practices, it is not surprising that child training practices would have a slightly larger effect within SCD studies. The skills children were being directly taught were often the same skills being assessed within studies, thus it might be expected that the impact of these interventions on these outcomes would be more immediate and pronounced. In contrast, training teachers and parents in behavior management strategies is an indirect process intended to help decrease student disruptive behaviors over time, and therefore, these strategies may not have the same immediate impact. However, we expect over time that teacher and parent training may produce more generalizable, and sustained behavior change. For instance, one study that followed children with early onset behavior problems who received an early childhood parenting intervention into adolescence found that the majority of youth were in the well-adjusted range (Webster-Stratton et al., 2011). Findings regarding interventions incorporating parent involvement are also noteworthy, and provide further support consistent with past research demonstrating the importance of parent involvement strategies in promoting children's social-emotional development (e.g., Sheridan et al., 2019).

**Research Question 3**

Lastly, several indicators, including child race and gender, whether the study was published in a journal, and whether the implementer was a researcher or not, were evaluated to determine if they moderated the findings. Only whether the study was published in a journal versus being a dissertation/thesis study was significant. In this case, those studies published in journals had a greater impact on student outcomes. This is not unexpected as published studies tend to be those in which significant outcomes were found, whereas studies with null findings are less likely to be published. This phenomenon is known as publication bias and research has demonstrated that effect size metrics are predictive of the difference between published and unpublished studies (see Chow & Ekholm, 2018).

**Implications for Research and Practice**

Importantly, the overall findings from this meta-analysis demonstrate that early childhood social-emotional interventions can positively impact key social-emotional and behavioral outcomes for young children in rural settings. The fact that only seven SCD studies met the criteria for inclusion is an indication that more research needs to be done in this area in the context of rural settings. Considering our larger meta-analytic database (i.e., including group-design and academic interventions) of 41 total intervention studies, we can estimate that SCD studies specific to social-emotional interventions account for roughly a quarter of studies in this area. This is a surprising finding given the increased use of SCD research in relevant applied areas, and may be due to the fact that many social-emotional interventions are manualized and targeted at the small-group or classroom level and assessed via group-design methodology. Further, much of the current literature focuses on a combination of contexts (e.g., suburban, rural, urban) and therefore findings may not be as relevant to rural settings given the unique features of living in rural America (Morales et al., 2020). Rural samples also tend to have fewer participants, making SCD an ideal method for understanding how intervention impact outcomes for young children in need of supports in rural settings. Thus, more SCD research in this area is warranted to address rural student concerns.

Another implication for research and practice is the need to focus on important findings from research directing interventions for young children in rural settings, while also considering the broader research literature to date. Important work from Webster-Stratton et al. (2011) found children at higher risk in early childhood (i.e., behavior problems in the top 10% of clinical range) had less positive long-term outcomes, when compared with their peers who were not in the clinical range. This indicates that children with more significant problems may need more intensive early supports. Given the heightened risk for social-emotional problems among children in rural settings, additional research that investigates the long-term outcomes of the types of interventions rural children receive is warranted.

These results also point to the need to combine the use of interventions identified as effective for young children in rural settings with what is known about barriers and cultural fit, to maximize the likelihood of positive outcomes for interventionists and participants. In order to do this, increased attention should be focused on the implementation of processes and systemic needs that support the intervention. It is possible that some of these elements, such as barrier reducing strategies, need to be part of the intervention. For instance, one common barrier in rural areas is a lack of trained service providers to support children's social-emotional development. Although the intervention implementer (i.e., parent/teacher compared to researcher/interventionist) was not found to significantly moderate results, it was promising to see that the majority of studies (i.e., 71%) involved parents and/or teachers as the individuals implementing social-emotional interventions. Given the lack of availability of highly-trained practitioners in rural areas, it is important to recognize that parents and teachers within these communities can be the agents of change used to provide critical interventions. Moving forward, efforts should be made to continue to train individuals in effective practices to support children's social-emotional development.

## Limitations

While this study yields important information regarding the overall effects of social-emotional interventions and different types of intervention components that contribute to positive outcomes for rural children, it is not without limitations. First, the overall number of studies that met inclusion criteria were few. As noted earlier, this is indicative of the need for additional research in this area using SCD. Because there were so few studies that met inclusion criteria, the findings may be somewhat skewed. A larger number of studies may produce different findings.

Second, although the current study assessed various intervention components, our research team did not assess the fidelity with which those intervention components were implemented. Intervention fidelity plays a significant role in terms of intervention effectiveness for students in practice. With parents and teachers, in particular, higher intervention fidelity is associated with greater intervention efficacy (Sheridan et al., 2016). Intervention fidelity may also be especially challenging to ensure in rural areas where resources are scarce. Future reviews in this area should consider and assess how fidelity may affect the effectiveness of social-emotional interventions.

The current study is also limited in its approach to intervention component analysis. In particular, we looked at whether or not each component was used within an intervention. However, it is very rare that social-emotional intervention components are delivered in isolation. Future studies should consider ways to investigate combinations of intervention practices that are used within social-emotional interventions to help continue to inform practices. Such research would create a greater understanding of the critical components necessary for social-emotional interventions implemented to support young children in rural areas.

Additionally, although we believe the LRR effect size index to be the best fit for the current study based on our data, it is also limited in that it does not account for trends in modeling single-case data. It is unknown whether using different effect size indices would have yielded different findings within the context of the current study. However, future research in this area should consider assessing intervention effects based on additional effect size indices that do account for trend (e.g., Tau-U, baseline correct Tau).

Finally, we used some restrictions within our inclusion criteria and search procedures that may have prevented some informative studies from being included. For instance, the current study only focused on studies including rural populations within the United States and published since the year 2000. It is possible that international studies and/or studies published prior to 2000 may yield important information regarding Pre-K social-emotional interventions implemented in rural areas that were not found within the context of the current study. Future studies in this area should consider expanding search parameters to attempt to locate older studies, and consider including studies focused on rural populations outside the United States.

## Conclusion

Overall, this meta-analysis found that social-emotional interventions were revealed to significantly and positively impact young children's social-emotional functioning (i.e., prosocial behavior, disruptive behavior) in rural areas. Additional research regarding the context of these interventions is important, given that rural settings bring unique challenges for young children. Young children in these settings are more likely to live in poverty with less access to needed services. As such, identifying the types of early childhood social-emotional interventions that produce positive effects can help guide the focus of rural mental health providers and potentially guide policies around training of providers. The meta-analysis identified three types of effective intervention components with young children in need of social-emotional supports (i.e., child skills training, teacher and parent behavior management training, and parent involvement/enhancement interventions). Further the interventions included in the analysis produced positive and significant effects for overall social-emotional functioning and for both prosocial behaviors and disruptive behaviors. The increase in prosocial behavior is particularly promising given its impact on school readiness. Continued research this area should explore how best to overcome identified barriers to young children and families accessing needed services in rural communities, and innovative ways to either deliver these services (e.g., telehealth) or to train providers who can better meet the needs of children in rural settings.

## References

NOTE: All references included in meta-analysis are denoted with an asterisk.

Bailey, R., Sharpe, D., Kwiatkowski, T., Watson, S., Dexter Samuels, A., & Hall, J. (2018). Mental health care disparities now and in the future. *Journal of Racial and Ethnic Health Disparities, 5*(2), 351–356. https://doi.org/10.1007/s40615-017-0377-6

*Beale, N. A. (2009). *Effects of utilizing educational TV shows and conversational recasting on language skills of preschoolers with specific language impairments* (Doctoral dissertation, Walden University).

Blewitt, C., Fuller-Tyszkiewicz, M., Nolan, A., Bergmeier, H., Vicary, D., Huang, T., ... & Skouteris, H. (2018). Social and emotional learning associated with universal curriculum-based interventions in early childhood education and care centers: a systematic review and meta-analysis. *JAMA network open, 1*(8), e185727-e185727.

Borenstein, M., Hedges, L. V, Higgins, J. P. T., & Rothstein, H. R. (2009). *Introduction to Meta-Analysis*. Chichester, UK: John Wiley & Sons, Ltd. https://doi.org/10.1002/9780470743386

Chow, J.C., & Ekholm, E. (2018). Do published studies yield larger effect sizes than unpublished studies in education and special education? A meta-review. *Educational Psychology Review, 30*, 727–744. https://doi.org/10.1007/s10648-018-9437-71

Conroy, M. A., Dunlap, G., Clarke, S., & Alter, P. J. (2005). A descriptive analysis of positive behavioral intervention research with young children with challenging behavior. *Topics in Early Childhood Special Education, 25*, 157-166.

Curby, T. W., Brown, C. A., Bassett, H. H., & Denham, S. A. (2015). Associations between preschoolers' social-emotional competence and preliteracy skills. *Infant and Child Development, 24*, 549–570. http://dx.doi.org/10.1002/icd.1899

Denham, S. A. (2006). Social-emotional competence as support for school readiness: what is it and how do we assess it? *Early Education and Development, 17*, 57–89. http://dx.doi.org/10.1207/s15566935eed17014

*Dufrene, B. A., Doggett, R. A., Henington, C., & Watson, T. S. (2007). Functional assessment and intervention for disruptive classroom behaviors in preschool and head start classrooms. *Journal of Behavioral Education, 16*(4), 368-388.

Farrigan, T. & Hertz, T. (2016). Understanding the rise in rural child poverty, 2003-2014. Washington, DC: Department of Agriculture, Economic Research Service. (https://www.ers.usda.gov/publications/pub-details/?pubid=45543. opens in new tab).

Hammond, D., & Gast, D. L. (2010). Descriptive analysis of single subject research designs: 1983—2007. *Education and Training in Autism and Developmental Disabilities, 45*, 187-202.

Hedges, L. V., Tipton, E., & Johnson, M. C. (2010). Robust variance estimation in meta-regression with dependent effect size estimates. *Research Synthesis Methods, 1*(1), 39-65. doi:10.1002/jrsm.5

Hoffman, T., Bennett, S., & Del Mar, C. (2013). Evidence-based practice: Across the health professions (2nd ed.). Chatswood, NSW: Elsevier.

*Hoffmann, A. N., Bogoev, B. K., & Sellers, T. P. (2019). Using telehealth and expert coaching to support early childhood special education parent-implemented assessment and intervention procedures. *Rural Special Education Quarterly, 38*(2), 95-106.

Lane, K. L., Kalberg, J. R., & Shepcaro, J. C. (2009). An examination of the evidence base for function-based interventions for students with emotional and/or behavioral disorders attending middle and high schools. *Exceptional Children, 75*, 321-340. doi:10.1177/001440290907500304

Luo, L., Reichow, B., Snyder, P., Harrington, J., & Polignano, J. (2020). Systematic review and meta-analysis of classroom-wide social–emotional interventions for preschool children. *Topics in Early Childhood Special Education*. Advance online publication. https://doi.org/10.1177/0271121420935579

*Mendoza, G. I. (2016). *Exploring gesturing as a natural approach to impact stages of second language development: A multiple baseline, single case study of a head start child* (Doctoral dissertation, East Tennessee State University).

Miller, P., Votruba-Drzal, E., & Setodji, C. M. (2013). Family income and early achievement across the urban–rural continuum. *Developmental Psychology, 49*(8), 1452-1465.

Moeyaert, M., Maggin, D., & Verkuilen, J. (2016). Reliability, validity, and usability of data extraction programs for single-case research designs. *Behavior Modification, 40*(6), 874-900.

Morales, D. A., Barksdale, C. L., & Beckel-Mitchener, A. C. (2020). A call to action to address rural mental health disparities. *Journal of Clinical and Translational Science, 4*(5), 463-467.

*Pasqua, J. L. (2016). *Evaluating the independent group contingency:" Mystery Student" on improving behaviors in Head Start classrooms* (Doctoral Dissertation, The University of Southern Mississippi).

Pustejovsky, J. E. (2021). clubSandwich: Cluster-robust (sandwich) variance estimators with small-sample corrections. Retrieved from https://cran.r-project.org/package=clubSandwich

Pustejovsky, J. E. (2018). Using response ratios for meta-analyzing single-case designs with behavioral outcomes. *Journal of School Psychology, 68,* 99–112. https://doi.org/10.1016/j.jsp.2018.02.003

Pustejovsky, J. E., & Ferron, J. M. (2017). Research synthesis and meta-analysis of single-case designs. In J. M. Kaufmann, D. P. Hallahan, & P. C. Pullen (Eds.), *Handbook of special education, 2nd edition* (p. 168-186). New York, NY: Routledge.

Pustejovsky, J. E., & Swan, D. M. (2018). *Effect size definitions and mathematical details.* https://cran.r-project.org/web/packages/SingleCaseES/vignettes/Effect-size-definitions.html

Raver, C. C. (2004). Placing emotional self-regulation in sociocultural and socioeconomic contexts. *Child Development, 75,* 346–353. http://dx.doi.org/10.1111/j.1467-8624.2004.00676.x

Reinke, W. M., Smith, T. E., & Herman, K. C. (2019). Family-school engagement across child and adolescent development. *School Psychology, 34*(4), 346-349. https://doi.org/10.1037/spq0000322

Rimm-Kaufman, S. E., Pianta, R. C., & Cox, M. J. (2000). Teachers' judgments of problems in the transition to kindergarten. *Early Childhood Research Quarterly, 15,* 147–166. http://dx.doi.org/10.1016/S0885-2006(00)00049-1

Robinson, L. R., Holbrook, J. R., Bitsko, R. H., Hartwig, S. A., Kaminski, J. W., Ghandour, R. M., ... & Boyle, C. A. (2017). Differences in health care, family, and community factors associated with mental, behavioral, and developmental disorders among children aged 2–8 years in rural and urban areas—United States, 2011–2012. *MMWR Surveillance Summaries, 66*(8), 1.

Rohatgi, A. (2014). *WebPlotDigitizer user manual version 3.4.* Retrieved from http://arohatgi.info/WebPlotDigitizer/userManual.pdf

Schindler, H. S., Kholoptseva, J., Oh, S. S., Yoshikawa, H., Duncan, G. J., Magnuson, K. A., & Shonkoff, J. P. (2015). Maximizing the potential of early childhood education to prevent externalizing behavior problems: A meta-analysis. *Journal of School Psychology, 53*(3), 243-263.

Sheridan, S. M., Knoche, L. L., Edwards, C. P., Bovaird, J. A., & Kupzyk, K. A. (2010). Parent engagement and school readiness: Effects of the Getting Ready intervention on preschool children's social–emotional competencies. *Early Education and Development, 21*(1), 125-156.

Sheridan, S. M., Holmes, S. R., Smith, T. E., & Moen, A. L. (2016). Complexities in field-based partnership research: Exemplars, challenges, and an agenda for the field. In S. M. Sheridan & E. M. Kim (Eds.), *Research on family-school partnerships: An interdisciplinary examination of state of the science and critical needs, Vol 3* (pp. 1–23). New York, NY: Springer.

Sheridan, S. M., Smith, T. E., Kim, E. M., Beretvas, S. N., & Park, S. (2019). A meta-analysis of family-school interventions and children's social-emotional functioning: Child and community influences and components of efficacy. *Review of Educational Research, 89*, 296-332.

Smith, T. E., Holmes, S. R., Sheridan, S. M., Cooper, J. M., Bloomfield, B. S., & Preast, J. L. (2021). The effects of consultation-based family-school engagement on student and parent outcomes: A meta-analysis. *Journal of Educational and Psychological Consultation, 31*(3), 278-306.

Smith, T. E., Reinke, W. M., Herman, K. C., & Huang, F. H. (2019). Understanding family–school engagement across and within elementary- and middle-school contexts. *School Psychology, 34*(4), 363-375. https://doi.org/10.1037/spq0000290

Smith, T. E., & Sheridan, S. M. (2019). The effects of teacher training on teachers' family engagement practices, attitudes, and knowledge: A meta-analysis. *Journal of Educational and Psychological Consultation, 29*, 128-157.

Smith, T. E., Sheridan, S. M., Kim, E. M., Park, S., & Beretvas, S. M. (2020). The effects of family-school partnership interventions on academic and social-emotional functioning: A meta-analysis exploring what works for whom. *Educational Psychology Review, 32*(2), 511-544. https://doi.org/10.1007/s10648-019-09509-w

Smith, T. E., Thompson, A. M., & Maynard, B. (2022). Self-management interventions for reducing challenging behaviors among school-age students: A systematic review. *Campbell Systematic Reviews, 18*(1), e1223. https://doi.org/10.1002/cl2.1223

*Stanton-Chapman, T. L., Denning, C. B., & Jamison, K. R. (2012). Communication skill building in young children with and without disabilities in a preschool classroom. *The Journal of Special Education, 46*(2), 78-93.

Stormont, M. (2021). *Kindergarten readiness for all: Strategies to support the transition to school.* Cambridge Scholars Publishing.

United States Census Bureau (2016). *New Census Data Show Differences Between Urban and Rural Populations.* Retrieved from United States Census Bureau: https://www.census.gov/newsroom/press-releases/2016/cb16-210.html.

Viechtbauer, W. (2010). Conducting meta-analyses in R with the metafor package. *Journal of Statistical Software, 36*(3), 1-48.

Webster-Stratton, C., Rinaldi, J., & Jamila, M. R. (2011). Long-Term outcomes of Incredible Years Parenting Program: Predictors of adolescent adjustment. *Child and Adolescent Mental Health, 16*(1), 38–46. https://doi.org/10.1111/j.1475-3588.2010.00576.x

What Works Clearinghouse. (2014). *Procedures and standards handbook* (Version 3.0). Retrieved from http://ies.ed.gov/ncee/wwc/pdf/reference_resources/wwc_procedures_v3_0_draft_standards_handbook.pdf

Wong, C., Odom, S. L., Hume, K. A., Cox, A. W., Fettig, A., Kucharczyk, S., ... Schultz, T. R. (2015). Evidence-based practices for children, youth, and young adults with autism spectrum disorder: A comprehensive review. *Journal of Autism and Developmental Disorders, 45*(7), 1951–1966. https://doi.org/10.1007/s10803-014-2351-z

*Wood, B. K., Ferro, J. B., Umbreit, J., & Liaupsin, C. J. (2011). Addressing the challenging behavior of young children through systematic function-based intervention. *Topics in Early Childhood Special Education, 30*(4), 221-232.

Yang, W., Datu, J. A. D., Lin, X., Lau, M. M., & Li, H. (2019). Can early childhood curriculum enhance social-emotional competence in low-income children? A meta-analysis of the educational effects. *Early Education & Development, 30* (1), 36–59. https://doi.org/10.1080/10409289.2018.1539557

# Addressing Barriers to Universal Screening for Social, Emotional, and Behavioral Risk in Elementary Schools

*Crystal N. Taylor, Rebecca W. Lovelace, Caitlyn M. Weaver, Sarah W. Harry, Terreca A. Cato, and Meleah M. Ackley*

## Abstract

Early identification of students in need of additional support in the classroom is an important structure for school districts to have in place. Universal screening for social-emotional and behavioral (SEB) risk is one method that schools can use to identify students in need of SEB support and to begin early intervention programing. Unfortunately, recommendations about universal screening and resources for universal screening for SEB risk are limited. As a result, barriers to screening are increased and interventions are delayed – sometimes indefinitely -- for those who need them most. This paper discusses the barriers and challenges experienced by elementary schools (grades K-5) in one school district in the South across a three-year consultative study. This district was supported by the researchers in identifying an appropriate SEB screener, in disseminating the screener, and in ensuring accuracy in its completion. Across the three years, data were evaluated from previous years, and recommendations to improve the district's screening initiative were made by the lead consultant and school psychology graduate students. Over time, positive changes were noted in screening practices, but it is evident that more work needs to be done. Specific solutions and future implications for early childhood are discussed.

*Keywords: universal screening, social-emotional, assessment*

## Addressing Barriers to Universal Screening for Social, Emotional, and Behavioral Risk in Elementary Schools

Early identification and intervention for social-emotional and behavioral (SEB) difficulties are particularly important in early childhood. Young children that exhibit SEB problems are at increased risk for negative, long-term outcomes such as academic problems, delinquency, and negative peer relationships (Reinke et al., 2008). Thus, higher rates of behavior problems can inhibit a child's behavior socially and emotionally and impact their academic success. Consequently, there is a need for an integration of behavioral supports in early childhood to improve student SEB outcomes as well as student academic outcomes (Lane et al., 2014). More recent legislation has shifted from being focused predominantly on reading performance, math scores, and teacher accountability, to a whole-child approach (Carlson, 2019). The introduction of the Every Student Succeeds (ESSA) Act in 2015 is seen as a primary source of funding for SEB support, and it has included the following strides toward supporting SEB development:

- broader definitions of student success (i.e., not exclusively academic indicators);
- language regarding the enhancement of student academic enabling skills (e.g., being prepared for class, participating in instruction, etc.) to support school readiness;
- broader definitions of professional development; and
- creation of specific school staff positions dedicated to improving school climate, safety, and student mental and behavioral health (Collaborative for Academic, Social and Emotional Learning; CASEL, 2021).

Thus, research and policy suggest the importance of supporting SEB growth in early childhood. SEB skills that are developed during early childhood include social skills such as relationship building, and emotional behavior skills such as emotion regulation and empathy (Darling-Churchill & Lippman, 2016). With more funding and a narrower focus on specific social and emotional skills, early childhood screening is becoming more popular as a proactive way to identify students needing additional SEB support (Elliott et al., 2021). Students identified as at-risk for SEB difficulties often benefit from social-emotional learning (SEL) programs, which, when integrated within the classroom, support generalization and provide a more robust approach than using stand-alone SEL curricula (Jones & Bouffard, 2012). Regardless of the process, however, early teaching and the fostering of SEB skills are known to lead to positive well-being and satisfactory educational outcomes in the short and long term (Djamnezhad et al., 2021).

Elementary schools are an ideal place to implement SEB support through their SEL and positive behavior interventions and supports (PBIS) programs. PBIS is a multi-tiered system of support (MTSS), in which students receive differentiated behavioral supports. Within this model, schools identify students in need of support beyond the universal interventions provided in Tier I. With universal screening schools can identify at-risk students (i.e., those not responding at Tier I) and provide further targeted service delivery early at Tier II (Kilgus & Eklund, 2016; Severson et al., 2007). Early identification of children who need more intensive Tier II supports for SEB difficulties is imperative in early childhood. The longer SEB difficulties go unidentified and untreated, the more stable these SEB difficulties appear, resulting in negative long-term outcomes (Gottlieb, 1991; Reinke et al., 2008).

Despite its importance, early identification of SEB risk, using universal screening procedures, is uncommon in elementary schools. This is likely due to the lack of recommendations for its implementation, further delaying services to those children that need it most (Briesch et al., 2018). Recent studies have examined the rates of universal screening in schools and found that 81% of schools administer screenings for academic concerns and 70% screen for health concerns, while only 9-12% of schools are using universal screening for SEB risk (Briesch, Chafouleas, Dineen, et al, 2021; Bruhn et al., 2014; Lane et al., 2015). A similar study in Australia found that 14.8% of surveyed schools used universal screening for mental health concerns (Burns & Rapee, 2021). In this study, Burns and Rapee identified three main barriers to mental health screening: (a) a lack of support for implementing universal screening protocols, (b) not knowing how to respond to at-risk students, and (c) lacking funding and resources to support at-risk students. Similar barriers have been described in other research studies such as that by Briesch, Chafouleas, Lovino et al, (2021). These perceived barriers impact schools' willingness to implement a SEB universal screening protocol in their schools. This paper sought to further understand the barriers and challenges associated with implementing a universal screening protocol for SEB risk, and to address challenges faced by elementary schools in a Southern United States school district.

## Purpose

A school district reached out to the primary author requesting consultation support for the implementation of universal screening practices in their elementary schools. Previously, the school district had used a self-developed screener without norms or criteria to identify those at risk for SEB difficulties, so they requested support to identify a psychometrically sound screening measure. The primary author of this paper, referred to as the lead consultant, supported the district's screening efforts across a three-year period. The school district used a top-down approach to implementing their screening initiative.

The purpose of the current paper was to address barriers and challenges this school district experienced in the first three years of implementing universal screening in their district. Understanding and addressing challenges to universal screening initiatives in early childhood is essential for providing practitioners and school personnel with recommendations to improve the implementation fidelity of universal screening, so they can provide intervention supports to at-risk children before problem behaviors worsen (Burns & Rapee, 2021; Severson et al., 2007).

## Research Questions

1. What challenges do elementary schools experience when initially administering universal screening for SEB risk?
2. When elementary schools receive consultation to address these challenges, will fidelity increase in terms of compliance for meeting deadlines and accuracy of data?

# Method

## Participants

Stakeholders from a school district in the Southern United States were considered the primary participants for this project. Stakeholders included the special education director, five school counselors from each elementary school, and school psychology graduate students. Teachers were considered secondary participants and were not involved in the consultation process. The decision to implement a universal screening initiative was made at the district level, to address the need to identify at-risk students in early elementary school and to align with special education policy.

No specific data were collected on the number of teachers that completed the screeners during 2019 (year one) due to a different focus (i.e., identify a universal screening measure and develop a screening protocol) for that first year. One hundred fifteen teachers completed screening for elementary students in 2020 (year two), and 97 teachers completed screening for elementary students in 2021 (year three). All participating elementary schools were considered Title 1 schools. Data obtained from the National Center for Education Statistics regarding the 2020-2021 year indicated that the district had approximately 2,000 elementary students. Most students identified as Black (85.23%), and there was an equal representation of male and female students. In this paper, the authors define early childhood as those under the age of eleven. This age range is slightly more inclusive as it includes children between nine and eleven years old.

## Measures
### Student Risk Screening Scale – Internalizing and Externalizing (SRSS-IE)

All elementary school students were rated using the SRSS-IE. Students were rated regardless of disability status, placement in the tiered system, or presence of any type of behavior support plan. The SRSS-IE (Drummond, 1994; Lane & Menzies, 2009) is used to identify students at risk for SEB problems. This instrument assesses internalizing and externalizing problems by having teachers rate students' behaviors on a Likert scale ranging from 0-3, with 0 indicating that the student never engages in the behaviors and 3 indicating that the student often engages in the behaviors. This measure is free and can be accessed online. The SRSS-IE has three forms: one for preschool students, one for elementary-aged students, and one for middle and high school students. For the purposes of this paper, the elementary version will be discussed. The SRSS-IE includes simple directions to guide teachers, but no formal training is required for teachers to complete it. In fact, Lane et al. (2015) noted the feasibility of completing the form. Directions specifically state to "use the above scale (0 = never, 1 = occasionally, 2 = sometimes, 3 = frequently) to rate each item for each student in your classroom." It has been mentioned that the original 7-item scale should take approximately 15 minutes for a teacher to rate an entire class (Lane et al., 2015). With the addition of 5 items on the SRSS-IE form used in this study, it was still assumed that the form would not be a time-intensive task for teachers to complete within the designated timeframe.

The externalizing scale of the SRSS-IE has 7 items (e.g., steal; lie, cheat, sneak; behavior problem; peer rejection; low academic achievement; negative attitude; and aggressive behavior). Scores ranging from 0-3 suggest low risk, 4-8 suggest moderate risk, and 9-21 suggest high risk. The internalizing scale has 5 items (e.g., emotionally flat; shy, withdrawn; sad, depressed; anxious, and lonely). Ratings from 0-1 on this scale suggest low risk, 2-3 suggest moderate risk, and 4-15 suggest high risk (Drummond, 1994; Lane & Menzies, 2009). Earlier research has supported the reliability of the SRSS-IE by showing strong internal consistency (>.80) and correct classification rates of 0.81 (Lane et al., 2015).

**Procedures**

During the fall semester of the 2019-2020 school year, stakeholders from a mid-size school district reached out to researchers and requested support with developing a plan for SEB universal screening procedures in their elementary schools. During year one, the district was specifically seeking guidance for identifying a universal screener to implement within their elementary schools. The district requested support with the implementation of the identified screener over the next two years of this study.

During this 3-year period, schools were only provided consultation regarding data collection. Brief reports were provided for intervention decision-making, but student and classroom outcome data were not collected. For the current study, all recommendations provided by the researchers for universal screening data collection were based on best practice models such as that from the School Mental Health Collaborative developed by Romer et al. (2020).

A professor in school psychology with nine years of experience in universal screening practices served as the lead consultant to identify and address challenges across all three years. The consultation was provided to the school district beginning in the fall of 2019. Consultation occurred once at the beginning of each school year prior to screening. During each consultation session, stakeholders from the school district identified challenges they experienced with their screening procedures, and the lead consultant identified solutions that each of the elementary schools could implement. Over the three-year process, conversations resulted in slow changes that positively affected the implementation of universal screening in this district. A description of screening procedures for each year is described below.

## Year One

In the fall of 2019, stakeholders at the district's elementary schools requested support from the lead consultant to improve their universal screening practices. The district then identified three challenges to their current universal screening procedures. First, the district wanted to better identify students that might need more SEB support, but they did not have the resources (i.e., experienced staff in early identification or universal screening). Second, because the district did not have experienced staff, the district was using a self-developed universal screener. This screener did not have norms, cut scores, or reliability and validity data. The district was seeking a universal screening tool that was reliable, valid, user-friendly, time-efficient, and cost-efficient. The final challenge experienced by this district was an ineffective implementation plan. In past years, implementation of their screening protocol was unsuccessful due to low buy-in, unclear expectations, and inconsistent use of the screening data.

During year one of this study, the lead consultant provided the district with a psychoeducational handout that described available universal screening measures, including the SRSS-IE (Drummond, 1994); the Social, Academic, and Emotional Behavior Risk Scale (Kilgus et al., 2014); the Strengths and Difficulties Questionnaire (Goodman, 1997); and the Behavior and Emotional Screening System (Kamphaus & Reynolds, 2015). From these options, the school district selected the SRSS-IE as their preferred screening measure because it was brief (only 12 items), free, and identified students with internalizing and externalizing risk. Next, the stakeholders chose teachers to be the informants because they spent most of their day with students and would, therefore, understand the typical behavioral expectations of children in that age group. Stakeholders identified October as the best time to screen students each year, as it was about two months after the start of the school year and would allow teachers to get to know their students before the screening began. This is consistent with best practice guidelines for universal screening, which recommends screening within four to six weeks of the beginning of the school year to ensure accurate ratings (Romer et al., 2020).

After this, one school psychology graduate student and the lead consultant acted as supports for the elementary schools as they went through their first year of universal screening. As part of the process, the graduate student provided the school counselors at each school with one folder of fillable Google Sheets for each classroom teacher to use to rate each student in their classroom. The graduate student met with the school counselors to discuss deadlines, expectations, and directions for the completion of the SRSS-IE. Teachers were given the option to complete the screener for all students in their classroom, or only for students that were believed to be at-risk. This was the district's method of conducting universal screeners in the past, so the stakeholders decided to maintain this practice to reduce the number of changes that occurred during year one. The counselors shared each Google Sheet with the teacher via email. The email explained the directions for completing the SRSS-IE and set a four-week deadline after the email was sent. School counselors were available to answer questions throughout the screening period. Once teachers received the Google Sheet, they entered the names of their students in the first column and were instructed to provide each student with a rating of zero to three for each behavior listed across on the first row of the Google Sheet.

After four weeks, school psychology graduate students scored the screeners and provided each school with a list of students that were at-risk on either the externalizing or internalizing scale. During the first year of the screening process, the elementary schools did not use their data to support at-risk students. This was due to incomplete and inaccurate screening data from some teachers and missing data from whole classrooms. Furthermore, intervention suggestions and screening reports were not provided by the consultant during year one because the district's request was to focus on identifying a screener and modifying expectations to further improve counselor and teacher buy-in.

### Year Two

During the fall of 2020 (year two), the lead consultant met face-to-face with district stakeholders to discuss and address challenges from their first year of screening. A primary challenge identified was that during the first year of screening, compliance was low and ratings from some teachers had missing data for their students. It is important to note that teachers were given the opportunity to only complete the screener on those they believed to be at-risk which might explain the missing data. Some school counselors also stated they did not see the benefit of screening, so they did not require teachers to complete the screener if they were resistant.

To address these concerns, two school psychology graduate students attended the district's monthly counselor meeting that was required for all counselors and behavior specialists. During this meeting, the graduate students gave a professional development-style presentation on the importance of universal screening, the specific features of the SRSS-IE, and instructions for completing the screener accurately. Furthermore, school counselors were informed that all teachers must screen all students in their respective classrooms. This was a change from previous years. At the end of the presentation, the screeners were distributed via Google Sheets, and the due date for SRSS-IE completion was provided. Stakeholders in the district decided on a shorter deadline of two weeks to help increase compliance.

Following the meeting, the counselor from each elementary school shared the online form with their schools' teachers via email and explained the directions and deadline for completing the SRSS-IE. Counselors and school psychology graduate students were available to answer teachers' questions during the screening period. Teachers were asked to complete the screener on every student in their classroom during the two-week timeframe. The

Google Sheets provided to the teachers in 2020 were identical to those provided in the previous year, and the process for the online forms remained consistent during both years. When student ratings were entered by the teachers into the Google Sheet, both externalizing and internalizing risk were automatically calculated. The line on the right side of the Google Sheet would turn green for low-risk, yellow for moderate-risk, and red for high-risk, to aid in visual analysis. These sheets were adapted from the Comprehensive Integrated Three-Tiered Model of Prevention screening website (Comprehensive Integrated Three-Tiered Model of Prevention; Ci3T, n.d.).

After the two-week screening period, graduate students evaluated the data with the lead consultant and provided a list of at-risk students (i.e., individuals flagged at high or moderate levels in either category) to each elementary school counselor. A formal written report was generated to describe rates of risk within each grade and throughout the whole school. The report included the percentage of students in each risk category and line graphs depicting the type of risk across grade levels. If the percentages of students at risk greatly exceeded 20%, as per the recommendations of Kilgus & Eklund (2016), the researchers provided the school with school-wide strategies to address SEB problems. Additionally, if one grade or one class had a significantly higher percentage of students at risk than other grades or classrooms intervention recommendations were supplied to that specific grade or classroom. These reports were provided to show school counselors the benefit of screening data and help them identify children in need of early intervention.

### Year Three

During the fall of 2021, the lead consultant met with the district stakeholders to discuss challenges seen in years one and two. The elementary schools indicated that fidelity (e.g., teachers completing the screener inaccurately, teachers not completing the screener by the deadline) was a major concern. Although issues with fidelity were directly related to teacher behaviors, researchers were not given access to teachers in a more formal manner. Instead, similar to the second year, the third year of the study began with a professional development at the monthly counselor meeting with the elementary schools' counselors and behavior specialists. This meeting was identical to the meeting from year two except it consisted of more explicit instructions for completing the SRSS-IE based on the errors that were made in the previous year. Counselors were instructed to provide additional support to teachers as necessary to improve the accuracy of the screening results. To further increase the accuracy of the behavior ratings and to increase the fidelity of the elementary schools' screening protocol, two school psychology graduate students followed-up with emails to the counselors that included explicit directions for completing the measures as well as the PowerPoint used during the professional development in the counselors' meeting. Counselors then shared the email which included the PowerPoint, instructions for completing the screener, the deadline, and the Google Sheets. The screening began in October, and teachers were given two weeks to complete their screening measures for their students.

To further increase fidelity, the importance of rating every behavior and not leaving any items blank was emphasized through emails and in-person when speaking with teachers. One week before the deadline, the school psychology graduate students sent reminder emails to the counselors and teachers with directions and emphasis on the importance of completing the screeners in a timely manner and accurately. Once the screeners were completed, the school psychology graduate students analyzed each school's results. Teacher ratings were combined, and results were analyzed by grade and school. A written report was generated using a template from year two and featured the percentage of students in each risk category and line graphs depicting the type of risk, percentage of risk, and how the risk varied across grade levels. The counselors were provided with these reports.

## Results

Data were analyzed at the district level for all elementary schools. Reported challenges were based on conversations between the lead consultant and district stakeholders across all three years. Challenges were also identified by school psychology graduate students' observations during the screening period. Additionally, fidelity data (i.e., timely and accurate completion of the SRSS-IE) were compared across years two and three. Year one's focus was more of a developmental phase during which elementary schools in the district identified a screener and solidified their screening practices. Fidelity data were not available during year one.

**Research Question One: What challenges do elementary schools experience when they begin administering universal screening for SEB risk?**

Three challenges to screening were most common in 2019 and 2020: limited or lack of buy-in, inaccurate and inconsistent responses to the SRSS-IE, and a need for training and explicit instructions in the implementation of universal screening procedures. These challenges were addressed in the fall of 2021.

### *Limited or Lack of Buy-In*

Reports from stakeholders in the district indicated that school counselors, school administrators, and teachers did not buy into the importance of universal screening. The lack of buy-in from upper administration and counselors resulted in incomplete screenings by some teachers. This was specifically problematic during the 2020 school year. Observations provided by the graduate students included a lack of engagement during the professional development held during the counselor's meeting, school personnel not encouraging teachers to adhere to deadlines, and a lack of follow-up with teachers to remind them to complete the screeners. This lack of follow-through from counselors and administrators likely resulted in less buy-in from teachers. To address the lack of buy-in, school psychology graduate students provided psychoeducation centered around universal screening during their professional development presentations at the counselors' meetings in year three. During these presentations, the importance of early identification using screening was highlighted. In addition, school psychology graduate students provided schools with reports that explained the results from the screening and offered intervention suggestions. These reports were provided in years two and three. It was anticipated that by providing support for using the data, school counselors would see the benefit of screening and encourage their teachers to complete the measures in future years.

### *Inaccurate and Inconsistent Responding to the SRSS-IE*

During the first year of screening (fall 2019), the district only required teachers to rate students that they suspected were at-risk. In the fall of 2020, teachers were instructed to complete ratings for every student in their classroom, but some teachers still only completed ratings for students they believed were at-risk. The different instructions between 2019 and 2020 may have contributed to this misunderstanding. In the third year of the study instructions were more explicit and were provided in multiple modalities such as on the Google Sheet and in an email with a PowerPoint attachment.

Another common error noted by the researchers was the inaccurate completion of the SRSS-IE. For example, some teachers submitted screening data with students receiving a rating of "6" on an item when the scale ranged from 0-3, or they reported students' total scores as 56 when the maximum total score, they could receive was 36. Similarly, some rating scales were returned with every item for each student marked with a zero, indicating that 100% of students in the class never engaged in any of the behaviors described on the rating scale. Additionally, some teachers only responded to questions they perceived as the most relevant to the student they were rating. These inaccurate and inconsistent ratings resulted in students with incomplete or missing data.

More explicit instruction and an emphasis on the importance of rating each behavior for all students and using the 0-3 Likert scale was provided to teachers during year two of the study. During year three, these instructions were further emphasized to school counselors at the presentation during the counselors' meeting. Moreover, a PowerPoint and email were provided to teachers that explained the purpose of universal screening and contained instructions for completing the screening measure in year three.

### *Need for Training and Explicit Instructions in Universal Screening Procedures*

According to stakeholders, training was necessary to teach school counselors the expectations for screening and to answer counselors' questions, before the counselors were required to ask teachers at their schools to complete the screener. Prior to screening in the fall of 2021, stakeholders also requested that the lead consultant and school psychology graduate students provide more explicit instructions directly to the teachers through emails and on the Google Sheets. A presentation during the monthly counselors' meeting that described the importance of screening and how to complete the screener was implemented in the fall of 2020. In the fall of 2021, the school counselors received the same training with further emphasis on the importance of gathering accurate and complete data to support student behavioral needs. Graduate students followed up with school counselors through email after the 2021 meeting. This email contained explicit instructions regarding the completion of the ratings and the importance of meeting deadlines. School psychology graduate students emphasized the importance of rating every behavior and answering each question, and the PowerPoint used during the meeting was provided for reference during the screening period. Finally, follow-up emails were sent by the school psychology graduate students to the counselors and teachers a week before the due date, to remind them of the deadline and to provide instructions for completing the SRSS-IE.

**Research Question Two: When elementary schools receive consultation to address challenges to their implementation of universal screening, will fidelity increase in terms of compliance for meeting deadlines and accuracy of data?**

In year two (the fall of 2020), a total of 113 teachers taught grades K-5 in the district. Of those teachers, 68 of them completed their screeners within the two-week period (60%). Overall completion rates ranged from 16 to 100% across all elementary schools in the district. In the fall of 2021, the district consisted of a total of 97 K-5 teachers, and of those teachers, 90 completed their screeners on time (92%). Overall completion rates in 2021 ranged from 81 to 100%. Percent increase in the completion rate was calculated by subtracting the 2020 completion rate and from the 2021 completion rate, dividing it by the 2021 completion rate, and multiplying by 100. This resulted in a 54% increase in completion between 2020 and 2021.

Errors were defined as any instance in which (1) a behavioral rating exceeded the maximum rating on the Likert scale; (2) when total scores exceeded the maximum possible score, (3) when all students in a classroom received an overall score of zero; or (4) when teachers had incomplete data for individual students (e.g., partially completed ratings for one student or no rating for individual students). Ratings exceeding 3 were determined to be intentional and not typographical errors. In 2020, the second year of screening, 37% of teachers had errors in their ratings. In the fall of 2021, only 9% of teachers had errors in their ratings. The percent decrease in error rate was calculated by subtracting the 2021 error rate from the 2020 error rate, dividing this by the 2020 error rate, and multiplying by 100. This resulted in a 76% decrease in errors between 2020 and 2021. Errors were only calculated for those teachers who completed the SRSS-IE.

## Discussion

Universal screening for SEB risk is a proactive method for early identification and intervention (Severson et al., 2007). By implementing universal screening within a prereferral, MTSS model, elementary schools would be able to provide early intervention, which would prevent negative outcomes associated with prolonged behavior problems (Reinke et al., 2008). However, there is little guidance or recommendations for implementation of universal screening protocols or the use of screening data once it is collected; these barriers may delay services for young children with SEB risk (Briesch, Chafouleas, Lovino et al., 2021). Across three years of implementing a screening protocol, elementary schools in a district encountered challenges associated with the screening process. The challenges experienced are like those encountered by other school districts (see Briesch et al., 2021; Burns & Rapee, 2021). The three main challenges experienced were issues with staff buy-in, inaccurate and inconsistent ratings, and a need for training. After addressing these barriers, the district saw improvements in their universal screening fidelity (i.e., teachers rating all students without errors).

During the first year, the district identified a universal screener (the SRSS-IE), an appropriate time to implement the screening (October), and the primary informant for the screener (teachers). School counselors were selected as the leaders in each elementary school to implement and facilitate the screening process. The district implemented the screening with little consultation and support during this first year. During the second year, stakeholders identified challenges from the previous year, and subsequently school psychology graduate students attended a meeting for all elementary school counselors in the district to address these challenges. During the third year, stakeholders determined that there were significant errors in the screening data completed by teachers in year two. These errors included rating students higher than was possible and skipping questions for some students. Additionally, some teachers did not complete the screeners on time. To address these issues, more explicit instructions and follow-up emails were provided during the third year. Between the second and third years of screening, there was a 54% increase in the number of completed screeners by the due date as well as a 76% decrease in the number of errors. Taken together, it is evident that minor changes aimed at providing more information and support to school districts can improve the fidelity of universal screening in elementary schools. Additional adjustments such as those described below might be made in the future to increase compliance and fidelity of universal screening initiatives.

**Implications for Practice**

Universal screening is an early identification procedure that is backed by research, but there is limited state guidance for the implementation of effective screening practices (Briesch et al., 2018). This paper illustrates the importance of buy-in, explicit instruction, and training when implementing screening within elementary schools. Simple changes to the implementation of screening protocols might help leaders and teachers understand the importance of the screening process, increasing buy-in and improving fidelity.

Within the current district, there was limited buy-in from school counselors, resulting in limited buy-in from teachers. Gaining support from those who have the task of asking teachers to complete the screening measures is important for the implementation fidelity of the screening protocol. The top-down approach may have also contributed to a lack of teacher buy-in. Including teachers in the screening process may be a better approach to implementing successful screening procedures. Therefore, elementary schools interested in implementing universal screening might consider including teachers in their initiatives to see more success. In this instance, the lead consultant and school psychology graduate students requested time to meet with teachers to provide professional development about screening and to help with the completion of the rating scales, but this did not occur due to the COVID-19 pandemic during years two and three of the study. As such, communication with teachers mostly occurred via email. School counselors were also available to assist with the screening. This approach was effective, but a meeting directly with teachers could be more beneficial. Moreover, elementary schools might ask for the screeners to be completed during teacher workdays or during faculty meetings. This would provide evidence of the school's commitment and value to the screening process, by providing teachers with specific times to complete the screeners and provide them the opportunity to receive in-person feedback and assistance from the school counselor and school psychology graduate students.

Elementary schools with limited resources, or those without access to experienced professionals with knowledge of screening, might consider using resources such as the Screening Coordinator Training Manual (Rollenhagen et al., 2021) or the Best Practice Universal Social, Emotional, and Behavioral Screening: An Implementation Guide (Romer et al., 2020). These resources provide suggestions for roles at the district and school levels, as well as guidance for the use of screening data to inform intervention. These are free resources that elementary schools might use if they do not have access to individuals with knowledge of universal screening. With these resources, school counselors and school psychologists could implement more efficient procedures for early identification and, therefore, improve school psychologists' and school counselors' ability to provide early intervention to young children.

**Limitations and Future Research**

This paper recognizes the importance of addressing challenges to universal screening to better support the implementation of screening protocols in elementary schools. However, there are some important limitations that must be addressed. First, this was a non-experimental paper examining the impact of consultation on screening practices. Future research, using an experimental design, is necessary to provide stronger support and empirical evidence for the need and direction of school-based universal screening practices. Furthermore, outcome data at the school and individual levels will provide further empirical evidence to support universal screening initiatives.

Second, some of the challenges experienced during the 2020-2021 school year may be attributed to the COVID-19 pandemic. In the fall of 2020, the elementary schools were hybrid with some students taking classes in the building and other students attending class virtually. The errors from the fall of 2020 were like those seen in 2019 (pre-COVID); however, it is unclear what impact hybrid schooling and, more broadly, the pandemic may have had on the screening process in the fall of 2020.

Third, teacher errors on the SRSS-IE were determined based on permanent products and do not reflect errors such as incorrect ratings of behaviors based on teacher bias or other extraneous variables. The term accuracy here refers to accurately entering data and providing complete (whole class) data. Future research is needed to further examine the accuracy of teachers' ratings of students' behaviors in the classroom. Researchers were not given access to teachers, so teachers did not receive direct training in completion of the screening measure. Current research regarding the need for teacher training for completing universal screening measures is limited (von der Embse et al., 2018), but further research regarding the importance of teacher training, and methods for training teachers to screen their students more accurately is warranted. Additional research examining the impact of training that addresses teacher bias and includes opportunities for self-reflection might be valuable in supporting more accurate teacher ratings (Dowdy et al., 2014). Current research suggests some teacher-level variance attributed to student scores on universal screening measures; thus, trainings for teachers might help improve screening outcomes

(McLean et al., 2019; Splett et al., 2018; Splett et al., 2020).

Lastly, a recent study by Brann et al. (2022) found limited research regarding the availability of culturally responsive universal screening measures, including the SRSS-IE. The elementary schools represented in the present study were considered Title I schools with large populations of students from racial minority groups. Therefore, the measure used with this group of children may not have been culturally relevant; the potential impact on results is unclear. It is possible that using a measure that is not culturally relevant could affect the social validity of the measure, which may have also impacted buy-in for the screening process. More research is needed in this area. Practitioners are encouraged to collect feedback from individuals in underrepresented communities regarding the acceptability and social validity of the measures being used to ensure the accurate identification of at-risk students (Brann et al. 2022; Dowdy & Kim, 2012).

## Summary

This paper described a three-year process of supporting a school district with its universal screening procedures at the elementary school level. Universal screening for SEB risk is imperative in early childhood. Elementary schools are an ideal place to identify children in need of additional SEB service delivery. Through consultation, elementary schools in this study were able to increase compliance and the accuracy of teacher ratings. Having a protocol for universal screening will allow elementary schools to provide early intervention to at-risk children and prevent long-term negative outcomes (Severson et al., 2007; Reinke et al., 2008). It is evident that more research and guidance are necessary to construct protocols for screening to be used by practitioners in elementary schools, but it is encouraging to observe that some change can be made in a short period. Overall, experts in this area are encouraged to continue to coach and consult with districts to address challenges to the implementation of universal screening. This type of support will help schools collect more accurate screening data, and help them make more informed intervention decisions for young children.

## References

Brann, K. L., Daniels, B., Chafouleas, S. M., & DiOrio, C. A. (2022) Usability of social, emotional, and behavioral assessments in schools: A systematic review from 2009 to 2019. *School Psychology Review, 51*(1), 6-24. https://doi.org/10.1080/2372966X.2020.1836518

Briesch, A. M., Chafouleas, S. M., & Chaffee, R. (2018). Analysis of state-level guidance regarding school-based universal screening for social, emotional, and behavioral risk. School Mental Health. *School Mental Health, 10,* 147-162. https://doi.org/10.1007/s12310-017-9232-5

Briesch, A.M., Chafouleas, S.M., Dineen, J.N., McCoach, B., & Donaldson, A. (2021). School building administrator reports of screening practices across academic, behavioral, and health domains. *Journal for Positive Behavior Interventions,* https://doi.org/10.1177%2F10983007211003335

Briesch, A.M., Chafouleas, S.M. Ivoino, E.A., Abdulkerim, N., Sherod, R.L., Oakes, W.P., Lane, K.L., Common, E.A., Royer, D.J., & Buckman, M. (2021). Exploring directions for professional learning to enhance behavior screening within a comprehensive, integrated, three-tiered model of prevention. *Journal of Positive Interventions, 00,* 1-11. https://doi.org/10.1177/10983007211050424

Bruhn, A.L., Woods-Groves, S., Huddle, S. (2014). A preliminary investigation of emotional and behavioral screening practices in K-12 schools. *Education and Treatment of Children, 37*(4), 611–634. https://doi.org/10.1353/etc.2014.0039

Burns, J. R., & Rapee, R. M. (2021). Barriers to universal mental health screening in schools: The perspective of school psychologists. *Journal of Applied School Psychology.* Advance online publication. https://doi.org/10.1080/15377903.2021.1941470

Carlson, D. (2019). No Child Left Behind, National Ambitions, and Local Realities: Implications for Social and Emotional Learning. *American Enterprise Institute.*

Collaborative for Academic, Social, and Emotional Learning (CASEL). (2021). SEL Policy at the Federal Level. Chicago, IL. Retrieved from https://casel.org/systemic-implementation/sel-policy-at-the-federal-level/

Comprehensive Integrated Three-Tiered Model of Prevention [Ci3T]. (n.d.). *Systematic Screening.* https://www.ci3t.org/screening

Darling-Churchill, K. E., & Lippman, L. (2016). Early childhood social and emotional development: Advancing the field of measurement. *Journal of Applied Developmental Psychology, 45,* 1-7. https://doi.org/10.1016/j.appdev.2016.02.002

Djamnezhad, Dariush & Koltcheva, Nadia & Dizdarevic, Alma & Mujezinovic, Amila & Peixoto, Carla & Coelho, Vera & Achten, Mart & Kolumbán, Erika & Machado, Francisco & Hofvander, Bjorn. (2021). Social and emotional learning in preschool settings: A systematic map of systematic reviews. *Frontiers in Education, 6.* https://doi.org/10.3389/feduc.2021.691670

Dowdy, E., & Kim, E. (2012). Choosing informants when conducting a universal screening for behavioral and emotional risk. *School Psychology Forum, 6*(4), 1-10.

Dowdy E., Kamphaus R.W., Twyford J.M., Dever B.V. (2014) Culturally Competent Behavioral and Emotional Screening. In: Weist M., Lever N., Bradshaw C., Owens J. (eds) *Handbook of school mental health. Issues in clinical child psychology* (pp. 311-321). Springer, Boston, MA. https://doi.org/10.1007/978-1-4614-7624-5_23

Drummond, T. (1994). The student risk screening scale (SRSS). Grants Pass, OR: Josephine County Mental Health Program.

Elliott, S. N., Lei, P. W., Anthony, C. J., & DiPerna, J. C. (2021). Screening the whole social-emotional child: Integrating emotional behavior concerns to expand the utility of the SSIS SEL brief scales. *School Psychology Review.* https://doi.org/10.1080/2372966X.2020.1857659

Goodman, R. (1997) The Strengths and Difficulties Questionnaire: A Research Note. *Journal of Child Psychology and Psychiatry, 38,* 581-586. https://doi.org/10.1111/j.1469-7610.1997.tb01545.x.

Gottlieb, G. (1991). Experiential canalization of behavioral development: Theory. *Developmental Psychology, 27*(1), 4-13. https://psycnet.apa.org/doi/10.1037/0012-1649.27.1.4

Jones, S. M., & Bouffard, S. M. (2012). Social and emotional learning in schools: From programs to strategies and commentaries. *Social policy report, 26*(4), 1-33.

Kamphaus, R. W., & Reynolds, C. R. (2015). Behavior Assessment System for Children—Third Edition (BASC-3): Behavioral and Emotional Screening System (BESS). Bloomington, MN: Pearson

Kilgus, S. P., Chafouleas, S. M., Riley-Tillman, T. C., & von der Embse, N. P. (2014). Social, Academic, and Emotional Behavior Risk Screener (SAEBRS). Minneapolis, MN: Theodore J.Christ & Colleagues.

Kilgus, S.P., & Eklund, K.R. (2016). Consideration of base rates within universal screening for behavioral and emotional risk: A novel procedural framework. *School Psychology Forum, 10*(1), 120-130.

Lane, K. L. & Menzies, H. M. (2009). Student Risk Screening Scale for Early Internalizing and Externalizing Behavior (SRSS-IE). Available at Ci3t.org/screening

Lane, K. L., Richards-Tutor, C., Oakes, W. P., & Connor, K. (2014). Initial evidence for the reliability and validity of the Student Risk Screening Scale with elementary age English learners. *Assessment for Effective Intervention, 39,* 219–232. https://doi.org/10.1177%2F1534508413496836

Lane, K. L., Oakes, W. P., Swogger, E. D., Schatschneider, C., Menzies, H., M., & Sanchez, J. (2015). Student risk screening scale for internalizing and externalizing behaviors: Preliminary cut scores to support data-informed decision making. *Behavioral Disorders, 40,* 159-170. https://doi.org/10.17988/0198-7429-40.3.159

McLean, D., Eklund, K., Kilgus, S. P., & Burns, M. K. (2019). Influence of teacher burnout and self-efficacy on teacher-related variance in social-emotional and behavioral screening scores. *School Psychology, 34*(5), 503-511. https://doi.apa.org/doi/10.1037/spq0000304

Reinke, W. M., Herman, K. C., Petras, H., & Ialongo, N. S. (2008). Empirically derived subtypes of child academic and behavior problems: co-occurrence and distal outcomes. *Journal of Abnormal Child Psychology, 36*(5), 759–770. https://doi.org/10.1007/s10802-007-9208-2

Rollenhagen, J., Buckman, M. M., Oakes, W. P., & Lane, K. L. (2021). Screening coordinator training manual – A guide for installing the Student Risk Screening Scale – Internalizing and Externalizing (SRSS-IE) in your school or district. Available at https://www.ci3t.org/wp-content/uploads/2021/03/SRSS-IE-Screening-Coordinator-Training-Manual-2021-03-03-F.pdf

Romer, N., von der Embse, N., Eklund, K., Kilgus, S., Perales, K., Splett, J. W., Sudlo, S., Wheeler, D. (2020). *Best practices in social, emotional, and behavioral screening: An implementation guide. Version 2.0.* School Mental Health Collaborative. https://smhcollaborative.org/wp-content/uploads/2019/11/universalscreening.pdf.

Severson, H. H., Walker, H. M., Hope-Doolittle, J., Kratochwill, T. R., & Gresham, F. M. (2007). Proactive, early screening to detect behaviorally at-risk students: Issues, approaches, emerging innovations, and professional practices. *Journal of School Psychology, 45*(2), 193-223. https://doi.org/10.1016/j.jsp.2006.11.003

Splett, J. W., Smith-Millman, M., Raborn, A., Brann, K. L., Flaspohler, P. D., Maras, M. A. (2018). Student, teacher, and classroom predictors of between-teacher variance of students' teacher-rated behavior. *School Psychology Quarterly, 33*(3), 460-468, https://doi.apa.org/doi/10.1037/spq0000241

Splett, J. W., Raborn, A., Brann, K., Smith-Millman, M. K., Halliday, C., & Weist, M. D. (2020). Between-teacher variance of students' teacher-rated risk for emotional, behavioral, and adaptive functioning. *Journal of School Psychology, 80,* 37-53. https://doi.org/10.1016/j.jsp.2020.04.001

Von der Embse, N.P., Kilgus, S.P., Eklund, K. Ake, E., Levi-Neilsen, S. (2018). Training teachers to facilitate early identification of mental and behavioral health risks. *School Psychology Review, 47,* 372-384. https://doi.org/10.17105/SPR-2017-0094.V47-4

# Building Foundations for Friendship: Preventing Bullying Behavior in Preschool

*Kara E. McGoey, Allison Aberson, Bridget Green, and Seana Bandi Stewart*

## Abstract

Early childhood is an essential time for social-emotional learning and the development of appropriate peer interactions. Preschool children also begin to use more physical and verbal forms of aggression and bullying within their relationships with peers. The Building Foundations for Friendship (BFF) curriculum was designed to teach preschool-aged children appropriate social skills to prevent bullying. The topics discussed in this curriculum include developing friendship skills, identifying various peer interactions, and learning how to appropriately respond to a peer's aggressive behavior. It was hypothesized that preschool students' social skills and social behavior would improve after implementation of the BFF curriculum. The participants in this study included 79 preschool students between the ages of 3 and 6. Data were collected pre- and post-intervention. Results indicated that there was a statistically significant increase in social skills and a decrease in problem behavior following intervention. There was not a statistically significant decrease in relational or overt aggression. Implications of the results and future directions are discussed.

**Keywords:** bullying, preschool, bullying in preschool, early childhood, social-emotional learning

The early childhood years are a critical period for social-emotional development. Social and emotional learning (SEL) was defined by the Collaborative for Academic, Social, and Emotional Learning (CASEL) as: an integral part of education and human development. SEL is the process through which all young people and adults acquire and apply the knowledge, skills, and attitudes to develop healthy identities, manage emotions, and achieve personal and collective goals, feel and show empathy for others, establish and maintain supportive relationships, and make responsible and caring decisions (CASEL, 2020).

SEL involves implementing evidence-based practices within an educational setting to enhance social, emotional, and cognitive growth. CASEL purposefully used the term learning as a way to reflect that the acquisition and establishment of these skills in children is a long-term process (Durlak et al., 2015).

In the CASEL model, SEL is comprised of five main behavioral, cognitive, and affective competencies: self-awareness, self-management, social awareness, relationship skills, and responsible decision-making (CASEL, 2020). Like other learning approaches, each of these competency domains is thought to develop early in life and build upon the integration of a student's interpersonal and intrapersonal knowledge, skills, and attitudes. The five competencies are supported by four critical settings in a person's life: classrooms, schools, families and caregivers, and communities (CASEL, 2020). Thus, early childhood classrooms play an integral role in the development and promotion of SEL.

Social interactions within a classroom setting are crucial to SEL. Children who are socially competent exhibit prosocial behavior by forming reciprocal friendships, displaying emotions that are responsive to group norms, and forming a balance between their needs and the needs of others. Friendships promote positive and healthy social-emotional development by providing an avenue to practice social-emotional skills and provide and receive feedback (Pressley & McCormick, 2006). When children typically enter preschool around the age of 3, they begin to prefer certain children over others. As these specific friendships begin to form, different patterns of social interaction start forming as well (Pressley & McCormick, 2006).

Unfortunately, young preschool children can also display physical and relational aggression (Ostrov & Keating, 2004). Research has supported a relationship between a child's diminished ability to regulate emotions and the increased likelihood of exhibiting relational and physical aggression. These findings further reveal that emotion dysregulation in childhood is a significant risk factor for later episodes of relational and physical aggression (Röll et al., 2012). As a result, the ability of young children to regulate their behaviors and emotions may influence their ability to express themselves without physical or relational aggression in social contexts, thus furthering the argument for implementing specific SEL in the preschool classroom.

The display of physical and relational aggression in early childhood can have other severe consequences extending into adolescence and adulthood. Research has revealed that children who have a strong tendency to be aggressive are less likely to maintain friendships, and are more likely to be rejected by their peers (Ettekal & Ladd, 2015; Vaughn et al., 2003). Children who were rejected early in their academic career had poor perceptions of school, higher levels of school avoidance, and low performance levels throughout the year (Ladd, 1990). Furthermore, children who have experienced rejection are more likely to become future targets of aggression. Difficulties forming and maintaining peer relationships in childhood are also associated with academic difficulties, criminal behavior, and mental health problems later in life (Harrist & Bradley, 2003). Moreover, children who display serious conduct problems, including aggression, can develop difficulties with self-help skills, socialization, and emotional regulation (McNeil & Hembree-Kigin, 2011).

**Bullying in Early Childhood**

Not all aggressive acts are forms of bullying. Bullying is typically defined as repeated aggressive actions performed by a domineering person toward a more vulnerable individual. Bullying has detrimental long-term effects for both the bully and the victim. Research has shown that bullying behavior is present and detrimental in young children as well. However, bullying in early childhood looks considerably different than in older children (Saracho, 2017). Often preschool children engage in bullying behaviors such as exclusion during play, calling names, and threats of betrayal of friendship. Definitions of bullying in early childhood should include broad descriptions of behavior, to encompass the initial risky but not persistent or intense forms of bullying behavior often seen in preschool classrooms.

Researchers have begun to identify the complexity of preschool bullying. This complexity is due to young individuals transitioning into different roles as the bully, victim, bystander, or bully-victim (Cameron & Kovac, 2016; Saracho, 2017) and whether the individuals meet the criteria of participating in bullying behaviors (Olweus, 1993). In preschool, most bullies show aggression towards peers through verbal (e.g., hurtful comments), and physical actions (e.g., physical aggression). Bully-victims are preschool students victimized by their peers who later become aggressive and impulsive within their friend group (Perren & Alsaker, 2006). Preschool children fulfill interchanging roles during bullying scenarios that are both predominant and peripheral. Like older children, bullies and victims in preschool have poor school adjustment, behavior problems, low self-esteem, depression, anxiety, and self-destructive thoughts, and are often rejected later in school. Young bullies are at risk for future anti-social behavior and criminal acts (Jenkins et al., 2017; Saracho, 2017).

The complexity and detrimental effects of bullying in early childhood require that early childhood professionals emphasize the importance of developing social skills needed by the bully, victim, bully-victim, and defender to create and maintain friendships and reduce isolation from peers (Saracho, 2017). However, it is not sufficient to intervene with bullies and victims. Direct, explicit, and intentional teaching of prosocial behaviors and responses to bullying behavior is imperative (Jenkins et al., 2017). SEL curricula must address bullying with a developmentally appropriate and feasible approach for early childhood populations. Few programs exist that address this need.

The most widely used programs for young children are (a) Olweus Bullying Prevention Program (Olweus, 1993), (b) Steps to Respect: A Bullying Prevention Program (Committee for Children, 2005), (c) Bernese Program against Victimization in Kindergarten and Elementary School (Alsaker, 2004), and (d) Second Step: A Bullying Prevention Program (Committee for Children, 2015; Saracho, 2017). The first three programs were designed for elementary age children, and the fourth was designed for ages 4 to 14. These common programs were designed for older children, and thus may not be developmentally appropriate or match the classroom environment and schedule of a preschool classroom. Programming designed with the preschool child and classroom in mind is needed to set the foundation and readiness for elementary programming.

Ostrov and colleagues (2015) created the Early Childhood Friendship Project as a bullying education and prevention program for preschool children. The Early Childhood Friendship Project is an eight-week program designed to be developmentally appropriate and used puppets, active engagement, and reinforcement throughout the classroom (Ostrov et. al., 2015). Evaluation of the program indicated that relational aggression was reduced in the intervention group compared to the control group. The study also found that relational and physical aggression were reduced for girls in the intervention group when compared to the control group girls. While the results of this program were positive, additional recommendations were made for future research. First, the program was initially implemented in NAEYC accredited preschools, which ensured high quality teaching and teacher-student interactions. The authors suggested that the program should also be tested in community preschools that may struggle with maintaining accreditation for various reasons. In addition, the study trained the teachers but did not include teacher support during the intervention.

This study investigated a developmentally-appropriate bullying prevention program for use in the early childhood classroom. In addition, the lessons and materials were created to be accessible, inexpensive, and easy to learn so that all early childhood centers could benefit from the program. The Building Foundations for Friendship (BFF) curriculum was developed to provide direct, explicit teaching to encourage prosocial behavior and guide bullying victims in responding appropriately to bullies. The study aimed to answer the following research questions: (a) Does the BFF curriculum increase prosocial behaviors (social skills, prosocial behavior), and decease problem behaviors (relational aggression, overt aggression, problem behaviors), in preschool children? and (b) Will teachers find the BFF curriculum acceptable? It was hypothesized that the curriculum would improve social skills and decrease the problem behaviors of preschool children and that teachers would find the curriculum acceptable.

# Method

## Participants

The participants in this study included 79 preschool children, 48 males and 31 females, across seven classrooms within four different early childhood centers in the southwest region of Pennsylvania. All children were enrolled in preschool at least one day per week and were between the ages of 3 and 6 years. Participants constituted a diverse sample of ethnic and socioeconomic groups that was representative of the surrounding area in which the study was conducted. All children at the center were asked to participate. One lead teacher per classroom also participated in this study by implementing the curriculum once a week for eight weeks.

## Measures

The Social Skills Improvement System Rating Scales-Teacher Form (SSiS; Gresham & Elliot, 2008) was used to determine participants' social behaviors in the preschool classroom as observed by the classroom teacher. The SSIS uses a four-point scale ranging from "never" to "almost always" to assess two distinct scales: the

Social Skills scale and the Problem Behavior scale. The Social Skills scale is composed of 46 items organized into seven subscales (communication, cooperation, assertion, responsibility, empathy, engagement, self-control), and a total Social Skills composite score. The Problem Behavior scale contains a total of 24 items that yield five subscales: externalizing, bullying, hyperactive-inattentive, internalizing, and autistic behavior, as well as a composite Problem Behaviors score. The teacher form also includes an Academic Competence Scale that assesses reading and math performance as well as motivation, parental support, and overall cognitive functioning. This scale is normed on elementary and secondary students and, as such, was not used in this study. The SSIS demonstrates high test-retest reliability coefficients of .82 for the Social Skills scale and .83 for the Problem Behaviors scale. There is moderate interrater reliability, with a coefficient of .68 on the Social Skills scale and .61 on the Problem Behavior scale. The SSIS also demonstrates moderate psychometric validity with median convergent validity coefficients at .40 for 3- to 5-year-olds and median discriminant validity coefficients at .34 for 3- to 5-year-olds. Data gathered via the Social Skills Improvement System Rating Scales-Teacher Form (SSiS) rating forms were analyzed for change from pre-intervention ratings to post-intervention ratings. The SSiS provides a measure of social behaviors in the preschool classroom as observed by the classroom teacher. For all preschool classrooms, data were analyzed for change from pre-intervention to post-intervention using a paired samples t-test. Per the research questions and hypothesis, the researchers analyzed the data to determine increase in observed social skills.

The Preschool Social Behavior Scale (PSBS; Crick et al., 1997) was used to assess social behavior in preschool-age children through the observations by the classroom teachers. The measure utilizes 23 items on a five-point Likert scale to address the teachers' perceptions of the individual child's aggressive and prosocial behaviors. The scale response anchors range from "never" to "almost always." The PSBS provides a measure of prosocial as well as aggressive behaviors, as observed by the classroom teacher. A PSBS was completed for each child by the same classroom teacher prior to the intervention and when the intervention was complete. For all preschool classrooms, data were analyzed for change from pre-intervention to post-intervention using a paired samples t-test.

The Behavior Intervention Rating Scale-Teacher Version (BIRS-T; Elliott & Treuting, 1991) was utilized to address this intervention's acceptability among classroom teachers. This questionnaire is a 24-item measure regarding the teacher's attitudes of the appropriateness of the implemented intervention. An example of a statement on this measure is "I like the procedures used in this intervention." Teachers are asked to circle a number on a six-point Likert scale, ranging from "strongly disagree" to "strongly agree." Factor analysis on the BIRS-T has yielded three distinct factors: acceptability, effectiveness, and time needed to implement the intervention. All three scales of this measure exhibit strong reliability with coefficient alpha's of .97, .92, and .87, respectively. Data gathered regarding the classroom teachers' acceptability of this intervention was collected post-intervention.

**Procedure**

Once all permission and consent forms were obtained, the classroom teachers completed the SSIS and PSBS for each participant in the classroom. Then, implementation of BFF began in the classroom. Sessions occurred once per week for eight weeks and lasted approximately 15-20 minutes. All of the materials needed for this study, such as pictures, books, and animal puppets, were provided at no cost. The materials were left with the early childhood centers to encourage the generalization of the prosocial skills learned in the curriculum. A school psychology graduate student observed approximately 75% of the sessions conducted in each setting to ensure treatment fidelity to the BFF curriculum. Treatment fidelity was 100%.

## *BFF Curriculum*

BFF curriculum addressed behaviors associated with relational aggression as it pertains to preschool-age children. The topics discussed in these lessons included developing friendship skills, identifying types of peer interactions, and learning how to respond to a peer's relationally aggressive behavior. The curriculum also included activities that are developmentally appropriate for early childhood and can easily be incorporated into typical aspects of a preschool classroom. Animal puppets, as well as pictures of the scenarios, were utilized throughout the intervention to engage children as well as help them understand the material. Concrete examples and stories were used throughout the curriculum to promote the acquisition and generalization of the concepts taught in the curriculum. Each session began and ended with a friendship song to maintain consistency across sessions, and to begin and end on positive notes. The curriculum also included phrases and activities that the teachers could easily embed into the daily routines to reinforce learned concepts or skills throughout the day.

In session one of the BFF curriculum, participants began by learning the opening and closing friendship songs. This lesson was primarily an introduction to the primary puppet character and narrator. Participants also began discussing what they liked to do with their friends. Session two began by discussing how the students would define "a good friend." After a few examples, the teacher then read a book about friendship to the participants. Following the book's reading, the teacher asked the participants to discuss how the characters in the books were each being a friend.

In session three, participants discussed being a kind friend and worked together to create a list of classroom rules for being a kind friend. The participants were encouraged to use their ideas and to be creative in making this list. Next, three short stories were presented in which a character breaks a friendship rule. Participants worked together to discuss and identify which friendship classroom rule was broken in each of the stories. The rules were posted throughout the preschool center to remind the children of these rules for the remainder of the school year. They were also reviewed in each session by the teachers to increase the participants' mastery.

Sessions four, five, and six all followed a similar structure. The puppet characters shared their own friendship story and asked for advice from the participants. Session four started with an aggressive character who responds to relationally aggressive peers in physically aggressive ways. Session five introduced a passive character who responded to relational aggression by being passive and withdrawn. In session six, the participants were introduced to an assertive character, who responded to relationally aggressive peers by being appropriately assertive. After the stories, participants worked together to identify which friendships rules were broken in each scenario.

Similar strategies from the previous three sessions were maintained in session seven. Participants were presented with more scenarios and were asked to discuss ways to respond to a relationally aggressive peer. This lesson aimed to increase the participants' ability to generalize and use the assertive strategies that were previously learned by applying them to the new friendship scenarios. Lesson eight, the final session, was described as a celebration of friendship and aimed to review what had been taught thus far about friendship.

After the conclusion of the BFF curriculum, the teachers again completed the SSIS and PSBS for each participant in the classroom. The teachers also completed the BIRS-T. Measures were completed within two weeks after the last session.

## Results

Pre- and post t-test measures were analyzed using paired sample t-tests for each dependent measure. Measures with missing data were excluded from analysis. Paired sample t-test results indicated significant differences in teachers' ratings between pre-intervention and post-intervention for observed social skills ($p = .00$) and problem behaviors ($p = .00$) as rated by the SSIS (see Table 1). The effect size for the change in social skills was .41 and the effect size for the change in problem behavior was .24. Thus, it was determined that teachers' ratings were significantly higher for observed social skills of the preschool children following participation in the program. Regarding observed problem behaviors, ratings were significantly lower for the preschool children following participation in the program. The PSBS indicated a statistically significant increase in scores for the observed depressed affect of the preschool children following participation in the program; however, the PSBS uses three items to rate depressed affect, so this result should be interpreted with caution. No significant differences were found between pre-intervention and post-intervention for observed relational aggression, overt physical aggression, and prosocial behaviors of the preschool children as rated on the PSBS.

The data from the BIRS-T were reviewed qualitatively for general feedback from the teachers and any criticisms or concerns of this intervention. Results revealed that while two teachers rated the intervention as neutral, (scores of 3 for every item on a 1 to 6 scale), the remainder of the teachers ($n=5$) either agreed or strongly agreed that the intervention was (a) acceptable for the child's problem behavior, (b) appropriate for a variety of children, (c) would prove effective in changing the child's problem behavior, and (d) an intervention the teacher would recommend to other teachers. No comments or concerns were provided.

**Table 1**
*Paired sample t test results for pre- and post-measures in each group*

|  | Mean | SD | SE Mean | Paired *t* test | | | Effect Size |
|---|---|---|---|---|---|---|---|
|  |  |  |  | *t* value | df | Sig (two-tailed) |  |
| Relational Aggression | .04 | 3.89 | .44 | .09 | 78 | .93 | NA |
| Overt Aggression | .67 | 3.39 | .38 | 1.76 | 78 | .08 | NA |
| Depressed Affect | -.51 | 1.66 | .19 | -2.72 | 78 | .01* | NA |
| Prosocial Behavior | .14 | 2.74 | .31 | .45 | 78 | .65 | NA |
| Social Skills | -5.99 | 10.85 | 1.26 | -4.75 | 73 | .00* | .41 |
| Problem Behavior | 3.96 | 10.10 | 1.17 | 3.37 | 73 | .00* | .24 |

**Note.** *Significant at the .01 level*

# Discussion

For many children, preschool is where they first learn how to effectively engage socially and emotionally with their peers and, ultimately, develop friendships. However, this is also a period when children develop behaviors that lead to physical and verbal aggression towards peers (Ostrov & Keating, 2004). Therefore, there is an immediate need for teachers to target the social and emotional skills in the preschool classroom (Jenkins et al., 2017).

Preschool provides multiple occasions to support SEL for students aged 3-5 years, to ensure that they understand and have opportunities to implement prosocial behaviors with their peers in the classroom. The BFF curriculum supported these opportunities and provided educators a unique method to target and help children develop social and emotional needs in order to alleviate bullying later in school, thus, supporting past recommendations by Jenkins et al. (2017). In the current study, teachers who used the BFF curriculum reported an increase in social skills observed in their classrooms and decreased problem behaviors by their students.

The effect size of the changes was small to moderate; however, BFF was designed as a prevention program, thus, the small to moderate effect sizes should be seen as notable. One would expect the foundational skills learned within the BFF program to be expanded upon in elementary school, furthering the possible effect of bullying prevention programs. The curriculum was implemented with the entire class which resulted in a low base-rate of bullying and aggressive behaviors, indicating that there was not room for great change in aggressive behavior. The growth of observed prosocial behaviors is an important finding, as improving prosocial skills early, such as in preschool and kindergarten, can reduce bullying experienced in middle school (Saracho, 2017).

While some bullying prevention programs decrease bullying behaviors (Bradshaw et al., 2009; Olweus, 1993), few target the cognitive and developmental periods to appropriately support preschool students' social and emotional skills (Saracho, 2017). However, the BFF curriculum was designed to be developmentally appropriate and meet the cognitive and emotional needs of children aged 3-5. In addition, the curriculum was specifically designed to fit into the typical preschool daily schedule. The BFF curriculum provided teachers with manipulatives, (e.g., puppets, pictures), so that the children could learn through specific scenarios that highlighted age-appropriate prosocial behavior. These lessons allowed the teachers' instruction to be purposeful and precise when discussing each topic. Further, the curriculum enabled the students to understand a variety of roles (e.g., bully, bystander) throughout the bullying-dynamic and how these roles may hurt the development of friendships.

In the BFF curriculum, three characters played specific roles to help participants understand the bully, victim, bully-victim, and defender. Angry Alligator was aggressive to peers, Shy-Squirrel was passive and did not support peers, and Cool Confident Cat taught students how to appropriately respond during the bullying dynamic. In this study, the teachers reported that these characters helped children understand the bully, victim, and bully-victim behaviors that impacted friendships. The teachers also stated that the characters supported students' learning of prosocial skills relating to friendships, and developed opportunities for students to change past maladaptive behaviors. Finally, participants stated that the characters created scenarios that allowed students to practice moving away from a peripheral role in the bullying dynamic (e.g., providing positive feedback to the bully or offering no input to the bully or victim), and taking on the defender's role in assisting in the elimination of bullying. Since the BFF program used Cool Confident Cat to demonstrate how to be a defender during the bullying event, the curriculum provided preschool students with opportunities to practice prosocial behaviors that could benefit the classroom community. Research has shown that the benefit for a victim of having a defender in a preschool classroom decreases anxiety and depression-like symptoms and promotes positive social networks (Sainio et al., 2011; Vlachou et al., 2013). Teachers must begin to implement opportunities to support social and emotional development in order to lessen the occurrence of bullying in their preschool classrooms.

**Implications for Practitioners**

SEL is key to early education. Many states have standards requiring early education programs to promote positive social and emotional development. Preschool teachers need support in purposefully using activities such as circle time to implement and practice social skill development. Further, teachers need to receive training on promoting prosocial skills through a universal design for learning (UDL) framework to ensure all learners understand the lessons.

Prosocial skills can alleviate classroom emotional and behavioral concerns that arise in preschool. The prevalence of mental health disabilities is increasing in school settings, and teachers may not have the skills needed to deal with the diverse emotional needs of young children. School psychologists and preschool teachers should work together to create trainings that targets preschool students' mental health, social, and behavior needs. These trainings can identify how teachers can use time during their classes to reinforce specific social, behavioral, and language skills which in turn decreases bullying (Horowitz et al., 2006; Jenkins et al., 2017).

**Future Research**

This initial validation of the BFF curriculum yielded many recommendations for future research. First, the study should be replicated in multiple classrooms across different regions to obtain a larger, more diverse sample of children and educators. Ideally, the study would be implemented to collect information regarding teachers' gender, education level, and age to see if there is any moderating effect on observed social, behavior, and emotions observed in a variety of classrooms.

A second recommendation would be to implement the study across multiple preschool classrooms, with some classrooms identified as a control group and the remaining receiving the BFF curriculum. Since the BFF curriculum is a prevention method to teach prosocial skills, the researchers did not collect data on maturation. Implementing the curriculum in multiple preschools during the school year with one classroom as a control group would provide insight on potential long-term effects on SEL. Furthermore, this would provide an opportunity to understand maturation related to bullying prevention programs and long-term social and emotional skills.

A third recommendation involves the implementation of the BFF curriculum in an inclusive preschool classroom. There is a need to understand how students who have difficulty interpreting social, emotional, and behavioral cues (i.e., students with autism spectrum disorder or intellectual disabilities) may benefit from conversations during and after each lesson. These students with disabilities may benefit from the curriculum as a preventative barrier for learned maladaptive isolating behaviors. Furthermore, future research needs to identify how this program provides students with disabilities with specific language skills to have conversations about perceived protection at school to ensure all students are safe.

Fourth, future research needs to identify how the program provides supports to the bystander. In preschool bullying, there is a paucity of research regarding the power of the bystander role in the bullying dynamic and how often preschoolers switch from the aggressor role of bullying to the observer (Vlachou et al., 2013). Repo and Sajaniemi (2015) emphasized the importance of teachers targeting and minimizing preschool bullying by paying particular attention to those who partake in peripheral bullying roles.

## Limitations

Four overarching limitations emerged from the study. First, there were only seven preschool classrooms involved in this study. Since most teachers were female, there could be a misrepresentation of bullying behaviors due to gender-related perceptions on bullying (Cameron & Kovac, 2016). Second, while 79 preschool students could participate, some students were only enrolled one day per week, which could hinder the opportunity for the student to learn from the BFF program.. Finally, the researchers did not collect data on teacher bias. Since the teachers were implementing the curriculum and also reporting on observation data from their classrooms, they could have reported higher social skills because they expected and knew what to look for based on the examples in the curriculum.

## Conclusion

In conclusion, SEL is essential to preschool. Bullying in preschool may be manifested differently than bullying seen in late elementary and middle schools. Therefore, to effectively address bullying in preschool, interventions should identify complex barriers (e.g., mental health needs, developmentally appropriate programs, perception of bullying) to ensure students' social and emotional development. Without addressing the need for positive supports in early childhood, there is an increased risk of maladaptive behaviors later in school (Espelage & Aisado, 2001; Prinstein & Cillessen, 2003).

Few programs offer targeted, developmentally appropriate support to facilitate prosocial behaviors in preschool students. The BFF curriculum provided multiple means of representation to ensure that teachers targeted preschool aggression and promoted positive emotional and social health. This study and the BFF curriculum contribute to the field by allowing preschool students to identify unhealthy behaviors in friendships through specific scenarios and clearly define and explain their perceptions of bullying. This study demonstrates the importance of age-appropriate activities to ensure all students develop social and emotional skills for future academic success.

## References

Alsaker, F. D. (2004). The Bernese program against victimization in kindergarten and elementary school (Be-Prox). In P. K. Smith, D. Pepler, & K. Rigby (Eds.), Bullying in schools: How successful can interventions be? (pp. 289–306). Cambridge: Cambridge University Press.

Bradshaw, C. P., Sawyer, A. L., & O'Brennan, L. M. (2009). A social disorganization perspective on bullying-related attitudes and behaviors: The influence of school context. *American Journal of Community Psychology, 43*(3), 204–220. (PubMed ID No. 19333749).

Cameron, D. L. & Kovac, V. B. (2016). An examination of parents' and preschool workers' perspectives on bullying in preschool. *Early Child Development and Care, 186*(12), 1961-1971. http://dx.doi.org/10.1080/03004430.2016.1138290

Collaborative for Academic, Social, and Emotional Learning (CASEL). (2020). Core SEL competencies. Retrieved from https://casel.org/core-competencies/.

Committee for Children. (2005). Steps to respect: Program guide. Seattle, WA: Author.

Committee for Children. (2014). Second step: Social-emotional skills for early learning. Retrieved from http://www.secondstep.org/Portals/0/EL/Research/EL_Review_Research.pdf.

Crick, N. R., Casas, J. F. & Mosher, M. (1997). Relational and overt aggression in preschool. *Developmental Psychology, 33*(4), 579-588.

Durlak, J.A., Domitrovich, C.E., Weissburg, R.P., Gullota, T.P. (2015). *Handbook of Social Emotional Learning: Research and Practice.* Guilford Press.

Elliott, S. N. & Treuting, M. V. (1991). The Behavior Intervention Rating Scale: Development and validation of a pretreatment acceptability and effectiveness measure. *Journal of School Psychology, 29,* 43-51. doi:10.1016/0022-4405(91)90014-I

Espelage, D. L., & Aisado, C. S. (2001). Conversations with middle school students about bullying and victimization: Should we be concerned? *Journal of Emotional Abuse, 2*(2), 49–62. https://doi.org/10.1300/J135v02n02_04

Ettekal, I., & Ladd, G. W. (2015). Costs and benefits of children's physical and relational aggression trajectories on peer rejection, acceptance, and friendships: Variations by aggression subtypes, gender, and age. *Developmental Psychology, 51*(12), 1756-1770. doi:10.1037/dev0000057

Gresham, F., & Elliott, S. N. (2008). Social skills improvement system rating scales. Minneapolis, MN: Pearson Assessments.

Harrist, A. W., & Bradley, K. D. (2003). "You can't say you can't play": Intervening in the process of social exclusion in the kindergarten classroom. *Early Childhood Research Quarterly, 8,* 185-205. doi:10.1016/S0885-2006(03)00024-3

Horowitz, L., Jansson, L., Ljungberg, T., Hedenbro, M. (2006). Interaction before conflict and conflict resolution in preschool boys with language impairment. *International Journal of Language & Communication Disorders, 23,* 1-16. Doi: 10.1080/08856250701791203

Jenkins, L. N., Mulvey, N., & Floress, M. T. (2017). Social and language skills as predictors of bullying roles in early childhood: A narrative summary of the literature. *Education and Treatment of Children, 40*(3), 401-418. Doi: 10.1353/ETC.2017.0017

Ladd, G. W. (1990). Having friends, keeping friends, and being liked by peers in the classroom:

Predictors of children's early school adjustment? *Child Development, 61*(4), 1081-1100. DOI: 0.1111/j.1467-8624.1990.tb02843.x

McNeil, C.B., & Hembree-Kigin, T.L. (2011). *Parent-Child Interaction Therapy.* Springer.

Olweus, D. (1993). *Bullying at school: What we know and what we can do.* Blackwell.

Ostrov, J. M., & Keating, C. F. (2004). Gender differences in preschool aggression during free play and structured interactions: An observational study. *Social Development, 13*(2), 255-277. doi:10.1111/j.1467-9507.2004.000266.x

Ostrov, J. M., Godleski, S. A., Kamper-DeMarco, K. E., Blakely-McClure, S. J., & Celenza, L. (2015) Replication and Extension of the Early Childhood Friendship Project: Effects on Physical and Relational Bullying, *School Psychology Review, 44*(4), 445-463. DOI: 10.17105/spr-15-0048.1

Perren, S., & Alsaker, F. D. (2006) Social behavior and peer relationships of victims, bully-victims, and bullies in kindergarten. *Journal of Child Psychology and Psychiatry, 47*(1), 45-57. doi: 10.1111/j.1469-7610.2005.01445.x.

Pressley, M., & McCormick, C. B. (2006). *Child and adolescent development for educators.* Guilford Press.

Prinstein, M. J., & Cillessen, A. H. N. (2003). Forms and functions of adolescent peer aggression associated with high levels of peer status. *Merrill-Palmer Quarterly, 49*, 310–342. https://www.jstor.org/stable/23096058

Repo, L. & Sajaniemi, N. (2015). Bystanders' roles and children with special educational needs in bullying situations among preschool-aged children. *Early Years, 35*(1), 5-21. DOI: 10.1080/09575146.2014.953917

Röll, J., Koglin, U., & Petermann, F. (2012). Emotion regulation and childhood aggression: Longitudinal associations. *Child Psychiatry and Human Development, 43*(6), 909-923. DOI: 10.1007/s10578-012-0303-4.

Sainio, M., Veenstra, R., Huitsing, G., & Salmivalli, C. (2011). Victims and their defenders: A dyadic approach. *International Journal of Behavioral Development, 35*(2), 144–151. https://doi.org/10.1177/0165025410378068

Saracho, O. (2017). Bullying: Young children's roles, social status, and prevention programmes. *Early Child Development and Care, 187*(1), 68-79. http://dx.doi.org/10.1080/03004430.2016.115027

Vaughn, S., Bos, C. S. & Schumm, J. S. (2003) *Teaching exceptional, diverse, and at-risk students in the general education classroom (3rd ed.).* Allyn & Bacon.

Vlachou, M., Botsoglou, K., & Didaskalou, E. (2013). Assessing bully/victim problems in preschool children: A multimethod approach. *Journal of Criminology, 8.* Article ID 301658

# Impact of Kindergarten Transition Practices in Promoting Positive Behavioral School Readiness Skills

*Tyler M. Szydlo and Elyse M. Farnsworth*

## Abstract

Successfully adjusting to the behavioral demands of kindergarten is a pivotal, yet challenging, developmental milestone for students, making it imperative that schools have a comprehensive menu of universal transition practices and targeted transition interventions available. This systematic review was conducted to synthesize and evaluate the existing research on the outcomes associated with universal transition practices and targeted transition interventions aimed at improving social-emotional behavioral skills important to the transition to kindergarten. 17 studies were identified that met the inclusion criteria. Results from this review highlight the utility of targeting self-regulation skills in students transitioning to kindergarten through multi-component interventions that incorporate caregiver involvement. Limitations, directions for future research, and implications for practice are discussed.

*Keywords:* kindergarten transition, behavioral intervention, social-emotional supports

## Impact of Kindergarten Transition Practices in Promoting Positive Behavioral School Readiness Skills

Successful adjustment to kindergarten is one of the earliest educational milestones for a student (Welchons & McIntyre, 2017). The transition to a formal learning environment introduces new academic and behavioral demands on students, with implications for educational success. Meeting these new demands is critical; research indicates a child's social-emotional behavioral skills in kindergarten, as well as their early school experiences, are key predictors of later school achievement (Cook & Coley, 2017; Rimm-

Kaufman et al., 2000). Still, many children struggle with this transition. Adjusting to the new behavioral demands of formal schooling may be especially profound for students who enter kindergarten already at-risk (Duncan et al., 2018; Eisenhower et al., 2016). Therefore, it is vital that there is a continuum of services available to support students preparing for and currently transitioning to kindergarten.

## Challenges Associated with Kindergarten Transition

The transition to kindergarten can be especially challenging as students experience a multitude of changes concurrently (Purtell et al., 2020). In addition to formalized academic demands, kindergarten students must adapt to new social, emotional, and behavioral demands introduced in the school environment. These include social interaction expectations with adults, cooperation with peers, increased independence, compliance with new routines, and increased attentional demands (Purtell et al., 2020; Rimm-Kaufman & Pianta, 2000).

Given the significant changes in behavioral expectations in kindergarten relative to preschool and the home environment, it is not surprising that many students struggle with this transition. Kindergarten teachers reported that 16% of students had severe adjustment problems, and 46% of teachers reported that up to half of their class displayed behavior problems (Rimm-Kaufman et al., 2000). Among the most common behavioral difficulties at school entry were difficulty following directions and working in a group, and increased externalizing issues such as defiance, aggression, and hyperactivity (Hart et al., 2016 Rimm-Kaufman et al., 2000). It is vital that schools identify and support students who struggle with the transition to kindergarten. Without effective strategies, these behavioral challenges may persist and result in elevated risk of low achievement, school failure, mental health problems, and substance abuse (Eisenhower et al., 2016; Garbacz et al., 2020; Hart et al., 2016).

The transition to kindergarten is even more challenging for students with elevated levels of risk of poor adjustment (e.g., students with disabilities, with no preschool experience, who are involved in the child welfare system, who live in low-income households, and who displayed externalizing issues in preschool; Duncan et al., 2018; Eisenhower et al., 2016; Hart et al., 2016; Mistry et al., 2008; Pears et al., 2013; Welchons & McIntyre, 2017). It is imperative that educators meet students where they are, by providing universal and targeted interventions to ease the transition to kindergarten, thus creating a foundation for future success.

## Core Components of School Readiness

Whereas preschool and early education centers are characterized by developmental and play-based approaches, entry into kindergarten often signifies a student's first experience with a formal learning environment (Welchons & McIntyre, 2017). Research suggests certain skills are vital for school readiness and a successful transition (Duncan et al., 2018; McClelland & Cameron, 2012; Pears et al., 2013). These necessary academic and behavioral skills allow students to better interact with their new environment and learn new skills (Duncan et al., 2007). For example, understanding number magnitude and relationships, phonological awareness, letter-sound knowledge, letter identification, and print concepts are some of the strongest predictors of later school outcomes and achievement (Duncan et al., 2018; Pears et al., 2013).

Academic skills, while important, only comprise one part of school readiness. Kindergarten introduces new behavioral demands on students, such as working independently, remaining on-task, and forming healthy relationships. Students must be able to meet these behavioral demands to engage in and benefit from academic instruction (Welchons & McIntyre, 2017). Key behavioral skills relevant to school readiness can be grouped into two related competencies: prosocial behaviors and self-regulation (Blair, 2002).

Prosocial behaviors are interpersonal behaviors that are exhibited to benefit others (Collie et al., 2018; Schmidt et al., 2002) and facilitate sharing, cooperation, group work, and interpretation of emotions (Pears et al., 2013). Not only do improved prosocial behavior skills allow for more success in developing positive attitudes about school, but they are also associated with improved achievement later in school (Denham, 2006; Nix et al., 2013). Perhaps prosocial behaviors allow students to better participate in collaborative learning experiences, cultivate positive relationships with teachers and peers, and promote a positive classroom environment (Collie et al., 2018; Nix et al., 2013).

Engaging in self-regulatory behaviors also fosters a positive transition to kindergarten. Self-regulation is a multidimensional set of skills, including the ability to regulate and direct attention, emotions, thoughts, and behaviors in order to act in a goal-oriented manner (Duncan et al., 2018; McClelland & Cameron, 2012; Pears et al., 2013). Successful self-regulation is reliant on three skills central to executive function: attentional flexibility, working memory, and inhibitory control (Blair et al., 2005). Together, these processes comprise self-regulation and enable students to meet the demands of common educational tasks like raising a hand instead of shouting, focusing on a project, persisting through difficult tasks, remembering classroom rules, following instructions, and transitioning between activities (Duncan et al., 2018; McClelland & Cameron, 2012). The integration of these skills is a robust predictor of academic engagement and success (Brock et al., 2009; McClelland & Cameron, 2012; Pears et al., 2013).

## The Dynamic Effects Model of Transition and the Use of Transition Interventions

The most widely accepted model of school transition, the Dynamic Effects Model (DEM), is an ecological-based, developmental model that emphasizes the interconnectedness of the child, their family, their preschool and school, peers, and community factors

(LoCasale-Crouch et al., 2008; Rimm-Kaufman & Pianta, 2000). A central tenet of this model is the development of relationships over time to facilitate a successful school transition. The DEM posits that interactions between these factors form relationships between individuals in the student's different environments which strongly affect student development (Rimm-Kaufman & Pianta, 2000). When there is alignment, high quality relationships are produced that help support the student through the kindergarten transition. Further, the transition process begins in the year prior to kindergarten and continues through kindergarten (Rimm-Kaufman & Pianta, 2000).

Based on the DEM, schools can best support students' behavioral adjustment to school when they utilize transition practices that intervene early, promote healthy relationships, and are implemented across environments (Berlin et al., 2011; Cook & Coley, 2017; LoCasale-Crouch et al., 2008). However, the most commonly used transition strategies are informal and tend not to start until the child has entered kindergarten (e.g., sending brochures home and hosting open houses; Berlin et al., 2011; Cook & Coley, 2017; Rimm-Kaufman et al., 2000).

Students are more likely to benefit from proactive universal and targeted transition interventions that engage parents and other key stakeholders (Berlin et al., 2011; LoCasale-Crouch et al., 2008). Transition interventions that are implemented across settings and that utilize more personalized components such as home visits, communication between preschool and kindergarten teachers, parent education, and relationship building have the potential to significantly improve the kindergarten transition, facilitating positive behavioral adjustment, especially for at-risk students (Berlin et al., 2011; Eisenhower et al., 2016; Garbacz et al., 2020).

## Present Study

Following the tenets of the DEM, students preparing for and currently transitioning to kindergarten should be provided with transition supports that are comprehensive, ecologically based, and facilitate high quality relationships between students, parents, and teachers. In order to be able to meet the needs of all students, schools need information about multi-tiered services with the greatest impact on behavioral outcomes during the kindergarten transition. Therefore, the purpose of the present review is to synthesize the existing evidence on the outcomes associated with the use of universal and targeted transition interventions to promote positive behavioral functioning during the kindergarten transition, by addressing two questions:

> 1. To what extent do universal transition practices promote positive behavior and school adjustment among students preparing for or currently transitioning to kindergarten?
> 2. To what extent do targeted transition interventions promote positive behavior and school adjustment among students preparing for or currently transitioning to kindergarten?

## Method

### Literature Search Procedure

A comprehensive search of the literature was conducted in the Education Source and Educational Resources Information Center (ERIC) databases using the following terms in the title, abstract, and key word indicators: "kindergarten," "transition," "school entry," "school readiness," "school adjustment," "kindergarten entry," "kindergarten readiness," "kindergarten adjustment," "behavior," and "self-regulation." The search produced 703 hits, and data were extracted into Zotero to remove duplicates A total of 577 unique records remained.

### Inclusion Criteria and Quality Assessment

These 577 records were uploaded into Rayyan (see Ouzzani et al., 2016) for screening. Studies had to meet the following inclusion criteria: (a) be published in a peer-reviewed journal, (b) be conducted in the United States, (c) utilize a randomized controlled trial methodology, a quasi-experimental design, or single-case experimental design, (d) include an intervention designed to improve student behavioral readiness for kindergarten, (e) include outcome measures that assess students' behavioral readiness skills or level of kindergarten adjustment, (f) participants were in preschool, kindergarten, parents of children in these grades, teachers of children in these grades, or a combination of these groups, and (g) interventions were conducted in school, home, or the community.

After reviewing titles and abstracts for relevancy, the full text was reviewed for 40 articles. Seventeen studies met the inclusion criteria and were included in the final review. The most common reason for exclusion was studies not meeting the criteria for study design. A detailed list of the studies that were excluded and for what reasons can be seen in Figure 1.

Prior to coding study characteristics, studies were appraised for methodological quality and risk of bias using the JBI Checklist for Randomized Controlled Trials (Tufanaru et al., 2020), JBI Checklist for Quasi-Experimental Studies (Tufanaru et al., 2020), and the WWC Standards for Single-Case Designs (Kratochwill et al., 2010). Given the inclusion of studies with various designs, studies were critically appraised focusing on their methodology. Each tool consisted of criteria related to its respective study design as well as a rating system for assessing whether each study met the criteria. No studies were excluded from the review based on poor quality; study quality was considered during the interpretation and discussion of results.

**Analysis of Included Studies**

Studies that met the inclusion criteria were coded with a protocol created by the authors. Data extraction included study and intervention variables. Study variables included design type, location (i.e., urbanicity, state, and/or census region), sample size, participant demographics (i.e., age of students, race/ethnicity, and biological sex or gender), student risk status (i.e., participants with elevated risk, participants with no risk, or participants from both risk groups), measurement tools, and outcomes (i.e., impact on behavioral functioning, prosocial behavior, self-regulation skills, student-teacher relationships, and/or on-task behavior). Notably, if groups previously identified in the empirical literature as experiencing elevated risk (e.g., students with disabilities, with no prior preschool experience, etc.) were included in the study sample, the risk status was coded as elevated risk. Intervention variables included intervention type (i.e., manualized program; universal/targeted practice), participants (i.e., students, families, educators, or multiple groups), duration (i.e., how long the intervention was implemented), and delivery context (i.e., home, school, community, or home/school combined).

Due to variability in study methodology, quantitative analysis was not applied. Narrative discussion and qualitative interpretation were used. Studies were initially categorized by transition practice characteristics: universal practices or targeted interventions. Studies that reported targeted interventions were further categorized dependent on the behavioral skills targeted.

**Second Coder Procedure and Interrater Agreement**

An Educational Psychology graduate student served as a secondary coder and was trained by the authors to apply the inclusion criteria and coding procedures during a one-hour meeting. The additional coder reviewed the abstracts and titles of 30% of the total articles. Initial interrater agreement between the authors and the second coder was 55%, with the most common discrepancy involving disagreements on the behavioral outcome inclusion criterion. All discrepancies were resolved through discussion and review of the inclusion criteria during a follow-up, one-hour session. Following this session, interrater agreement was 100%.

## Results

The participant and intervention context characteristics are described in Table 1, and intervention descriptions and participant outcomes are provided in Table 2.

## Participant and Setting Characteristics

Total participants (N = 2,893) represented diverse racial and ethnic backgrounds and were conducted in kindergarten classrooms, preschool classrooms, Head Start classrooms, and community centers. Participants ranged from age 4 to 6 years and came from 5 different United States regions, representing both urban and rural areas. One study (Hains, 1992) did not provide information on study location. The majority of participants had elevated risk levels; only one study (i.e., Wenz-Gross et al., 2018) contained a participant sample that included individuals without elevated risk.

Of the 17 studies, five reported interventions conducted exclusively in schools (Duncan et al., 2018; Eisenhower et al., 2016; Hains, 1992; Stormshak et al., 2020; Wenz-Gross et al., 2018), four reported interventions implemented at both school and another educational setting (Bierman et al., 2013; Nix et al., 2013; Hart et al., 2016; Sprague & Perkins, 2009), and the remaining eight reported interventions completely implemented in a community-based settings.

Eight studies reported interventions that were implemented before kindergarten. Four of these studies reported on interventions conducted exclusively during children's preschool year (Bierman et al., 2013; Hains, 1992; Nix et al., 2013; Wenz-Gross et al., 2018), while the other four studies reported interventions conducted during the summer before kindergarten (Duncan et al., 2018; Graziano & Hart, 2016; Hart et al., 2019; McLeod et al., 2017). Four studies reported on interventions that started during kindergarten (Eisenhower et al., 2016; Hart et al., 2019 Sprague & Perkins, 2009; Stormshak et al., 2020). The remaining six studies utilized a developmental approach consistent with the DEM and were implemented during the children's preschool year and continued through kindergarten (Hart et al., 2016, 2019; Lynch et al., 2017; McDermott et al., 2017; Pears et al., 2012, 2013, 2014).

## Table 1
*Participant Characteristics*

| Authors | n | Biological Sex of Students | M Age of Students | Racial and Ethnic Identities of Students | Risk Status of Students |
|---|---|---|---|---|---|
| Bierman et al. (2013) | 356 | 54% F, 46% M | 4.59 | 25% B, 17% L, 58% W | Elevated Risk |
| Duncan et al. (2018) | 125 | Not provided | C: 5.29 I: 5.25 | Not provided | Elevated Risk |
| Eisenhower et al. (2016) | 97 | 26% F, 74% M | 5.33 | 5% A, 3% B, 16% L, 57% W, 16% O | Elevated Risk |
| Graziano & Hart (2016) | 45 | 24% F, 76% M | 5.16 | 4% B, 84% L, 9% W, 4% O | Elevated Risk |
| Hains (1992) | 11 | 18% F, 82% M | | Not provided | Elevated Risk |
| Hart et al. (2016) | 50 | 22% F, 78% M | 5.08 | 52% Latino | Elevated Risk |
| Hart et al. (2019) | 45 | 18% F, 82% M | 5.16 | 93% Latino | Elevated Risk |
| Lynch et al. (2017) | 192 | C: 54% F, 46% M I: 48% F, 52% M | 5.25 | C: 2% AI, 1% B, 30% L, 2% PI, 55% W, 10% O I: 31% L, 51% W, 18% O | Elevated Risk |
| McDermott et al. (2017) | 41 | C: 33% F, 67% M I: 15% F, 85% M | C: 5.24 I: 5.26 | C: 10% L, 71% W, 19% O I: 15% L, 85% W | Elevated Risk |
| McLeod et al. (2017) | 25 | 44% F, 56% M | Not provided | 100% B | Elevated Risk |
| Nix et al. (2013) | 356 | 54% F, 46% M | 4.59 | 25% B, 17% L, 58% W | Elevated Risk |
| Pears et al. (2012) | 192 | C: 54% F, 46% M I: 48% F, 52% M | C: 5.25 I: 5.26 | C: 31% L, 51% W, 18% O I: 2% AI, 1% B, 30% L, 2% PI, 55% W, 10% O | Elevated Risk |

## Table 1 (continued)

| Authors | n | Biological Sex of Students | Mean Age of Students | Racial and Ethnic Identities of Students | Risk Status of Students |
|---|---|---|---|---|---|
| Pears et al. (2013) | 192 | C: 54% F, 46% M<br>I: 48% F, 52% M | C: 5.25<br>I: 5.26 | C: 31% L, 51% W, 18% O<br>I: 2% AI, 1% B, 30% L, 2% PI, 55% W, 10% O | Elevated Risk |
| Pears et al. (2014) | 209 | C: 23% F, 77% M<br>I: 23% F, 77% M | C: 5.28<br>I: 5.26 | C: 1% A, 2% AI, 2% B, 14% L, 67% W, 14% O<br>I: 1% A, 1% AI, 1% B, 14% L, 71% W, 12% O | Elevated Risk |
| Sprague & Perkins (2009) | 4 | 25% F, 75% M | 5.4 | 100% W | Elevated Risk |
| Stormshak et al. (2020) | 365 | 46% F, 54% M | 5.45 | 2% A, 2% B, 13% L, .3% PI, 59% W, 23% O | Elevated Risk |
| Wenz-Gross et al. (2018) | 972 | 49% F, 51% M | 4.42 | 26% B, 40% L, 42% W | |

**Table 2**

*Intervention Descriptions and Outcomes*

| Authors | Design | Groups Targeted | Behavioral Skills | Findings |
|---|---|---|---|---|
| Bierman et al. (2013) | RCT | Parents, Students | BF, PB, MD | BF: students receiving intervention displayed fewer aggressive behaviors at home and school<br>PB: students receiving intervention displayed improved social-problem solving abilities<br>MD: students receiving the intervention were rated by teachers as more engaged and motivated in kindergarten |
| Duncan et al. (2018) | RCT | Students | SR | Students receiving the intervention demonstrated significant growth in self-regulation; estimated to be equal to four months of normal development |
| Eisenhower et al. (2016) | RCT | Parents, Teachers | BF, STR | BF: fewer teacher and parent reported externalizing and internalizing concerns in kindergarten<br>STR: no direct effect of intervention on improved STR quality for all students in the study, but there was an effect for for student who had low-quality initial relationships |
| Graziano & Hart, 2016 | RCT | Parents, Students | BF, PB, SR | BF: significant reduction in teacher reported behavior impairment<br>PB: significant increase in emotion knowledge<br>SR: increased executive functioning as measured by objective measures |
| Hains, 1992 | SCD | Students | OTB | Three of the four students receiving intervention displayed increased academic engaged time |
| Hart et al. (2016) | RCT | Parents, Students | BF, PB, STR | BF: Both high and low intensity versions of intervention resulted in reduced teacher report of behavior problems, but the high intensity version resulted in more rapid improvement<br>PB: no significant effects of high or low intensity intervention on improved prosocial behaviors<br>STR: both versions resulted in reduced conflict with teachers, but the high intensity version displayed greatest reduction |

**Table 2** (continued)

| | | | | |
|---|---|---|---|---|
| Hart et al. (2019) | RCT | Parents, Students | BF, PB, SR | BF: students in both 4W and 8W intervention groups displayed reduced parent reported behavior concerns, but no significant difference between groups<br>PB: students in 8W group displayed greatest growth in emotion knowledge, but results were not maintained at follow-up<br>SR: students in 4W and 8W group both demonstrated significant growth in SR skills, but no difference between groups |
| Lynch et al. (2017) | RCT | Parents, Students | BF | Students receiving intervention demonstrated significantly more days free of externalizing and internalizing concerns |
| McDermott et al. (2017) | RCT | Parents, Students | SR | Students receiving intervention displayed enhanced response monitoring time on a series of neural reactivity tasks |
| McLeod et al. (2017) | QA | Students | PB | Students receiving intervention did not display significant growth in prosocial behavior skills |
| Nix et al. (2013) | RCT | Parents, Students | PB, MD | PB: gains in prosocial behavior made during Head Start REDI in preschool were maintained through kindergarten<br>MD: growth in behavior skills made during Head Start REDI in preschool were predictive of learning engagement in kindergarten |
| Pears et al. (2012) | RCT | Parents, Students | BF | Students receiving intervention displayed reduced teacher ratings of aggressive and oppositional behavior |
| Pears et al. (2013) | RCT | Parents, Students | PB, SR | PB: no direct effect of the intervention on growth in PB<br>SR: students receiving intervention displayed improved SR skills at the end of preschool and were maintained through kindergarten |
| Pears et al. (2014) | RCT | Parents, Students | SR | Students receiving the intervention displayed significant gains in SR skills by the end of kindergarten |

### Targeted Domains of Functioning

All studies reported on interventions that aimed to increase social-emotional behavioral readiness skills and promote positive school adjustment. Eleven studies assessed multiple areas of functioning, while the other studies assessed one domain of behavioral readiness. In total, eight studies included measures of behavioral functioning, seven studies included measures of prosocial behavior, six studies included measures of self-regulation skills, three studies included measures of student-teacher relationships, two studies included measures of on-task behavior, and four studies included multi-domain measures of behavioral readiness for kindergarten.

### Universal Transition Practices

Notably, only one study reported on a universal transition practice. Wenz-Gross et al. (2018) utilized a cohort randomized trial design to test the effectiveness of The Second Step Early Learning Curriculum (SSEL; Committee for Children, 2011) for promoting behavioral readiness of preschoolers preparing for kindergarten. Wenz-Gross et al. (2018) reported that there was no direct effect of SSEL on overall kindergarten readiness or social-emotional skills, but participation did result in significantly increased executive functioning. Authors noted that a lack of significant effect on social-emotional skills might have been due to concurrent social-emotional skill building in control classrooms.

### Targeted and Intensive Transition Interventions

Social-emotional behavioral skills targeted by these interventions included behavioral functioning, prosocial behavior, self-regulation, student-teacher relationships, and on-task behavior, with most interventions targeting multiple skills. Some studies included multi-domain measures of behavioral readiness for school, rating students' capacities across a range of behavioral skills. Most targeted interventions were delivered to both students and parents.

## Behavioral Functioning Outcomes

Eight studies included measures of behavioral functioning. Studies varied in how behavioral functioning was defined and assessed, ranging from measures of overall externalizing and internalizing behavior to more focused measures of aggressive, disruptive, and oppositional behaviors. Targeted transition interventions showed a positive impact on improving students' behavioral functioning. For studies reporting effect sizes, effect sizes ranged from -1.34 (Graziano & Hart, 2016) to 0.33 (Pears et al., 2012). Seven studies utilized interventions that were multi-component and included caregiver involvement (Bierman et al., 2013; Graziano & Hart, 2016; Hart et al., 2016; Hart et al., 2019; Lynch et al., 2017; Pears et al., 2012; Sprague & Perkins, 2009). Three studies (Graziano & Hart, 2016; Hart et al., 2016; Hart et al., 2019) reported on the Kindergarten Summer Readiness Classroom (KSRC; see Hart et al., 2010).

Hart et al. (2016) compared a high intensity version of the KSRC to a low intensity version. They reported that students in both groups displayed significant reductions in teacher reported behavior problems, but the high intensity group experienced greater improvement (d= -0.43). Similarly, Graziano and Hart (2016) tested the impact of adding 30-minutes of daily self-regulation training to the KSRC. Students receiving the self-regulation enhanced KSRC displayed significant reductions in behavior impairment as rated by their teachers (d = -1.34), but the improvement in behavioral functioning was not significantly different from students receiving the traditional KSRC (d = -0.93). Further, Hart et al. (2019) attempted to identify the ideal length of the self-regulation enhanced KSRC intervention, comparing a 4-week and 8-week version to traditional school behavioral consultation. Students in both the 4-week and 8-week self-regulation enhanced KSRC displayed significant reductions in behavior problems compared to students receiving school-based consultation on parent reported behavioral functioning, and these reductions were maintained through follow-up (d = -0.61; d = -0.46, respectively). However, there was not a significant difference between the 4-week and 8-week groups. Overall, KSRC implementation was associated with moderate to large decreases in externalizing behavior for children at-risk of poor behavioral functioning at kindergarten entry.

Similarly, Kids in Transition to School ([KITS]; see Pears et al., 2018) was associated with positive effects. Pears et al. (2012) assessed the impact of KITS on reducing aggressive and oppositional behaviors and found that teacher ratings of these behaviors at the end of kindergarten were significantly lower for students receiving the intervention compared to students in the control group (d = 0.33). The positive impact of KITS is also supported by Lynch et al. (2017), who reported that students receiving the intervention displayed significantly fewer externalizing and internalizing symptoms than those who did not participate in KITS. Similarly, Bierman and colleagues (2013) reviewed Head Start Research-Based, Developmentally Informed (REDI) and reported positive effects, with students who received the intervention displaying fewer aggressive behaviors at home and school one year after the intervention compared to the control group, as measured by both parent and teacher reports ($\beta$ = -0.26; $\beta$ = -0.23, respectively). In contrast to the previously mentioned interventions, Sprague and Perkins (2009) reviewed First Step to Success (Walker et al., 1998), a targeted transition intervention that begins after students enter kindergarten. The researchers observed that students receiving the First Step to Success intervention demonstrated an immediate reduction in problem behaviors compared to their baseline performance, with the number of problem behaviors observed decreasing by 5.5 instances per day on average. These results were maintained at follow-up.

While the prior interventions have all included direct services to students and caregivers, Starting Strong is an intensive transition intervention that targets parents and teachers rather than students (see Eisenhower et al., 2016). Starting Strong had a positive effect on student's behaviors with fewer teacher- and parent-reported externalizing and internalizing concerns ($d = -0.19$; $d = -0.35$, respectively; Eisenhower et al., 2016). Findings indicate that participation was associated with small to moderate reductions in problem behaviors.

Collectively, transition interventions targeting behavioral functioning were associated with a range of reductions (small to large) in undesired behaviors. These results were observed for both parent- and teacher-reported behavioral functioning. Most studies included multiple components and caregiver involvement, suggesting these may be important elements of kindergarten transition services for children at-risk of behavioral problems.

**Prosocial Behavior Outcomes**

Prosocial behavior was another commonly targeted skill, with seven studies addressing this area (Bierman et al., 2013; Graziano & Hart, 2016; Hart et al., 2016; Hart et al., 2019; McLeod et al., 2017; Nix et al., 2013; Pears et al., 2013). Definitions and measures varied across studies, including measures of prosocial behavior, social competence, emotion understanding, social-emotional skills, and social problem-solving. Targeted interventions were associated with mixed results on improving prosocial behavior. Three studies (Hart et al., 2016; McLeod et al., 2017; Pears et al., 2013) reported null effects on prosocial behavior. Studies reporting effect sizes reported a range of positive effects from 0.26 (Nix et al., 2013) to 1.50 (Graziano & Hart, 2016). Findings suggest that participation in prosocial behavior interventions is linked to null to large effects. Interestingly, targeting prosocial behavior may have a positive effect on school readiness for students with externalizing behavior concerns.

Graziano and Hart (2016) investigated the effectiveness of adding 30 minutes of daily self-regulation training to the KSRC intervention. Results indicated that students in the experimental group had significantly higher emotion knowledge ($d = 1.50$). Hart et al.'s (2019) evaluation of the 4-week and 8-week version of the self-regulation enhanced KSRC found that although the 8-week group displayed the greatest improvement in emotion knowledge at the time of post-assessment (g= 1.23), all groups displayed comparable knowledge by the end of kindergarten. Hart et al.'s (2016) review of the high- and low-intensity versions of the KSRC compared to parent training alone found no significant differences between the three groups on prosocial behavior. Likewise, Pears et al. (2013) reported that there was no significant difference in prosocial behavior between students receiving KITS and in the control group. Together, these results indicate that comprehensive transition services with parent education components may increase prosocial behaviors for some, but not all children transitioning to kindergarten.

Transition interventions targeting improvement in prosocial behaviors for students from economically disadvantaged households demonstrated mixed results. Bierman et al. (2013) reported that students receiving the Head Start REDI intervention displayed improved social-problem solving skills compared to students in the control group ($\beta = 0.40$). Nix et al. (2013) provided evidence that these gains were maintained through kindergarten. They reported that prosocial behavior gains made during the Head Start REDI intervention were predictive of positive social behavior in kindergarten ($\beta = 0.26$). McLeod et al. (2017) also reviewed a community-based transition intervention administered with students from economically disadvantaged households (i.e., adapted lessons of the Incredible Years Classroom Dinosaur Curriculum; see Webster-Stratton, 1990). Results indicated that students receiving the intervention did not display any significant growth in prosocial behavior skills.

Collectively, some studies found that participation in transition services targeting prosocial behaviors was associated with small to large improvements in these behaviors, while others reported null effects. No studies indicated negative or iatrogenic effects. Across studies reporting positive effects, most included an emotional or self-regulation component, suggesting that targeting prosocial and regulatory skills together may bolster kindergarten readiness.

**Self-Regulation Outcomes**

Self-regulation was also targeted by intensive transition interventions, with six studies including outcome measures related to this domain. Despite differences in time of implementation, dosage, and target groups, interventions targeting self-regulation skills reported consistently positive effects. For studies reporting effect sizes, effects ranged from small (i.e., 0.18; Pears et al., 2013) to large (i.e.,1.23; Graziano & Hart, 2016). An important trend with this category of interventions was their broad utility.

Pears et al. (2013) reported that children receiving the KITS intervention displayed small, but statistically significant, improved self-regulation skills compared to the control group (d = 0.18). Similarly, Pears et al. (2014) evaluated the impact of KITS on students with developmental disabilities, finding higher self-regulation skills among intervention participants compared to the control group (d = 0.29). These results are supported by McDermott et al. (2017), who found that students receiving the KITS intervention showed an improved ability to alter their performance and respond to feedback ($\eta^2_p$= 0.15).

Interventions targeting the improvement of self-regulation skills for students displaying externalizing behavior concerns also had a positive impact. Graziano and Hart (2016) reported that students receiving the self-regulation enhanced version of the KSRC displayed greater growth in emotional executive functioning compared to students receiving the traditional KSRC and parent services alone (d = 1.23). Increasing the duration of the intervention, however, did not result in significantly more self-regulation growth. Comparing a 4-week and 8-week version of the KSRC, Hart et al. (2019) reported that while both groups displayed significantly improved self-regulation across a series of measures compared to the control group, there was minimal difference in growth between groups.

There is also emerging evidence that supports the use of intensive transition interventions targeting self-regulation for children with no preschool experience. Duncan et al. (2018) reported on the effects of adding a self-regulation intervention, Red Light Purple Light ([RLPL]; see Tominey & McClelland, 2011), to a summer kindergarten readiness program (i.e., Bridge to Kindergarten; [B2K]; see Yoshikawa et al., 2013). Students receiving the RLPL intervention displayed significant gains in self-regulation compared to students receiving the traditional kindergarten readiness program, with growth estimated to be equivalent to four months of expected development. In sum, targeted transition interventions showed small to large positive effects on self-regulation skills with a range of student groups, including children with no previous school experience, children at-risk of behavior problems, children in the child welfare system, and children with developmental disabilities. Findings provide promising evidence that transition interventions targeting self-regulation are likely to support a successful transition to kindergarten.

**Student-Teacher Relationship Outcomes**

Three studies included in this review reported the effects of targeted transition interventions on the quality of student-teacher relationships in kindergarten (Eisenhower et al., 2016; Hart et al., 2016; Sprague & Perkins, 2009). Results in this domain were mixed, with two studies reporting positive outcomes (Hart et al., 2016; Sprague & Perkins, 2009), and one study reporting no direct effects (Eisenhower et al., 2016).

Studies reporting positive effects both implemented direct services with students. Hart et al. (2016) reported that students in both the 4-week and 8-week version of the KSRC displayed fewer conflicts with their teachers compared to the control group, but students in the 8-week version experienced the greatest reduction in student-teacher conflicts (d = -0.45). Likewise, Sprague and Perkins (2009) reported positive effects of the First Step to Success intervention on improving the quality of student-teacher relationships during the kindergarten transition. Students receiving the intervention displayed an increase of nearly five positive student-teacher interactions per day following intervention. Similarly, the number of negative student-teacher interactions decreased by about five interactions per day. Conversely, Eisenhower et al. (2016) reported overall participation in Starting Strong had no direct effect on student-teacher relationship quality (d = -0.002). However, it is important to note that students who began the intervention with low quality student-teacher relationships at baseline experienced significantly higher quality student-teacher relationships after intervention, compared to the control group.

Collectively, targeted transition interventions demonstrated emerging evidence of moderately positive impacts on student-teacher relationship quality. The most effective interventions were those that administered direct services to students. Evidence suggested that stronger impacts may result for students with low-quality initial student-teacher relationships.

**On-Task Behavior Outcomes**

Two studies examined targeted transition interventions for improving on-task behavior. Hains (1992) investigated a checklist intervention with students with developmental disabilities, finding that three out of the four students receiving the intervention demonstrated improvements in on-task behavior. Sprague and Perkins (2009) reported that academic engaged time for four students receiving First Step to Success was 64% at baseline and 89% after intervention. Increases were maintained at 91% of observed intervals during follow-up. These studies provide emerging evidence that transition interventions targeting on-task behavior may be beneficial.

**Multi-Domain Behavioral Readiness Outcomes**

Three studies included multi-domain measures of behavioral readiness for kindergarten. These measures evaluated students' capacities across behavioral skills relevant to kindergarten transition. Kindergarten transition interventions targeting multiple domains were associated with small, but significant, positive effects. This was true for interventions providing direct support to children as well as those targeting parenting skills to support children's behavioral functioning.

Two studies examined the effects of a targeted transition intervention on students' learning engagement (i.e., self-regulation, attention, motivation, and engagement). Bierman et al. (2013) reported that students who participated in the Head Start REDI intervention were rated by their teachers as more engaged and motivated in the classroom ($\beta = 0.28$). These results were supported by Nix et al. (2013), who reported that the growth of targeted behavior skills during the Head Start REDI intervention had a significant effect on student's learning engagement in kindergarten. Growth in prosocial behavior was found to have the largest impact on learning engagement ($\beta = 0.26$). These findings suggest that participation in the Head Start REDI program is associated with small, but significant, increases in learning engagement behaviors.

Stormshak and colleagues (2020) reported on the effects of the Family Check-Up (FCU; Stormshak et al., 2010). The researchers reported a small effect of the intervention on the reduction of child behavioral concerns in kindergarten ($d = 0.20$), providing emerging evidence that behavioral outcomes can be targeted through improvements in parenting techniques.

**Study Quality**

Studies were also coded for methodological quality to assess risk of bias using the JBI Checklist for Randomized Controlled Trials, JBI Checklist for Quasi-Experimental Studies, and the WWC Standards for Single-Case Designs. 14 studies were assessed using the JBI Checklist for Randomized Controlled Trials, with scores ranging from 8/13 to 10/13.

## Table 3

*Study Quality for Randomized Controlled Trials*

| Authors | C1 | C2 | C3 | C4 | C5 | C6 | C7 | C8 | C9 | C10 | C11 | C12 | C13 | Total |
|---|---|---|---|---|---|---|---|---|---|---|---|---|---|---|
| Bierman et al. (2013) | 1 | 0 | 1 | 0 | 0 | 1 | 1 | 1 | 1 | 1 | 1 | 1 | 1 | 9 |
| Duncan et al. (2018) | 1 | 0 | 0 | 0 | 0 | 0 | 1 | 1 | 1 | 1 | 1 | 1 | 1 | 8 |
| Eisenhower et al. (2016) | 1 | 0 | 0 | 0 | 0 | 0 | 1 | 1 | 1 | 1 | 1 | 1 | 1 | 8 |
| Graziano & Hart (2016) | 1 | 0 | 1 | 0 | 0 | 0 | 1 | 1 | 1 | 1 | 1 | 1 | 1 | 9 |
| Hart et al. (2016) | 1 | 0 | 1 | 0 | 0 | 0 | 1 | 1 | 1 | 1 | 1 | 1 | 1 | 9 |
| Hart et al. (2019) | 1 | 0 | 1 | 0 | 0 | 0 | 1 | 1 | 1 | 1 | 1 | 1 | 1 | 9 |
| Lynch et al. (2017) | 1 | 0 | 1 | 0 | 0 | 0 | 1 | 1 | 1 | 1 | 1 | 1 | 1 | 9 |
| McDermott et al. (2017) | 1 | 0 | 1 | 0 | 0 | 0 | 1 | 1 | 1 | 1 | 1 | 1 | 1 | 9 |
| Nix et al. (2013) | 1 | 0 | 1 | 0 | 0 | 0 | 1 | 1 | 1 | 1 | 1 | 1 | 1 | 9 |
| Pears et al. (2012) | 1 | 0 | 1 | 0 | 0 | 0 | 1 | 1 | 1 | 1 | 1 | 1 | 1 | 9 |
| Pears et al. (2013) | 1 | 0 | 1 | 0 | 0 | 0 | 1 | 1 | 1 | 1 | 1 | 1 | 1 | 9 |
| Pears et al. (2014) | 1 | 0 | 1 | 0 | 0 | 0 | 1 | 1 | 1 | 1 | 1 | 1 | 1 | 9 |
| Stormshak et al. (2020) | 1 | 0 | 0 | 0 | 0 | 0 | 1 | 1 | 1 | 1 | 1 | 1 | 1 | 8 |
| Wenz-Gross et al. (2018) | 1 | 0 | 1 | 0 | 0 | 1 | 1 | 1 | 1 | 1 | 1 | 1 | 1 | 10 |

*Note.* See Appendix B for full description of criteria. The 13 criteria listed here map onto the 13 criteria listed on the checklist.

A detailed breakdown of study quality is in Table 3. An area that was consistently rated poorly involved keeping outcome assessors blind to treatment assignment, with only one study meeting this criterion (i.e., Wenz-Gross et al., 2018). Consistent strengths were the similarity of treatment groups at baseline, the use of robust outcome measures, and the utilization of follow-up procedures. McLeod et al. (2017) was the only study utilizing a quasi-experimental design and thus was evaluated using the JBI Checklist for Quasi-Experimental Designs. This study obtained a score of 5/7 (C4 and C7 omitted for relevance), with a poor rating for a lack of multiple measurements before and after intervention, as the researchers only used a single measure to assess behavioral outcomes. Finally, the methodological quality of two studies (Hains, 1992; Sprague & Perkins, 2009) was assessed using the What Works Clearinghouse (WWC) Standards for Single-Case Designs. Table 4 provides an overview of specific criteria. Both studies were scored 4/4, indicating that they met 100% of the quality indicators for single-case designs.

## Discussion

This review synthesized the existing research on interventions designed to improve students' behavioral transition to kindergarten. Reviewed interventions varied on setting, duration, dosage, period of implementation, behavioral skills targeted, and groups targeted. Nevertheless, 15 out of 17 studies reported positive effects. Those studies not finding positive outcomes reported null effects. Further, the studies reviewed included participants who varied on race, ethnicity, socioeconomic status, disability status, and risk status for poor kindergarten adjustment. An important finding from this review was that transition practices were effective with a wide range of students, including students who are involved in the foster care system, with developmental disabilities, from economically disadvantaged households, and with no prior preschool experience.

**Table 4**
*Study Quality for Single-Case Designs*

| Authors | C1 | C2 | C3 | C4 | Total |
|---|---|---|---|---|---|
| Hains, 1992 | 1 | 1 | 1 | 1 | 4 |
| Sprague & Perkins, 2009 | 1 | 1 | 1 | 1 | 4 |

**Note.** See Appendix D for full description of criteria. The criteria listed her map onto the four criteria listed under the "Criteria for Designs that Meet Evidence Standards" section.

## Universal Transition Practices

One primary aim of this study was to synthesize the available research on universal transition practices. However, only one study reporting such a strategy met the inclusion criteria for the present review (Wenz-Gross et al., 2018). Wenz-Gross et al. reported that the Second Step Early Learning Curriculum was associated with improved executive functioning skills in students transitioning to kindergarten. Although these authors did not report improved global kindergarten readiness outcomes, executive functioning is a critical skill for school readiness, suggesting the Second Step Early Learning Curriculum may be a potential option for schools targeting executive functioning with all incoming kindergarteners. However, due to the limited evidence presented here, this intervention should be implemented with caution.

## Targeted Transition Interventions

A second aim of this review was to understand the extent to which targeted interventions promoted positive behavioral school readiness. Overall, the included studies suggested promising results, with effect sizes ranging from -1.34 for reduction of undesired behaviors (Graziano & Hart, 2016) to 1.50 for improvement of desired behaviors (Graziano & Hart, 2016). Reviewed targeted interventions provided supports to parents, students, teachers, and multiple groups. The most common approach, which was also the approach with the greatest empirical support, involved those interventions that targeted multiple groups. Eleven studies reported on interventions that targeted a combination of students and caregivers, with all reporting positive effects on student behavioral outcomes. This pattern of positive outcomes was unique to this group of interventions, as interventions targeting only students or only parents displayed more mixed results. Given the importance of the involvement of families, these results are consistent with the underlying theory of the DEM (Rimm-Kaufman & Pianta, 2000), which holds that high quality relationships can help address challenges faced by a student during the transition to kindergarten.

Although behavioral functioning was the most common outcome measure, self-regulation appears to be the most critical underlying behavioral skill pertinent to kindergarten transition. Interventions that included self-regulation training were not only effective in improving self-regulation capacities, but there is evidence that these self-regulation gains contributed to improvements in behavioral functioning, prosocial behavior, and student-teacher relationship quality. Another relevant factor in promoting behavioral readiness for kindergarten is the importance of developmental timing. Fourteen studies reported on interventions that were implemented prior to kindergarten entry, underscoring the significance of this developmental period for skill development.

A potential limitation of these interventions is their intensive implementation and resource requirements. Interventions that begin prior to kindergarten require strong collaboration between school districts, families, and communities, as well as the availability of resources, which may be a barrier to implementation. The Head Start REDI intervention and checklist intervention outlined by Hains (1992) may act as good models for schools wishing to provide transition services to students but unable to deliver more intensive interventions due to these constraints. Both require minimal resources and can be implemented by classroom teachers.

## Limitations

This review is not without its limitations. Relevant articles may have been omitted due to the search strategy, inclusion criteria, or search terms. If other inclusion criteria or search terms were utilized, different studies might be identified. Gray literature (e.g., dissertations, theses, books, technical reports) was not included, yet there may be relevant findings in the gray literature that could inform school-based practices. Therefore, it is possible the studies included in this review do not represent the full scope of available research on this topic.

There were also limited findings identified related to universal kindergarten transition supports. Thus, it was challenging to draw conclusions regarding the effects associated with universal transition services. No informal, universal transition supports (e.g., open houses) were identified in the current review, making evaluation of these commonly used practices impossible. Further, transition programs exist that have yet to be evaluated in the empirical literature (e.g., see Cappelloni, 2012; Mashburn et al., 2018). Without empirical investigations, the impact of these programs on children's behavioral functioning at kindergarten entry cannot be determined. More research on universal supports and other programs is necessary to draw reliable conclusions.

Finally, while many positive outcomes were associated with targeted transition interventions for specific groups (e.g., children involved in the child welfare system), these results may not hold for other kindergarteners. It is important to consider each study sample when applying the results presented in this review, as the generalizability of the findings in this review is limited to students similar to the students included in the reviewed studies.

**Implications for Practice**

It is imperative that schools have a menu of transition services and interventions that can be utilized in a multi-tiered system of support (MTSS) delivery model. This includes universal transition practices that can improve the behavioral readiness of all students, as well as targeted interventions that meet the needs of students entering kindergarten at elevated levels of risk. While the evidence on universal transition interventions was scant, findings provide strong support for the impact of targeted transition interventions for improving behavioral kindergarten readiness. Schools should aim to collaborate with families to provide early intervention for students at elevated risk of poor behavioral adjustment to kindergarten, specifically targeting self-regulation skills. These interventions should be comprehensive and multimodal, targeting both students and parents. Namely, efforts should be made to strengthen not only the behavioral skills of students, but also the skills of parents, who play a pivotal role in the kindergarten transition process. When partnering with families, however, it is essential to understand for whom and under what conditions empirical support exists for the various intervention strategies discussed in this review (see Tables 1 and 2) as outcomes may vary. Further, practitioners should be aware that not all families share similar views regarding readiness for kindergarten, behavioral expectations, or academic goals. Practitioners are encouraged to use the results presented here as a starting place to discuss strategies with families, and to co-create a targeted intervention plan that is mutually acceptable to both the educators and the family. With that in mind, we acknowledge that facilitating successful behavioral readiness for kindergarten is a complicated process involving many components, and this review provides guidance on key skills to target and how to best target them in an effort to strengthen schools' ability to support the needs of all kindergarteners.

## Recommendations for Future Research

A prominent finding of this review was the disparity in extant research between universal transition practices and targeted interventions. Out of the 17 studies reviewed, 16 reported on interventions designed to be implemented students with elevated levels of risk. Still, the transition to kindergarten may be difficult for all students (Rimm-Kaufman et al., 2000). Further research is needed on the impact of universal transition practices used to foster behavioral skills relevant to successful transition for all students. Further research is also needed to explore the impact of transition interventions implemented in kindergarten. The vast majority of literature focuses on transition interventions that begin prior to kindergarten, and these interventions may not be possible for all school districts due to barriers (e.g., access to student, finances, resources, etc.). In order to promote equity, it is essential that school districts facing these obstacles have access to evidence-based transition interventions that are less resource-intensive.

## References

Berlin, L.J., Dunning, R.D., & Dodge, K.A. (2011). Enhancing the transition to kindergarten: A randomized controlled trial to test the efficacy of the "stars" summer kindergarten orientation program. *Early Childhood Research Quarterly, 26*, 247-254. doi: 10.1016/j.ecresq.2010.07.004

Blair, C. (2002). School readiness: Integrating cognition and emotion in a neurobiological conceptualization of children's functioning at school entry. *American Psychologist, 57*, 111-127. doi: 10.1037/0003-066X.57.2.111

Blair, C., Zelazo, P.D., & Greenberg, M.T. (2005). The measurement of executive function in early childhood. *Developmental Neuropsychology, 28*(2), 561-571. doi: 10.1207/s15326942dn2802_1

Bierman, K. L., Nix, R. L., Heinrichs, B. S., Domitrovich, C. E., Gest, S. D., Welsh, J. A., & Gill, S. (2013). Effects of Head Start REDI on children's outcomes 1 year later in different kindergarten contexts. *Child Development, 85*(1), 140–159. doi:10.1111/cdev.12117

Brock, L.L., Rimm-Kaufman, S.E., Nathanson, L., & Grimm, K.J. (2009). The contribution of 'hot' and 'cool' executive function to children's academic achievement, learning-related behaviors, and engagement in kindergarten. *Early Childhood Research Quarterly, 24*, 337-349. doi: 10.1016/j.ecresq.2009.06.001

Cappelloni, N. (2012). *Kindergarten readiness.* Corwin Press.

Collie, R.J., Martin, A.J., Roberts, C.L., & Nassar, N. (2018). The roles of anxious and prosocial behavior in early academic performance: A population-based study examining unique and moderated effects. *Learning and Individual Differences, 62*, 141-152. doi: 10.1016/j.lindif.2018.02.004

Committee for Children (2011). *Second Step Learning Program.* Seattle, WA: Committee for Children.

Cook, K.D., & Coley, R.L. (2017). School transition practices and children's social and academic adjustment in kindergarten. *Journal of Educational Psychology, 109*(2), 166-177. doi: 10.1037/edu0000139

Denham, S.A. (2006). Social-emotional competence as support for school readiness: What is it and how do we assess it? *Early Education and Development, 17*(1), 57-89. doi: 10.1207/s15566935eed1701_4

Duncan, G.J., Dowsett, C.J., Claessons, A., Magnuson, K., Huston A.C., Klebanov, P., Pagani, L.S., Feinstein, L., Engel, M., Brooks-Gunn, J., Sexton, H., & Duckworth, K. (2007). School readiness and later achievement. *Developmental Psychology, 43*(6), 1428-1446. doi: 10.1037/0012-1649.43.6.1428

Duncan, R.J, Schmitt, S.A., Burke, M., & McClelland, M.M. (2018). Combining a kindergarten readiness summer program with a self-regulation intervention improves school readiness. *Early Childhood Research Quarterly, 42,* 291-300. doi: 10.1016/j.ecresq.2017.10.012

Eisenhower, A., Taylor, H., & Baker, B.L. (2016). Starting strong: A school-based indicated prevention program during the transition to kindergarten. *School Psychology Review, 45*(2), 141-170.

Garbacz, S.A., McIntyre, L.L., Stormshak, E.A., & Kosty, D.B. (2020). The efficacy of the family check-up on children's emotional and behavior problems in early elementary school. *Journal of Emotional and Behavioral Disorders, 28*(2), 67-79. doi: 10.1177/1063426618806258

Graziano, P. A., & Hart, K. (2016). Beyond behavior modification: Benefits of social-emotional/self-regulation training for preschoolers with behavior problems. *Journal of School Psychology, 58,* 91–111. doi: 10.1016/j.jsp.2016.07.004

Hains, A. H. (1992). Strategies for Preparing Preschool Children with Special Needs for the Kindergarten Mainstream. *Journal of Early Intervention, 16*(4), 320–333. doi:10.1177/105381519201600403

Hart, K. C., Graziano, P. A., Kent, K. M., Garcia, A., Gnagy, E. M., Greiner, A. R., Pelham, W. E. (2010). *Kindergarten summer readiness classroom program manual* (Unpublished manual). Center for Children and Families, Department of Psychology, Florida International University.

Hart, K.C., Graziano, P.A., Kent, K.M., Kuriyan, A., Garcia, A., Rodriguez, M., & Pelham, Jr., W.E. (2016). Early intervention for children with behavior problems in summer settings: Results from a pilot evaluation in head start preschools. *Journal of Early Intervention, 38*(2), 92-117. doi: 10.1177/1053815116645923

Hart, K. C., Maharaj, A. V., & Graziano, P. A. (2019). Does dose of early intervention matter for preschoolers with externalizing behavior problems? A pilot randomized trial comparing intensive summer programming to school consultation. *Journal of School Psychology, 72,* 112–133. doi: 10.1016/j.jsp.2018.12.007

Kratochwill, T.R., Hitchcock, J., Horner, R.H., Levin, J.R., Odom, S.L., Rindskopf, D.M., & Shadish, W.R. (2010). *Single-case designs technical documentation*. Retrieved from What Works Clearinghous website: http://ies.ed.gov/ncee/wwc/pdf/wwc_scd.pdf

LoCasale-Crouch, J., Mashburn, A.J., Downer, J.T., & Pianta, R.C. (2008). Pre-kindergarten teachers' use of transition practices and children's adjustment to kindergarten. Early Childhood Research Quarterly, 23, 124-139. doi: 10.1016/j.ecresq.2007.06.001

Lynch, F. L., Dickerson, J. F., Pears, K. C., & Fisher, P. A. (2017). Cost effectiveness of a school readiness intervention for foster children. *Children and Youth Services Review, 81,* 63–71. doi: 10.1016/j.childyouth.2017.07.011

Mashburn, A. J., LoCasale-Crouch, J., & Pears, K. C. (2018). *Kindergarten transition and readiness*. Springer International Publishing. https://doi.org/10.1007/978-3-319-90200-5.

McClelland, M.M., & Cameron, C.E. (2012). Self-regulation in early childhood: Improving conceptual clarity and developing ecologically valid measures. *Child Development Perspectives*, 6(2), 136-142. doi: 10.1111/j.1750-8606.2011.00191.x

McDermott, J. M., Pears, K. C., Bruce, J., Kim, H. K., Roos, L., Yoerger, K. L., & Fisher, P. A. (2017). Improving kindergarten readiness in children with developmental disabilities: Changes in neural correlates of response monitoring. *Applied Neuropsychology: Child*, 7(3), 187-199. doi:10.1080/21622965.2017.1286239

McLeod, R., Kim, S., Tomek, S., & McDaniel, S. (2017). Effects of a summer school-readiness programme on measures of literacy and behaviour growth: a pilot study. *Early Child Development and Care*, 1-8. doi:10.1080/03004430.2017.1374259

Mistry, R.S., Biesanz, J.C., Chien, N., Howes, C., & Benner, A.D. (2008). Socioeconomic status, parental investments, and the cognitive and behavioral outcomes of low-income children from immigrant and native households. *Early Childhood Research Quarterly*, 23, 193-212. doi: doi.org/10.1016/j.ecresq.2008.01.002

Nix, R. L., Bierman, K. L., Domitrovich, C. E., & Gill, S. (2013). Promoting children's social-emotional skills in preschool can enhance academic and behavioral functioning in kindergarten: Findings from Head Start REDI. *Early Education & Development*, 24(7), 1000-1019. doi:10.1080/10409289.2013.825565

Ouzzani, M., Hammady, H., Fedorowicz, Z., & Elmagarmid, A. (2016). Rayyan—a web and mobile app for systematic reviews. *Systematic Reviews*, 5(1), 1-10.

Pears, K. C., Carpenter, L., Kim, H. K., Peterson, E., & Fisher, P. A. (2018). The kids in transition to school program. In *Kindergarten transition and readiness* (p. 283-302). Springer.

Pears, K. C., Kim, H. K., & Fisher, P. A. (2012). Effects of a school readiness intervention for children in foster care on oppositional and aggressive behaviors in kindergarten. *Children and Youth Services Review*, 34(12), 2361-2366. doi: 10.1016/j.childyouth.2012.08.015

Pears, K.C., Fisher, P.A., Kim, H.K., Bruce, J., Healey, C.V., & Yoerger, K. (2013). Immediate effects of a school readiness intervention for children in foster care. *Early Education and Development*, 24, 771-791. doi: 10.1080/10409289.2013.736037

Pears, K. C., Kim, H. K., Healey, C. V., Yoerger, K., & Fisher, P. A. (2014). Improving child self-regulation and parenting in families of pre-kindergarten children with developmental disabilities and behavioral difficulties. *Prevention Science*, 16(2), 222-232. doi:10.1007/s11121-014-0482-2

Purtell, K.M., Valauri, A., Rhoad-Drogalis, A., Jiang, H., Justice, L.M., Lin, T.J., & Logan, J.A.R. (2020). Understanding policies and practices that support successful transitions to kindergarten. *Early Childhood Research Quarterly, 52*, 5-14. doi: 10.1016/j.ecresq.2019.09.003

Rimm-Kaufman, S.E., & Pianta, R.C. (2000). An ecological perspective on the transition to kindergarten: A theoretical framework to guide empirical research. *Journal of Applied Developmental Psychology, 21*(5), 491-511. doi: 10.1016/S0193-3973(00)00051-4

Rimm-Kaufman, S.E., Pianta, R.C., & Cox, M.J. (2000). Teachers' judgments of problems in the transition to kindergarten. *Early Childhood Research Quarterly, 15*(2), 147-166. doi: 10.1016/S0885-2006(00)00049-1

Schmidt, M., Demulder, E., & Denham, S. (2002). Kindergarten social-emotional competence: Developmental predictors and psychosocial implications. *Early Childhood Development and Care, 172*(5), 451-462. doi: 10.1080/03004430214550

Sprague, J., & Perkins, K. (2009). Direct and collateral effects of the First Step to Success program. *Journal of Positive Behavior Interventions, 11*(4), 208–221. doi:10.1177/1098300708330935

Stormshak, E. A., DeGarmo, D., Garbacz, S. A., McIntyre, L. L., & Caruthers, A. (2020). Using motivational interviewing to improve parenting skills and prevent problem behavior during the transition to kindergarten. *Prevention Science.* doi:10.1007/s11121-020-01102-w

Stormshak, E. A., Fosco, G. M., & Dishion, T. J. (2010). Implementing interventions with families in schools to increase youth school engagement: The Family Check-Up model. *School Mental Health, 2*(2), 82-92.

Tominey, S. L., & McClelland, M. M. (2011). Red light, purple light: Findings from a randomized trial using circle time games to improve behavioral self-regulation in preschool. *Early Education & Development, 22*(3), 489-519.

Tufanaru, C., Munn, Z., Aromataris, E., Campbell, J., & Hopp, L. (2020). Chapter 3: Systematic reviews of effectiveness. In Aromataris, E. & Munn, Z. (Eds.). *JBI Manual for Evidence Synthesis.* Available from https://synthesismanual.jbi.global

Walker, H. M., Stiller, B., Severson, H. H., Feil, E. G., Golly, A. (1998). First step to success: Intervening at the point of school entry to prevent antisocial behavior patterns. *Psychology in the Schools, 35*, 259-269. doi:10.1002/(SICI)1520-6807(199807)35:3<259::AID-PITS6>3.0.CO;2-I

Webster-Stratton, C. (1990). *Dina Dinosaur's Social Skills and Problem-Solving Curriculum.* Incredible Years.

Welchons, L. W., & McIntyre, L. L. (2017). The transition to kindergarten: Predicting sociobehavioral outcomes for children with and without disabilities. *Early Childhood Education Journal, 45*(1), 83-93.

Wenz-Gross, M., Yoo, Y., Upshur, C. C., & Gambino, A. J. (2018). Pathways to kindergarten readiness: The roles of Second Step Early Learning Curriculum and social emotional, executive functioning, preschool academic and task behavior skills. *Frontiers in Psychology, 9.* doi:10.3389/fpsyg.2018.01886

Yoshikawa, H., Weiland, C., Brooks-Gunn, J., Burchinal, M. R., Espinosa, L. M., Gormley, W. T., ... & Zaslow, M. J. (2013). *Investing in Our Future: The Evidence Base on Preschool Education.* Society for Research in Child Development.

# List of Contributors

*\* indicates corresponding author and inclusion of contact information.*

**Allison Aberson**, PhD, is currently a Psychologist at the Cognitive Behavior Institute in Cranberry Township, PA. She is a licensed psychologist in the state of Pennsylvania. She is passionate about utilizing and disseminating evidence-based practice for direct services. Her research interests include scientifically-based interventions in outpatient settings to improve the social-emotional functioning of young children, families, and adolescents.

**Meleah M. Ackley** is a fifth-year student in the School Psychology program at The University of Southern Mississippi. She is a Board Certified Behavior Analyst, currently completing an APA accredited internship with the Munroe Meyer Institute (MMI) in Pediatric Feeding. Meleah is primarily interested in examining caregiver treatment integrity of pediatric feeding interventions, the efficacy of feeding tools, component analyses, and translational research.

**\*Kayla Bates-Brantley**, PhD, BCBA-D, NCSP is an assistant professor in the school psychology program at Mississippi State University. She is a Licensed Board-Certified Behavior Analyst, Doctoral as well as a National Certified School Psychologist. Her research interests include academic and behavioral consultation in applied settings, applied behavior analysis, and early intervention for developmental disabilities. *Email: Keb240@msstate.edu*

**Terreca A. Cato** is a third-year student in the School Psychology program at the University of Southern Mississippi. She is a New Orleans, LA native. Terreca received her B.S. in Psychology with a Minor in Biology from Xavier University of Louisiana and her M.S. in Psychology with a specialization in Applied Behavior Analysis from Capella University. She currently has an assistantship as a Behavioral Consultant with Pearl River Valley Opportunity Inc (PRVO). Her primary research interest relates to parent training, early intervention, and behavioral assessment. Terreca also serves as a Student Representative and the Diversity Committee Chair for the School Psychology Organization of Graduate Students (SPOGS).

**Dr. Evan H. Dart**, PhD, is an associate professor in the school psychology program at the University of South Florida. He is a licensed psychologist and a board certified behavior analyst. His research broadly involves the identification and evaluation of evidence-based intervention strategies for individuals with or at-risk for behavior disorders.

**James R. Derieux**, PhD, graduated from the University of Southern Mississippi with a doctoral degree in School Psychology. He completed his pre-doctoral internship at Kennedy Krieger Institute and John Hopkins School of Medicine in the Applied Behavior Analysis track consisting of one 6-month stint in the Pediatric Developmental Disabilities Clinic and one 6-month stint in the Pediatric Feeding Disorders Program. He is currently completing his post-doctoral fellowship in the Pediatric Feeding Disorders Program. His work encompasses the application of behaviorally-oriented interventions with individuals with developmental disabilities and feeding concerns within clinic and hospital settings.

**Mallie Donald** is a second-year doctoral candidate in the school psychology program at Mississippi State University. While at Mississippi State, she has worked in both the school and clinic setting using academic and behavioral evidenced-based interventions. Her research interests include academic and behavioral interventions for autism or related disorders, pediatric feeding disorders, and parent consultation involving behavior analytic principles.

**\*Mikayla Drymond,** EdS, is a doctoral candidate in the school psychology program at the University of South Florida. While at USF, Mikayla worked in several school districts providing individual and group therapies, as well as universal school-based services to children and adolescents with diverse needs. Mikayla is a Nationally Certified School Psychologist who is currently working as a school-based school psychologist and also works in private practice providing therapeutic services to young children and their families. Mikayla's research focuses on school mental health, including early identification and intervention for children who have social-emotional and behavioral concerns, social emotional learning, and trauma-informed care. *Email: mdrymood@usf.edu*

**Brad A. Dufrene**, PhD, is a Professor of Psychology at The University of Southern Mississippi. He is primarily interested in increasing access to evidence-based practices for underserved populations. In particular, Dr. Dufrene is interested in the treatment integrity of evidence-based interventions for preschoolers at-risk for emotional and behavioral disorders.

**Nathaniel P. von der Embse**, PhD, is an associate professor of school psychology at the University of South Florida. Dr. von der Embse serves as an associate editor for the Journal of School Psychology and his research interests include universal screening for behavioral and mental health, teacher stress and student test anxiety, and training educators in population-based mental health services. He received the 2018 Lightner Witmer Award for early career scholarship from Division 16 of the American Psychological Association and is a primary and co-investigator on multiple federally funded research grants. Dr. von der Embse is the co-author of the Social, Academic, and Emotional Behavior Risk Screener.

**\*Elyse M. Farnsworth**, PhD, LP, NCSP is an Assistant Professor in the school psychology program at Minnesota State University, Mankato. Her research team examines how public policy, academic enablers, and early intervention influence school-based cognitive and non-cognitive outcomes for PK12 students with a special interest in hope and school readiness. *Email: elyse.farnsworth@mnsu.edu*

**Gabrielle Francis**, M.A. is a third-year doctoral student in the School Psychology program at the University of South Florida. During her time at USF she has provided evidence-based interventions, counselling services and consultation in primary and secondary school settings as well as in clinical settings. Gabrielle has also supported graduate course instruction and is an instructor for an undergraduate class on mental health stigma. Her interests include early childhood education and the cultural relevance of evidence-based interventions.

**Bridget Green**, Ed.D is an assistant professor of Special Education in the Department of Counseling, Psychology, and Special Education at Duquesne University. Her research focuses on understanding the needs of students who have disabilities transitioning into college and employment, transition assessment, and developing best practices to ensure students with and without disabilities have access to meaningful career-based assessments in the general education classroom.

**Sarah W. Harry**, PhD, HSPP, BCBA-D, NCSP is an assistant professor in the educational psychology department at Ball State University. She functions as a core faculty member in the School Psychology program. Dr. Harry is a licensed clinical psychologist in the state of Indiana, board certified behavior analyst at the doctoral level and a nationally certified school psychologist. She focuses her research in areas of academic assessment and intervention as well as class-wide behavior interventions.

**\*Lynda B. Hayes**, PhD, is a Postdoctoral Psychology Fellow at the University of Nebraska Medical Center's Munroe-Meyer Institute. She provides outpatient behavioral health assessment and evidence-based treatments to diverse populations and age groups, including youth and adults with intellectual and developmental disabilities. *Email: lynda.hayes@unmc.edu*

**\*Kate Helbig**, PhD, BCBA-D is an Assistant Professor in the School Psychology Program at the University of South Dakota. Dr. Helbig's research interests are focused on the application of behaviorally oriented interventions within educational environments. Dr. Helbig is particularly interested in the areas of social skills teaching, peer-management interventions, and transition services for individuals with developmental disabilities. *Email: kate.helbig@usd.edu*

**Samin Khallaghi**, B.A. is a first-year doctoral student in the school psychology program at the University of South Florida (USF). She also attended USF for her undergraduate and majored in psychology. During her undergraduate career, Samin has worked in public elementary schools as a teacher's assistant and has collected data for multiple research teams. Her current research interests include influencing systems change, early childhood risk identification, and how to increase subjective well-being for students through positive psychology.

**\*Zachary C. LaBrot**, Ph.D, is an Assistant Professor of School Psychology at the University of Southern Mississippi. Dr. LaBrot's research interests include consultation in early childhood education settings, class wide interventions, and behavioral parent training. Additionally, Dr. LaBrot is proudly a practicing licensed psychologist.
*Email: zachary.labrot@usm.edu*

**Rebecca W. Lovelace** is a third-year student in the School Psychology program at The University of Southern Mississippi. She is primarily interested in examining social-emotional and behavioral assessment and intervention, including the treatment utility of universal screening.

**\*Kara McGoey**, PhD, is currently a professor of school psychology at Duquesne University. She is a Pennsylvania and Nationally Certified School Psychologist. She teaches courses on behavioral assessment and intervention, child and adolescent psychopathology and early childhood assessment and intervention. She is active in the early childhood education mental health consultant community by providing supervision and support to early childhood centers throughout the Pittsburgh region. Her research interests include translating scientifically sound interventions into the school setting to improve the social-emotional functioning of young children, implementation science, reducing the barriers to intervention fidelity, and preschool mental health.
*Email: mcgoey@duq.edu*

**Rylee McHenry** is a first-year school psychology doctoral student at Mississippi State University. Her research interests include postsecondary preparedness for individuals with Intellectual and/or Developmental Disabilities (IDDs) and social skills interventions for adolescents and young adults with IDDs.

**D. Joe Olmi**, PhD, is in his 30th year as faculty in the USM School of Psychology. He served as Director of the School for ten years prior to returning to his role as Professor in the School of Psychology. He is a faculty member in the School Psychology Program and a licensed Psychologist in Mississippi with approximately 40 years' experience in educational settings.

**Keith C Radley**, PhD, BCBA-D., NCSP is an Associate Professor and Director of the School Psychology Program at the University of Utah. Dr. Radley's research interests center on the application of behavioral interventions within academic settings, particularly for individuals with developmental disabilities. Further, his research focuses on data collection, visualization, and analysis in research and applied contexts.

**\*Hailey Ripple**, PhD, BCBA-D is an assistant professor in the school psychology program at Mississippi State University. She is a Board-Certified Behavior Analyst, Doctoral and her research interests include pediatric feeding disorders, functional analysis of problem behavior in individuals with sensory impairments, the effectiveness of interventions rooted in applied behavior analysis, and CHARGE Syndrome. *Email: her156@msstate.edu*

**Dorie Ross**, M.A. is a second-year doctoral student in the School Psychology program at the University of South Florida. Prior to graduate school, she worked as a teaching assistant at a therapeutic school. Her primary research interests include the development of progress monitoring tools and interventions to improve mental health outcomes of middle school and high school students with internalizing concerns, multi-informant decision making in mental health assessment, and threat identification and assessment in schools.

**Alexis Sánchez**, M.A. is a fourth-year doctoral candidate in the school psychology program at the University of South Florida (USF). During their time at USF, Alexis has worked in primary, secondary, and clinic settings in multiple counties providing school-based consultation, evidence-based interventions, and data-based decision making. Alexis' research interests include social justice for minoritized populations, advocacy and policy change that promotes success in education, promotion of youth mental health supports for students, and multi-tiered systems of support.

**Stefanie Schrieber**, PhD, BCBA graduated from the University of Southern Mississippi with a doctoral degree in School Psychology. She completed her pre-doctoral internship at the May Institute's school for autism and developmental disabilities and is currently a post-doctoral fellow in the Psychology Department at the Munroe Meyer Institute and University of Nebraska Medical Center. Her work is generally encompassed by the application of behaviorally-oriented interventions to address student behavioral health in educational settings at both the individual and systems level.

**\*Hallie Smith** PhD, BCBA-D, is an assistant professor in the applied behavior analysis program at Mississippi State University. She is a Board-Certified Behavior Analyst, Doctoral as well as a licensed psychologist. Her research interests include the assessment and treatment of pediatric feeding disorders as well as the development of behavioral interventions for individuals with development disabilities. *Email: hms238@msstate.edu*

**Jasmine Sorrell** is a fourth-year school psychology doctoral student at Mississippi State University. She is currently a Board-Certified Behavior Analyst and a Licensed Psychometrist in the state of Mississippi. Jasmine serves as Clinical Coordinator at the TK Martin Center's Ignite Reading Clinic. Her primary research interests include training non-professionals to implement applied behavior analytic assessment and intervention procedures as well as identifying effective and efficient academic interventions for students of all ages.

**Meredith Staggers** is a fourth-year school psychology doctoral student at Mississippi State University (MSU) and is a Board-Certified Behavior Analyst. While at MSU, Meredith has worked in both the school and clinical settings providing evidence-based intervention services rooted in Applied Behavior Analysis to children with autism spectrum disorder, developmental disabilities, and behavioral disorders. Her research interests include the application of behavioral analysis to individuals with ASD, Developmental Disabilities, pediatric feeding disorders, and rare genetic disorders.

**Seana Bandi Stewart**, PhD, NCSP is a licensed psychologist and nationally certified school psychologist. Dr. Bandi practices in psychological assessment and individual and group counseling for a wide range of questions for children and adolescents, including autism, ADHD, anxiety, depression, intellectual disabilities, learning disabilities, developmental delays, and behavioral concerns. Dr. Bandi also has experience collaborating and consulting with public and private schools and completing psychoeducational evaluations for special education and giftedness.

**Tyler M. Szydlo,** MA, is a graduate student in the school psychology program at the University of Minnesota. His research interests include early childhood, behavioral intervention, and social emotional learning. Tyler plans to practice as an early childhood or elementary school psychologist upon completion of his graduate training.

**\*Crystal N. Taylor**, PhD, is an assistant professor of School Psychology at the University of Southern Mississippi. Her primary interests include social-emotional and behavioral assessment and intervention. She has received awards from APA-Division 16 and the Society for the Study of School Psychology. She is a Nationally Certified School Psychologist. *Email: crystal.n.taylor@usm.edu*

**Leonard Troughton** , PhD, is an educator and researcher with 20+ years of experience working with individuals with emotional and behavioral disabilities. His research is primarily focused on cognitive-behavioral and social skills interventions for students with emotional/behavioral disorders.

**Caitlyn M. Weaver**. is a fourth-year student in the School Psychology program at The University of Southern Mississippi. She is primarily interested in studying the treatment integrity of behavioral intervention and the implementation of targeted behavioral interventions within multitiered systems of support frameworks.

## *Perspectives on Early Childhood Psychology and Education*

PECPE publishes twice a year, in the fall and spring. These two issues on specific focuses are typically guest-edited and can also include a few general articles.

## Editorial Policy and Submission Guidelines

*Perspectives on Early Childhood Psychology and Education* focuses on publishing original contributions from a broad range of psychological and educational perspectives relevant to infants, young children (to age 8 years), families, and caregivers. Manuscripts incorporating evidence-based research, theory, and practice within clinical, community, developmental, neurological, and school psychology perspectives are considered. In addition, the journal accepts test and book reviews, literature reviews, program descriptions and evaluations, clinical studies, and other professional materials of interest to psychologists and educators working with young children. Proposals for special focus topics may be made to the Editor.

**Format:** Manuscripts should be original work not currently submitted for publication to other journals. Authors must follow the guidelines of the Publication Manual of the American Psychological Association (Sixth Edition). Manuscripts may not exceed 35 double-spaced pages in length, including the cover page, abstract, references, tables, and figures.

**Submission:** Submit an electronic copy of the manuscript for editorial review. Avoid including any identifying author information in the text. Selection of manuscripts is based on blind peer review. Include a cover page with the following information: the title of article, author(s) full name(s), title(s), institution or professional affiliations, and mailing and email address of primary author. The cover page will not be sent to reviewers.

## Selection Criteria:

- Importance of topic in early childhood psychology and education
- Theory and research related to content
- Contribution to professional practice in early childhood psychology and education
- Clear and concise writing

Submit manuscripts to the Editor electronically at the following email address: PECPE@bsu.edu.

Volume 7, Issue 1 of
Perspectives on Early Childhood Psychology and Education
was published in Spring 2022
by Pace University Press

Cover and interior layout by: Adjei Kwesi Boateng
The journal was typeset in Minnion and Myriad and printed
by Lightning Source

Pace University Press
Director: Manuela Soares
Associate Director: Erica Johnson
Design Consultant: Joseph Caserto
Marketing Consultant: Tina McIntyre

Graduate Assistants: Wairimu Muriithi and Adjei Kwesi
Boateng
Graduate Student Aide: Rachel Smithline

www.ingramcontent.com/pod-product-compliance
Lightning Source LLC
Chambersburg PA
CBHW061439300426
44114CB00014B/1746